高职高专英语专业系列教材　　　　　　　　　　总主编：常红梅

新世纪
英语阅读教程

主　编：薛　冰
副主编：韩晓美　李傲君　许　冬
编　委：（以姓氏笔画为序）
　　　　刘　鹏　许　冬　李广义
　　　　李傲君　秦小雅　夏　丹
　　　　韩晓美　薛　冰

北京大学出版社
PEKING UNIVERSITY PRESS

图书在版编目(CIP)数据

新世纪英语阅读教程/薛冰主编. —北京：北京大学出版社，2010.1
（高职高专英语专业系列教材）
ISBN 978-7-301-09979-7

Ⅰ. 新… Ⅱ. 薛… Ⅲ. 英语—阅读教学—高等学校：技术学校—教材 Ⅳ. H319.4

中国版本图书馆CIP数据核字(2009)第107514号

书　　　名：	新世纪英语阅读教程
著作责任者：	薛　冰　主编
责 任 编 辑：	孙　莹
标 准 书 号：	ISBN 978-7-301-09979-7/H·2280
出 版 发 行：	北京大学出版社
地　　　址：	北京市海淀区成府路205号　100871
网　　　址：	http://www.pup.cn　新浪微博:@北京大学出版社
电　　　话：	邮购部 62752015　发行部 62750672　编辑部 62759634　出版部 62756370
电 子 邮 箱：	zbing@pup.pku.edu.cn
印 　刷 　者：	北京大学印刷厂
经 　销 　者：	新华书店
	787毫米×1092毫米　16开本　17印张　412千字
	2010年1月第1版　2019年9月第3次印刷
定　　　价：	33.00元

未经许可，不得以任何方式复制或抄袭本书之部分或全部内容。
版权所有，侵权必究　举报电话：010-62752024
　　　　　　　　　　　　电子邮箱：fd@pup.pku.edu.cn

丛书编写说明

　　高等职业教育是我国高等教育体系的重要组成部分，为满足我国社会发展和经济建设需要，促进高等职业教育持续健康发展，教育部积极推进高等职业教育改革，颁布了《高职高专教育英语课程教学基本要求》。北京经济管理职业学院外语系近年来在外语教学上进行了一系列的改革和创新，贯彻先进的教育教学理念，按照岗位要求设置课程、整合教学内容，建立了两门北京市级精品课程"实用英语写作"、"商务英语翻译"，以及院级精品课程"实用英语语法"，"英语阅读"课程也在积极建设之中。高职高专英语专业系列教材正是几年来根据高职教育培养目标的要求，在实践中进行教学内容和课程体系改革的成果。

　　本套教材力图体现我国高职高专英语专业教学实践的特点，遵循高职高专教育"实用为主"、"够用为度"的总体指导方针；教材的设计充分考虑高职高专英语专业的课程设置、课时、教学要求与高职高专英语专业人才培养的要求与目标，强调英语语言基本技能训练与培养实际英语语言能力并重；充分体现了基础性、实用性、够用性和科学性。基础性是指注重语言基础知识，巩固并拓展学生中学阶段的英语知识和能力；实用性是指教材紧扣高职学生的职业方向；够用性是指教材尽可能控制难度，学一点、会一点、用一点，确保学生接受语言信息输入的效果；科学性是指该教材吸收先进的教学理念和方法，符合语言学习规律，恰当、充分地利用现代教育技术手段，有利于教师使用，有利于学生学习。为方便自学，书后提供了练习参考答案。全套四本教材在遵循总的编写原则的同时，又根据各自课程的特点自成体系。

　　高职高专英语专业系列教材包括《新世纪英语写作教程》、《新世纪英语翻译教程》、《新世纪英语阅读教程》和《新世纪英语语法教程》共四本。北京经济管理职业学院的常红梅教授担任总主编以及《新世纪英语写作教程》的主编，《新世纪英语语法教程》由卢玲蓉（北京经济管理职业学院）主编，《新世纪英语翻译教程》由孙海红（广东女子职业技术学院）主编，《新世纪英语阅读教程》由薛冰（北京服装学院）主编。

　　高职高专英语专业系列教材涵盖了英语专业及相关专业的骨干课程，旨在构建以核心职业能力培养为主线的理论与实践相结合的特色鲜明的课程教材体系。该系列教材的编写内容是完全根据高职生特点以及职业岗位需求选取的,既考虑了高职学生英语基础薄弱,又贯彻了《高职高专英语课程基本要求》对该课程的具体要求,同时体现了高等职业教育的特色,不仅非常适合高职高专的学生学习,也供普通高校学生、成人学生以及同等英语水平的学生学习和参考。

  高职高专英语专业系列教材是身处教学改革第一线的教师们,在深入研究高职教育思想,广泛汲取国内外优秀教材精华的基础上,以创新的意识和大胆改革、勇于实践的精神,经过集体研讨、反复实验而编写完成的。我们期待着这一成果能为推动高职教学改革作出贡献。

编写组
2009 年 3 月

前 言

1. 本书的意义

《新世纪英语阅读教程》以高职高专层次的英语阅读为着眼点,以教育部颁布的《高职高专教育英语课程教学基本要求》为理论依据,以"实用为主,够用为度"为指导原则,突破多年来阅读教材的传统编写模式,将原汁原味的英美国家短文分门别类、重新编排,配以英美文化背景入门以及难易适中的单词、阅读练习题等。将国外先进的外语教学理念和我国高职高专英语教学的现状相结合,既重视语言基础的学习,更重视学生应用能力的培养。指导学生在夯实阅读能力、掌握阅读技巧的同时,提升写作和翻译水平,兼备应用和应试能力。

2. 本书的特点

(1) 形式"三位一体"

《新世纪英语阅读教程》将目前阅读普遍使用的精读、泛读和快速阅读分类教学融为一体。三个部分的阅读要求不尽相同,训练项目也各有所异。这样编排既能保证内容丰厚,又能保证思路明晰;既能丰富语言知识和表达方式,又能拓宽阅读视野和背景常识,从而做到有的放矢,融会贯通。

(2) 内容"三位一体"

《新世纪英语阅读教程》将英语阅读中常见的文化信息、常听的语言理论、常用的应试技巧融为一体,突出体现了高职高专教材的实用性和实践性。所选篇章涉及面广,时效性强,涵盖经济、贸易、科技、环境、法律、人文、文化等多个层面。

(3) 目标"三位一体"

《新世纪英语阅读教程》除了精读、泛读、快速阅读篇章以外,还归纳总结了阅读实践和应试环节中需注意的阅读技巧,并附有近年来的高职高专A/B级考试以及参考答案。因此本书不仅适合高职高专层次学生,还可为有意参加四六级、考研、托福、雅思等考试的同学在阅读方面打下坚实的基础。这样就最大限度地保证了目标的"三位一体":以课文学习为纲,辅以练习为主的消化吸收,和以考试为主的应用实践。在练习的编写上力求多元化,如采用下定义、词汇填空、判断正误、多项选择等多种题型,适度增加"写"和"译"的练习内容,务求使学生在英语的"读"、"写"、"译"多个技能上得到一体发展。

《新世纪英语阅读教程》由北京服装学院与北京经济管理职业学院共同编写。由总主编常红梅进行总体指导;薛冰担任主编,负责统稿,审定修改全文,并承担了 Unit One—Three 的编写;许冬、李傲君、刘鹏、韩晓美分别负责 Unit four—five, Unit Six—Ten, Unit Eleven—Fifteen, Unit Sixteen—Eighteen 的编写,夏丹、李广义和秦小雅分别参加了 Unit Nine、Unit Twelve、Unit Thirteen 的编写工作,在此一并表示感谢。

本教材在编写过程中,参考了较多的相关著作和教材,并借鉴了其中一些内容,在此,谨向有关作者表示诚挚的谢意。

由于编者心长力绌、绠短汲深,其中纰漏瑕疵,在所难免。敬希外语界同仁明鉴厘正,不吝赐教。

薛 冰
2009 年 3 月

Contents（目录）

Unit One ··· 1
   Text 1   Planning for Study in the United States 留学美国的规划 / 1
   Text 2   The English Character 英国人的性格 / 6
   Text 3   Language Teaching 语言教学 / 10

Unit Two ··· 13
   Text 1   Tertiary Education in the UK 英国的高等教育 / 13
   Text 2   Who Am I? 我是谁？/ 18
   Text 3   London: Pollution at its Worst 伦敦：最糟糕的污染 / 22

Unit Three ·· 25
   Text 1   Live and Let Live—A New Strategy 互不相扰——一种新策略 / 25
   Text 2   This is New York 这就是纽约 / 31
   Text 3   Road Rage: A Western Phenomenon? 道路泄愤：西方现象吗？/ 35

Unit Four ··· 38
   Text 1   A Race to Conquer Racism 消除种族歧视的战斗 / 38
   Text 2   Going to School—Why? 为什么要上学？/ 43
   Text 3   The Calendar 日历 / 47

Unit Five ··· 50
   Text 1   A Nation of Sports 体育国度 / 50
   Text 2   Parents—A Soul Harbor 父母——心灵的港湾 / 55
   Text 3   The "Mommy Track" "妈妈的未来" / 59

Unit Six ··· 63
   Text 1   An Open-classroom System 开放的教室 / 63
   Text 2   A Handful of History 扑克——手中的历史 / 67
   Text 3   Food Politics 食物政治 / 71

Unit Seven 74
- Text 1 What's in a Name? 名字的内涵？/ 74
- Text 2 Oral and Non-material Cultural Heritage 口头与非物质文化遗产 / 79
- Text 3 Baseball 棒球的故事 / 83

Unit Eight 86
- Text 1 American Constitution 美国宪法的由来 / 86
- Text 2 Mister Imagination 想象先生 / 91
- Text 3 The Truth about Cats and Dogs 有关猫与狗的真理 / 94

Unit Nine 97
- Text 1 "For skin like peaches and cream" "如桃子和奶油般的皮肤" / 97
- Text 2 Life in Death 生死消长 / 101
- Text 3 Abraham Lincoln 亚伯拉罕·林肯 / 104

Unit Ten 107
- Text 1 Teenagers, Television and Depression 青少年、电视和抑郁症 / 107
- Text 2 Conquer Yellow Fever 战胜黄热病 / 111
- Text 3 The Story of "John Henry" "约翰·亨利"的故事 / 115

Unit Eleven 118
- Text 1 The Personal Qualities of a Teacher 教师的个性 / 118
- Text 2 Mammals in the Sea 海洋中的哺乳动物 / 123
- Text 3 Energy from the Sun 来自太阳的能量 / 126

Unit Twelve 130
- Text 1 Work 工作 / 130
- Text 2 Zoo 动物园 / 135
- Text 3 Sleeping and Dreaming 睡眠与做梦 / 138

Unit Thirteen 142
- Text 1 It's Never Too Late for Success 成功之路，永不言迟 / 142
- Text 2 Meet the President 认识总统 / 147
- Text 3 The Lion, the Witch, and the Wardrobe 狮子，女巫和衣橱 / 150

Unit Fourteen 154
- Text 1 The English and the Americans 英国人和美国人 / 154
- Text 2 Stargazing Basics 观星常识 / 159
- Text 3 The Strange Voyage of the Mary Celeste "玛丽·莎莉丝特"号奇怪的航行 / 162

Contents

Unit Fifteen ... 165
- Text 1 Work and Happiness 工作和快乐 / 165
- Text 2 The Scientific Method 科学研究的方法 / 170
- Text 3 Fishing 垂钓 / 174

Unit Sixteen ... 177
- Text 1 McDonald's Targets Starbucks 麦当劳叫板星巴克 / 178
- Text 2 Is EU Lost in Translation? 欧盟在翻译中迷失了吗？/ 182
- Text 3 Secrets of Self-Made Millionaires 成为百万富翁的秘密 / 186

Unit Seventeen ... 190
- Text 1 Want to Stay Warm in Winters? Think COLD
  在冬天想要保暖,想想"COLD"吧 / 190
- Text 2 Pockety Women Unite 穿口袋服装的女士们团结起来 / 194
- Text 3 The Role of Supplements in Health and Nutrition
  添加剂在健康和营养中的角色 / 198

Unit Eighteen ... 201
- Text 1 Numerology—Using Numbers to Predict the Future
  数字命理学—使用数字预测未来 / 201
- Text 2 Internet Addiction 网络成瘾 / 206
- Text 3 Can Animals Sense Earthquakes? 动物能感知地震吗？/ 210

附录（Appendix） ... 213

参考答案（Keys） ... 241

参考文献（References） ... 261

Unit One

Text 1 (Intensive Reading)

Background Tips: Ivy League

Ivy League, eight long-established colleges and universities in the United States with prestigious academic and social reputations. Members of the Ivy League are **Brown University** in Providence, Rhode Island; **Columbia University** in New York City; **Cornell University** in Ithaca, New York; **Dartmouth College** in Hanover, New Hampshire; **Harvard University** in Cambridge, Massachusetts; **University of Pennsylvania** in Philadelphia; Princeton University in Princeton, New Jersey; and **Yale University** in New Haven, Connecticut. The members of the Ivy League compete in intercollegiate athletics.

Planning for Study in the United States
留学美国的规划

Applying to college in the United States from another country can be exciting and challenging. It also can be frustrating—but it need not be difficult if you get accurate information and follow the required procedures carefully.

There are almost a half million students from other countries enrolled at nearly 3,000 two-year and four-year colleges and graduate institutions in the United States. This represents a little over 3 percent of the U.S. higher education enrollment each year. Many of these institutions have more applicants than they can accept in any year. As a result, college admission can be very competitive, especially for applicants from outside the United States.

The key to successful admission lies in careful planning and timely completion of the required steps. Keep in mind the following advice during your college planning.

Begin planning about 18 months before the date you wish to start studying in the United States. Contact universities that interest you at least one year in advance.

Identify the things that are most important to you when looking for a college in the United States. Make a list of those characteristics to help you compare among the colleges that interest you.

If you have access to the Internet, college web sites are a rich source of information about degrees and courses offered, costs, students services, financial aid, and some even provide a virtual campus tour!

Consult an educational advising center. Locate the one nearest you in the list of international advising centers.

Talk with students in the country who have studies in the United States to get practical advice.

Start planning your college budget. Be realistic about how you will pay for your education.

If you plan to apply for scholarships, do so before leaving home. Little financial help is available once the school year starts, even for U.S. students.

Be sure that the source of your information is current and correct. It is best not to rely on hearsay or someone else's experience. Contact the admission office of the university directly to get information and instructions about admission.

Complete all the steps in the admission and financial aid process as early as possible. If you do not understand why a college asks for particular information or requires a particular process, ask them for more information about it.

(383 words)

Word List

challenging	[ˈtʃælɪndʒɪŋ]	adj.	具有挑战性的
frustrating	[frʌˈstreitɪŋ]	adj.	令人沮丧的
accurate	[ˈækjʊrət]	adj.	精确的, 准确的
procedure	[prəˈsiːdʒə]	n.	程序, 步骤
enroll	[ɪnˈrəʊl]	v.	注册, 登记
represent	[ˌriːprɪzent]	v.	代表
applicant	[ˈæplɪkənt]	n.	申请人
admission	[ədˈmɪʃən]	n.	录取, 承认
competitive	[kəmˈpetɪtɪv]	adj.	具有竞争性的
timely	[ˈtaɪmlɪ]	adj.	及时的
contact	[ˈkɒntækt]	v.	联系
identify	[aɪˈdentɪfaɪ]	v.	辨认, 识别
characteristic	[ˌkærɪktəˈrɪstɪk]	n.	特色, 特点
compare	[kəmˈpeə]	v.	比较, 对比
financial	[faɪˈnænʃəl]	adj.	经济的, 金融的
aid	[eɪd]	n.	资助, 帮助
virtual	[ˈvɜːtʃuəl]	adj.	实际的, 真正的
locate	[ləʊˈkeɪt]	v.	确定, 定位
budget	[ˈbʌdʒɪt]	n.	预算
realistic	[rɪəˈlɪstɪk]	adj.	务实的, 现实的
current	[ˈkʌrənt]	adj.	当前的, 现今的

Unit One

Idioms & Expressions

as a result	因此	lie in	存在于,缘于
keep sth in mind	牢记	in advance	提前
have access to	接触,得到		

Exercises

1. [Definitions]

Match the words in the box with their meanings. Write the word that stands for the definition in the appropriate answer space.

frustrating	accurate	enroll	represent	applicant
admission	competitive	identify	characteristic	consult
budget	realistic	scholarship	available	hearsay

1) _____: someone who has formally asked, usually in writing, for a job, university place, etc.

2) _____: permission given to someone to enter a building or place, or to become a member of a school, club etc.

3) _____: to officially speak or take action for another person or group of people.

4) _____: something that you have heard through another rather than directly.

5) _____: to officially arrange to join a school, university, or course, or to arrange for someone else to do this.

6) _____: correct and true in every detail.

7) _____: an amount of money that is given to someone by an educational organization to help pay for their education.

8) _____: to recognize and correctly name someone or something.

9) _____: a quality or feature of something or someone that is typical of them and easy to recognize.

10) _____: to ask for information or advice from someone because it is their job to know something.

11) _____: the money that is available to an organization or person, or a plan of how it will be spent.

12) _____: judging and dealing with situations in a practical way according to what is actually possible rather than what you would like to happen.

13) _____: determined or trying very hard to be more successful than other people or businesses.

14) _____: be able to be used or can easily be bought or found.

15) _____: making you feel annoyed, upset, or impatient because you cannot do what you want to do.

2. [Sample Sentences]

Use the new words you have learned from the box in the following sentence. Change the form where necessary.

1) I _____ at the University of Vienna.

2) Can you _____ your umbrella among this lot?

3) Stop daydreaming and be _____.

4) Judgment should be based on facts, not on _____.

5) Ambition is a _____ of all successful businessmen.

6) _____ to British universities depends on examination results.

7) Nobody can entirely keep away from this _____ world.

8) After two hours' _____ delay, our train at last arrived.

9) As the wages were low, there were few _____ for the job.

10) I will have to _____ my principals before I can give you an answer on that.

11) Congress has approved the new educational _____.

12) We might have a free press, but that doesn't mean all reporting is true and _____.

13) She has been awarded a _____ to study at Harvard.

14) You will be informed when the book becomes _____.

15) This essay _____ a considerable improvement on your recent work.

3. [Translation]

A. Translate the following English sentences into Chinese.

1) Applying to college in the United States from another country can be exciting and challenging.

2) College admission can be very competitive, especially for applicants from outside the United States.

3) The key to successful admission lies in careful planning and timely completion of the required steps.

4) Little financial help is available once the school year starts, even for U.S. students.

5) It is best not to rely on hearsay or someone else's experience.

B. Translate the following Chinese sentences into English by using the word in the bracket.

1) 如今,许多大学毕业生都在积极报名上 MBA 课程。(enroll)

2) 玫瑰是英格兰的象征。(represent)

3) 指望经济马上复苏很不现实。(realistic)

4) 那本书一到就通知你。(available)

5) 下一年度的预算将大幅度削减。(budget)

4.【Writing】

Suppose your friend Wang Kai is planning to study abroad, write him a letter of 150-200 words in English about your advice on his application. You should emphasize the following points:

1) A brief introduction about the requirements by foreign universities.
2) Some detailed procedures needed for a successful application.
3) The importance of English in the application process.

Reading Skills：生词破解法(1)

英语词汇浩如烟海,层出不穷。因此,在阅读文章的过程中遭遇生词在所难免。如果不能理解生词,文章理解就会受阻。但是,一遇到生词就查阅字典,会占用很多时间,特别是考试中也不允许这样做。有鉴于此,学会在不同的语境中猜测生词含义对于增强阅读理解、提升阅读速度是不可或缺的。下面介绍几种比较常用的猜词方法。

1. 定义解释法：

顾名思义,该方法就是通过对某一名词(通常是专有名词或术语名词)进行解释,说明其内容或特点。破解该名词的关键就是寻找具有下定义属性的词汇以及该词前后的某些关键词汇。常见的下定义的标记词有：

be concerned with, be regarded as, be defined as, be termed/called, refer to, mean, 等。

例 1：The animals whose temperature is regulated by internal metabolic process are called **endotherms** and those whose temperature is regulated by the environment, and who get most of their heat from the environment are called **ectotherms**.

句中出现了关键词组 **are called**,说明这是一个下定义句。通过定义可知,**endotherm** 是一种动物,其体温由体内的新陈代谢过程来调节,即"恒温动物、温血动物"。同理,体温由外部环境来调节的动物即"变温动物、冷血动物"。

例2：The science of **meteorology** is concerned with the study of the structure, state, and behaviour of the atmosphere.

句中出现了关键词组 **is concerned with**，说明这也是一个下定义句。通过定义可知，**meteorology** 是研究大气的结构、状态以及行为的科学，即"气象学"。

2. 对比推测法：

对比推测法就是寻找具有对比、比较意义的词汇，其前后的内容必定相反，这样就可通过已知信息推出生词的大致含义。常见的表比较、对照的词或短语有：**but, however, unlike, although, rather than, instead of, on the other hand,** 等。

例1：Unlike his **gregarious** brother, Albert is very shy, not liking to go to parties, or making new friends.

句中出现了关键词 **unlike**，可以迅速推出 **gregarious** 与后面的 **shy** 等内容意义相反，所以 **gregarious** 的含义是"爱社交的，合群的"。

例2：He is usually **loquacious**, but today he is quite silent.

句中 **but** 之后的 **silent** 是已知信息，由此推断，**loquacious** 的含义与之相反，即"健谈的，爱说话的"。

Text 2 (Extensive Reading)

The English Character
英国人的性格

To other Europeans, the best known quality of the British, and in particular of the English, is "reserved." A reserved person is one who does not talk very much to strangers, does not show much emotion, and seldom gets excited. It is difficult to get to know a reserved person: he never tells you anything about himself, and you may work with him for years without ever knowing where he lives, how many children he has, and what his interests are. English people tend to be like that.

If they are making a journey by bus they will do their best to find an empty seat; if by train, an empty apartment. If they have to share an apartment with a stranger, they may travel many miles without starting a conversation. If a conversation does start, personal questions like "How old are you?" or even "What is your name?" are not easily asked.

This reluctance to communicate with others is an unfortunate quality in some ways since it tends to give the impression of coldness, and it is true that the English (except perhaps in the North) are not noted for their generosity and hospitality. On the other hand, they are perfectly human behind their barrier of reserve, and may be quite pleased when a friendly stranger or foreigner succeeds for some time in breaking the barrier down. We may also mention at this point that the people of the North and West, especially the Welsh, are much less reserved than those of the South and East.

Closely related to English reserve is English modesty. Within their hearts, the English are perhaps no less conceited than anybody else, but in their relations with others they value at least a show of modesty. Self-praise is felt to be impolite. If a person is, let us say, very good at tennis and someone asks him if he is a good player, he will seldom reply "Yes," because people will think him conceited. He will probably give an answer like, "I'm not bad," or "I think I am very good," or "Well, I'm very keen on tennis." Even if he had managed to reach the finals in last year's local championships, he would say it in such a way as to suggest that it was only due to a piece of good luck.

The famous English sense of humor is similar. Its starting-point is self-dispraise, and its great enemy is conceit. Its object is the ability to laugh at oneself—at one's own faults, one's own failure, even at one's own ideals. The criticism, "He has no sense of humor" is very commonly heard in Britain, where humor is highly prized. A sense of humor is an attitude to life rather than the mere ability to laugh at jokes. This attitude is never cruel or disrespectful or malicious. The English do not laugh at a cripple or a madman, or a tragedy or an honorable failure.

Since reserve, a show of modesty and a sense of humor are part of his own nature, the typical Englishman trends to expect them in others. He secretly looks down on more excitable nations, and likes to think of himself as more reliable than they. He doesn't trust big promises and open shows of feelings, especially if they are expressed in flowery language. He doesn't trust self-praise of any kind. This applies not only to what other people may tell him about themselves orally, but to the letters they may write to him. To those who are fond of flowery expressions, the Englishman may appear uncomfortably cold.

Finally, sportsmanship. Like a sense of humor, this is an English ideal which not all Englishmen live up to. It must be realized that sport in its modern form is almost entirely a British invention. Boxing, rugby, football, hockey, tennis and cricket were all first organized and given rules in Britain. Rules are the essence of sport, and sportsmanship is the ability to practice a sport according to its rules, while also showing generosity to one's opponent and good temper in defeat. The high pressure of modern international sport makes these ideals difficult to keep, but they are at least highly valued in Britain and are certainly achieved there more commonly than among more excitable peoples. Moreover, sportsmanship as an ideal is applied to life in general. This is proved by the number of sporting terms used in ordinary speech. Everyone talks of "fair play" and "playing the game" or "playing fair." Borrowed from boxing, "straight from the shoulder" is used to describe a well-aimed, strong criticism and "below the belt" is used to describe an unfair one. One of the most elementary rules of life is "never hit a man when he is down"—in other words, never take advantage of a person's misfortune. English schoolboys often show this sense of sportsmanship to a surprisingly high degree in their relations with each other.

(824 words)

Word List

reserved	[rɪˈzɜːvd]	adj.	矜持的,缄默的
reserve	[rɪˈzɜːv]	n.	矜持,缄默
emotion	[ɪˈməʊʃən]	n.	感情,激情
reluctance	[rɪˈlʌktəns]	n.	不情愿,不乐意
communicate	[kəˈmjuːnɪkeɪt]	v.	交流,交际
unfortunate	[ʌnˈfɔːtʃənɪt]	adj.	不幸的
generosity	[ˌdʒenəˈrɒsɪtɪ]	n.	慷慨,大方
hospitality	[ˌhɒspɪˈtælɪtɪ]	n.	热情好客
barrier	[ˈbærɪə]	n.	障碍
modesty	[ˈmɒdɪstɪ]	n.	谦卑,谦逊
conceited	[kənˈsiːtɪd]	adj.	骄傲的,自负的
championship	[ˈtʃæmpɪənʃɪp]	n.	锦标赛,冠军称号
ideal	[aɪˈdɪəl]	n.	理想,崇尚之物
mere	[mɪə]	adj.	仅仅的,不过
disrespectful	[ˌdɪsrɪsˈpektfʊl]	adj.	无礼的,不尊重的
malicious	[məˈlɪʃəs]	adj.	恶毒的
cripple	[ˈkrɪpəl]	n.	瘸子,残疾人
honorable	[ˈɒnərəbl]	adj.	高尚的,可敬的
excitable	[ɪkˈsaɪtəbl]	adj.	易兴奋的,易激动的
flowery	[ˈflaʊərɪ]	adj.	(语言)矫饰的,过于华丽的
sportsmanship	[ˈspɔːtsmənʃɪp]	n.	运动员风范,运动员资格
opponent	[əˈpəʊnənt]	n.	对手,敌手
elementary	[ˌelɪˈmentərɪ]	adj.	基础的,基本的
misfortune	[mɪsˈfɔːtʃən]	n.	不幸,厄运

Idioms & Expressions

in particular	特别是,尤其是	communicate with	与……交流
on the other hand	另一方面	break down	克服,冲破
be good at	擅长……	be fond of	喜欢
live up to	达到……的标准;遵照	in other words	换言之
to ... degree	达到……的程度	take advantage of	占……的便宜,利用

8

Unit One

Exercises

1. [Questions]

Based on the information provided in the text, answer the following questions briefly.

1) What are the typical characteristics of being "reserved"?

2) Give examples to show that the English are "reserved."

3) What is the starting-point of the English sense of humor?

4) In summary, what are the most striking qualities of the English?

5) What is sportsmanship? How should this ideal be applied to life in general?

2. [Multiple Choices]

Choose the right answer from the four choices marked A, B, C, and D.

1) Other Europeans normally regard the English as _____.
   A. open-minded   B. radical
   C. frugal   D. reserved

2) The author thinks the English are reluctant to communicate with others is unfortunate because _____.
   A. they may lose the chance of knowing more friends
   B. this reluctance will lead to insularity
   C. other people may feel them to be very cold
   D. they will lose passion and enthusiasm

3) Another noted quality of the English is _____.
   A. modesty   B. arrogance
   C. frugality   D. extravagance

4) The Englishman may appear uncomfortably cold to _____.
   A. those who are unfriendly
   B. those who like to use beautiful yet superficial expressions
   C. those who are selfish
   D. those who are frugal

5) Which of the following sporting terms is NOT directly borrowed from boxing?
   A. playing the game   B. never hit a man when he is down
   C. below the belt   D. straight from the shoulder

Text 3 (Fast Reading)

Language Teaching
语言教学

Foreign languages, have, of course, been taught in schools, colleges, and universities for generations. Moreover, in all education systems, in all countries throughout the world, the importance of being able to speak a second language is gaining recognition. More often than not, the language is English, given its importance as the language of international communication. Yet, traditionally the concept of teaching language with the aim of developing students ability to use the language effectively to communicate ideas and thoughts has taken second place to the acquisition of language as a knowledge that can easily be tested using formal examinations. The need for effective and efficient forms of communication, however, is of vital importance to a modern economic system that is built upon international trade. This has facilitated much research in the field of language learning and teaching and has resulted in a swing from the traditional grammar translation method that can easily be tested, to a modern-day communicative approach that cannot.

The communicative approach to language teaching focuses on students using new language structures, vocabulary and stylistic texts (formal, informal, etc) presented by the teacher. Thus, under the teacher's guidance students become involved in situational appropriate activities in the classroom (role-plays, debates, etc)—a method of teaching that has proven itself to be a far more effective way of developing communication skills than the traditional grammar translation method. Further research, however, has developed other hypotheses about language acquisition. The most recent concerns the working of the memory which has traditionally been neglected, even in the modern communicative approach. Yet it is precisely the working of the human memory that may hold the key to further developments in language teaching, leading to even greater success in the classroom.

The success of the communicative approach has been linked to student motivation, contextual language learning and memorization of sentences through "doing", the effectiveness of which is not in doubt. Moreover, and possibly more relevant, is that the communicative approach neglects to "teach" grammar. Instead, a grammar structure is presented by the teacher as a focus for students' attention. Other than this the structure is presented by the students during discussions and role-plays. Indeed, there are often academic discussions as to whether the teaching of grammar should form part of language learning at all!

The real key for language learning, however, is accuracy. Without accuracy communication becomes strained and severely limited. Yet accurate use of any language relies upon the accurate and appropriate use of the grammar structure, and this is where the new theory differs from the previous ones. In the new "skills based approach", grammar is seen not as a knowledge, but as a skill, which contradicts both the traditional grammar translation method and the modern communicative approach.

The skills based approach views the learning of grammar as a skill just like any other, such as playing a piano or riding a bicycle. In fact, research with patients who have suffered severe memory loss due to accident or illness shows that they never forget skills they'd previously learnt such as playing the piano, riding a bicycle and language. This is even the case in very severe incidences where a lifetime of memories has been deleted, even up to the point of not knowing their own identity!

It is well documented that there is a memory for knowledge and a memory for skills that operate as two very distinct sources of memories in separate parts of the brain. However, for memories to become automated skills, those skills must be preceded by knowledge. A good example would be learning to type. If you are taught how to operate a computer key board, where certain keys are pressed by certain fingers, then with practice the skill of typing becomes extremely fast, accurate and easy—it no longer requires thinking about where to place your fingers. Yet without the initial knowledge one's typing ability will never succeed beyond the clumsy, inaccurate and painfully slow stage, regardless of practice: the new theory simply translates this approach into language learning.

In the new approach grammar structures are taught, and students are allowed to practice the structure under the guidance of a teacher until the skills of using the structure becomes automated. Although the approach sounds laborious, and may open itself to criticism for failing to motivate students, several structures can be practiced simultaneously to allow students a better "feel" for the language, while at the same time teaching new vocabulary and making the classroom exercises interesting and stimulating for the learning.

Vocabulary, however, is still taught as knowledge for the simple reason that the new approach assumes this to be case. Indeed, even when communicating using your own language it is often the case that you may have to search for appropriate words or phrases to precisely express your meaning. This is because you have to search through your long-term memory store—vocabulary is stored as knowledge, and not as an automated skill. However, if grammar is taught as subject knowledge to be tested in a formal examination it will always be stored as such, leading to the production of clumsy, inaccurate sentence structures regardless of how much practice the student allows him or herself.   (868 words)

Exercises

1. [Questions]

Decide whether the following statements are True, False or Not Given.

T (for True) if the statement agrees with the information given in the passage;

F (for False) if the statement doesn't agree with the information given in the passage;

NG (for Not Given) if the information is not given in the passage.

1) The passage talks about two new approaches to teaching a foreign language.
2) All countries consider the teaching of English to be very important.
3) The traditional grammar translation method was commonly used because it is easily tested in examinations.
4) Modern approaches to language learning consider how the memory works.
5) The communicative approach teaches language in context.
6) Students find the skill based approach interesting and stimulating.
7) In the skill based approach, vocabulary is treated as knowledge rather than a skill.

2. [Blank-Filling]

For questions 1)–3), complete the sentences with the information given in the passage.

1) In the communicative approach, under the teacher's guidance, students are engaged in _____ activities in the classroom.
2) In order for memories to become automated skills, _____ should be memorized first before the memory of skills.
3) In the skill based approach, grammar is taught to students until _____ becomes automated.

Unit Two

Text 1 (Intensive Reading)

Background Tips: British Universities

Britain has more than 90 universities. British universities can be divided into several categories. The foremost universities are the University of Oxford and the University of Cambridge, both founded in the Middle Ages. The term Oxbridge is used to refer to both schools as a single entity, much as Americans would use the term Ivy League in reference to the group of prestigious East Coast universities. Scotland has equivalent ancient institutions at Edinburgh, Glasgow, and St. Andrews. Another type of university is the so-called redbrick variety—old and solid schools built in the 19th century when bricks were the standard building material. The large number of ultramodern universities that sprouted up in the last half of the 20th century are often called cement block and plateglass universities. London has its own great schools, the enormous University of London and its world-famous college, the London School of Economics.

Tertiary Education in the UK
英国的高等教育

University teaching in the United Kingdom is very different at both undergraduate and graduate levels from that of many overseas countries.

An undergraduate course consists of a series of lectures, seminars and tutorials, and, in science and engineering, laboratory classes which in total account for about 15 hours per week. Arts students may well find that their official contact with teachers is less than this average, while science and engineering students may be expected to be timetabled for up to 20 hours per week. Students studying for a particular degree will take a series of lecture courses which run in parallel at a fixed time in each week and may last one academic term or the whole year. Associated with each lecture course are seminars, tutorials and laboratory classes which draw upon, analyze, illustrate or amplify the topics presented in the lectures. Lecture classes can vary in size from 20 to 200 although larger sized lectures tend to decrease as students progress into the second and third year and more options become available. Seminars and tutorials are on the whole much smaller than lecture classes and in some departments can be on a one-to-one basis (that is, one member of staff to one student).

Students are normally expected to prepare work in advance for seminars and tutorials and this can take the form of researching a topic for discussion, by writing essays or by solving problems. Lectures, seminars and tutorials are all one hour in length, while laboratory classes usually last either 2 or 3 hours. Much emphasis is put on how to spend as much time if not more studying by themselves as being taught. In the UK it is still common for people to say they are "reading" for a degree! Each student has a tutor whom they can consult on any matter whether academic or personal. Although the tutor will help, motivation for study is expected to come from the student.

(324 words)

Word List

tertiary	[ˈtɜːʃərɪ]	adj.	第三的,高等教育的
undergraduate	[ˌʌndəˈɡrædʒueɪt]	n.	大学生
graduate	[ˈɡrædʒueɪt]	n.	研究生
lecture	[ˈlektʃə]	n.	讲课,讲座
seminar	[ˈsemɪnɑː]	n.	专题研讨会
tutorial	[tjuːˈtɔːrɪəl]	n.	(大学导师的)辅导课
engineering	[ˌendʒɪˈnɪərɪŋ]	n.	工科,工程学
timetable	[ˈtaɪmˌteɪbəl]	v.	为……定时间表
analyze	[ˈænəlaɪz]	v.	分析
illustrate	[ˈɪləstreɪt]	v.	阐述,解释
amplify	[ˈæmplɪˌfaɪ]	v.	放大,增强
vary	[ˈveərɪ]	v.	变化,不同
option	[ˈɒpʃən]	n.	选择
available	[əˈveɪləbəl]	adj.	可提供的,可得到的
staff	[stɑːf]	n.	(全体)员工
consult	[kənˈsʌlt]	v.	咨询
academic	[ˌækəˈdemɪk]	adj.	学术的
motivation	[ˌməʊtɪˈveɪʃən]	n.	动机,动力

Idioms & Expressions

consist of	由……组成,包括	a series of	一系列
in total	总共	account for	占(比例)
up to	多达	in parallel	平行,并列
academic term	学期	on the whole	总体上
on a one-to-one basis	一对一	in advance	提前
take the form of	采用……的形式		

14

Unit Two

Exercises

1. [Definitions]

Match the words in the box with their meanings. Write the word that stands for the definition in the appropriate answer space.

tertiary	undergraduate	seminar	tutorial	engineering
timetable	parallel	analyze	illustrate	amplify
vary	option	available	staff	motivation

1) _____: a period of teaching and discussion with a tutor, especially in a British university.
2) _____: increase in size, volume or significance.
3) _____: eagerness and willingness to do something without needing to be told or forced to do it.
4) _____: be able to be used or can easily be bought or found.
5) _____: a university student who has not yet received a first degree.
6) _____: coming next after the second and just before the fourth in position.
7) _____: to examine or think about something carefully, in order to understand it.
8) _____: a class at a university or college for a small group of students and a teacher to study or discuss a particular subject.
9) _____: to make the meaning of something clearer by giving examples.
10) _____: (of two or more straight lines) being the same distance apart along all their length.
11) _____: to change or be different, esp. from one occasion to another or from one item to another within a group, or to cause this to happen.
12) _____: a group of people who work for an organization, often for a special purpose, or who work for a manager within an organization.
13) _____: to arrange the times at which classes will take place in a school or college.
14) _____: a choice one makes in a particular situation.
15) _____: the work involved in designing and building roads, bridges, machines etc.

2. [Sample Sentences]

Use the new words you have learned from the box in the following sentence. Change the form where necessary.

1) One's attendance at a professor's _____ and seminar is very important.
2) These stories only _____ her fears.
3) Jack is an intelligent pupil, but he lacks _____.

4) You need to sit down and _____ why you feel so upset.

5) A course of study for graduate and advanced _____ students in a college or university, conducted in the manner of a seminar.

6) Many students like the _____ given by professor John.

7) She pointed at the diagram to _____ her point.

8) Take the road running _____ to the main road just after the village.

9) The value of stocks will _____ from month to month.

10) Our department has a _____ of fifty.

11) The carnival parade is _____ for 9:00 am.

12) Teenage mothers often have no _____ but to live with their parents.

13) My major is the subject of chemical _____.

14) Escape from reality can be a strong _____ for travel.

15) _____ education normally means higher education in the UK.

3. 【Translation】

A. Translate the following English sentences into Chinese.

1) Medical care varies greatly from country to country.

2) There are plenty of jobs available in the area.

3) She illustrated her point with diagrams.

4) The painting is parallel to the greatest artistic level.

5) The pyramids are a testimony to the Ancient Egyptians' engineering skills.

B. Translate the following Chinese sentences into English by using the word in the bracket.

1) 在这件事情上，我的经验和你的类似。(parallel)

2) 这门课安排在每周一。(timetable)

3) 遗传工程将对人类产生深远的影响。(engineering)

4) 他除了同意之外别无选择。(option)

5) 你当老师的动机是什么？(motivation)

4.【Writing】

Write an article of 150-200 words in English. Use the ideas given below.

Title: Why do many Chinese students love to go abroad?
Introduction: An increasing number of Chinese students choose to go abroad.
Development: The reasons for this phenomenon are diversified.
Conclusion: Whether to stay at home or go abroad is up to the student himself. But this choice should be rational and well-thought.

Reading Skills: 生词破解法(2)

1. 相关信息法：

有时，一个句子里的生词无法用前文提到的定义解释进行识别，也不能用对比对照等方法进行破解。我们需要另辟蹊径，这里介绍的相关信息法就是其中之一。顾名思义，相关信息就是句间的逻辑关系，通过一定的逻辑关系，生词就可以迎刃而解，至少可以推导出其大致含义，使得阅读能够自然顺畅。

例1：Smith is considered an **autocratic** administrator because he makes decisions without seeking the opinions of others.

这里的 **autocratic** 具有一定的难度，但是其后 **because** 引导的原因状语从句告诉我们："该管理者做决策时从不征询他人意见"，因此其行为特点就是 **autocratic**，即"独断专行的"。

例2：Knowing that a small error may mean losing the job, Tom **gingerly** carried the expensive artware out of the room.

该句可以分为两部分，**knowing... the job** 是原因状语，即"他知道一个小失误就可能意味着被炒鱿鱼"，后面的 **Tom... the room** 是主干部分，是前面原因状语产生的结果，即"（于是）他就……拿着那件艺术品走出房间"。根据上下逻辑，可以推断所空缺的部分，即 **gingerly** 大致的意思是"谨慎地，小心翼翼地"。

例3：Jane **piqued** Hanks by refusing his invitation.

该句也可看作两部分，**by** 引导的是方式状语，大意是"**Jane** 拒绝了 **Hanks** 的邀请"；**Jane piqued Hanks** 是主干部分，其中的 **pique** 是生词。不过借助方式状语，我们还是能够推导出 **Jane** 使得 **Hanks...**，空缺处的生词 **pique** 一定是贬义词，由此可知其大意是"使生气，使恼火"。

例4：The purpose of the campaign was to catch "**ringers**", students who take tests for other students.

ringer 是比较生僻的词汇，但根据语法知识，可知其后的 **students... other students** 是其同位语，大意是"替人考试者"，因此，这就是 **ringer** 的本意，即俗称的"枪手"。

2. 一词多义的理解：

1) The play had **run** for only a week.
2) **run** a business
3) **run** a computer
4) **run** a temperature
5) **run** one's own life
6) **run** lights

在阅读过程中，经常也会遇到熟词生义的现象，以上的 **run** 即是这个问题。6个例句中 **run** 的意思分别是：1) 连续上映；2) 经营，管理；3) 操作，使用；4) 发（烧）；5) 过（日子）；6) 闯（红灯）。要提高这方面的能力，就要勤查字典，尤其关注一些小词多重含义的现象，也就是尽可能多留心这些小词之后列出的多个词条。日积月累，循环往复，词汇识别能力就会渐有提高。

Text 2 (Extensive Reading)

Who Am I?
我是谁？

In 1880 my great-grandfather, an illiterate peasant, left his small village in southern China for San Francisco, California, in search of his father, who had disappeared during the construction of the transcontinental road. At about the same time, Angelia's family crossed America in a covered wagon and settled in Washington. By the late 1890s, after years of hard labor, my great-grandfather set up his own small firm. Angelia had run away from home and ended up in San Francisco. When no one would hire a single, uneducated woman, she drifted into Chinatown and my great-grandfather's firm, where she begged him for a job. He hired her, one thing led to another, and they decided to get married.

It was against the law in California and many other states for Chinese and Caucasians to marry. It was also against the law for Chinese to own property in California, and unlawful at the federal level for Chinese to become naturalized citizens. When Chinese had literally been driven from western towns—when they weren't hung, shot, burned or stabbed by members of the white community, the latter had no fear of retribution because Chinese couldn't testify in court against Caucasians.

But with a contract marriage drawn up by a lawyer, my great-grandparents set out to achieve the American Dream. My great-grandfather and Angelia raised five children and ran four stores in southern California. He was the first Chinese to own an automobile and was one of the few Chinese to do business with the white community. Despite these successes, my great-grandfather's four sons—all American-born citizens—had to go to Mexico to marry their Caucasian fiancés.

　　Drop down another two generations. I am only one-eighth Chinese, with red hair and freckles. People often ask me where I fit in and how I define myself. My answer has to do with where I grew up and what I saw around me. My great-grandfather had four wives, as Chinese traditional codes dictate for men with great wealth and prowess, so the Chinese side of my family in Los Angeles numbers close to 400, with only a handful that look like me. It's been 130 years since my great-great-grandfather left China, and we've become educated, changed our way of dress and lost our Cantonese. But there's a deep core that connects to our peasant ancestors.

　　Many small rituals in my daily life mirror what I experienced as a child. I tell my sons to put only what they're going to eat on their plates, and I still pick at their discarded chicken bones. When they want comfort food, I cook them rice.(Shortly after going to college, my older son called to announce happily that the girls next door had a rice cooker.) When my younger son boasted that he'd told his chemistry teacher to stop checking her e-mail during class, I made him go back the next day with a gift of a perfect orange and apology.

　　I do look different, and nothing will ever change that or people's reactions. At my baby shower, some friends mistook my father, a professor, for a Chinese waiter. I've had Chinese Americans and Chinese-in-China talk about me as though I weren't there: "I had a cousin from the south who looked like her, but her hair is disgusting." On book tours, Caucasians will often ask pointblank, "Why would you choose to be Chinese when you have all the privileges of being white?" Given my family and the era in which I grew up, I don't know I had a choice.

　　The last of America's miscegenation laws were overturned in 1965. Intermarriage is common, and if you walk into a classroom today, it's impossible to tell a child's exact race, or what race or ethnicity he or she may identify with. You certainly can't with my own sons, who are only-sixteenth Chinese and otherwise Irish, English, Scottish, Spanish, Russian, German, Austrian and Polish. I tell it's up to them to choose their own identity—just so long as they marry nice Chinese girls. They think I'm kidding. I'm not, really. Who, I wonder, is going to cook them nice rice?

(689 words)

Word List

- illiterate [ɪˈlɪtərɪt] *adj.* 没文化的,不识字的
- transcontinental [ˌtrænzkɒntɪˈnentəl] *adj.* 跨州的
- Caucasian [kɔːˈkeɪzɪən] *n.* 白种人,高加索人
- property [ˈprɒpəti] *n.* 财产,房产
- naturalize [ˈnætʃərəlaɪz] *v.* 使(外国人)入国籍
- literally [ˈlɪtərəli] *adv.* 实际上

retribution	[ˌretrɪˈbjuːʃən]	n.	惩罚,报应
testify	[ˈtestɪfaɪ]	v.	作证,证明
freckle	[ˈfrekəl]	n.	雀斑
define	[dɪˈfaɪn]	v.	定义,界定
code	[kəʊd]	n.	准则,原则
dictate	[dɪkˈteɪt]	v.	规定,指定
prowess	[ˈpraʊɪs]	n.	才能,技能
Cantonese	[ˌkæntəˈniːz]	n.	广东话
ancestor	[ˈænsəstə]	n.	祖先
discard	[dɪsˈkɑːd]	v.	遗弃,抛弃
boast	[bəʊst]	v.	吹嘘,夸耀
apology	[əˈpɒlədʒɪ]	n.	道歉
reaction	[riːˈækʃən]	n.	反应
disgusting	[dɪsˈɡʌstɪŋ]	adj.	令人厌恶的
privilege	[ˈprɪvɪlɪdʒ]	n.	特权,优势
era	[ˈɪərə]	n.	时代
miscegenation	[ˌmɪsɪdʒəˈneɪʃən]	n.	种族通婚
overturn	[ˌəʊvəˈtɜːn]	v.	推翻
intermarriage	[ˌɪntəˈmærɪ]	n.	异族通婚
ethnicity	[ˈeθnɪsɪtɪ]	n.	种族划分
kid	[kɪd]	v.	开玩笑,逗乐

Idioms & Expressions

draw up	起草,制定	set out to do	开始做某事,着手做某事
shortly after...	不久,很快	baby shower	(基督教)婴儿受洗礼
mistake... for...	把……误认为……	as though	似乎,好像
book tour	巡回书展	be up to...	由……决定
so long as	只要		

Exercises

1.【Questions】

Based on the information provided in the text, answer the following questions briefly.

1) Why did my great-grandfather leave his hometown for San Francisco?

2) What caused my great-grandfather to marry Angelia?

3) Describe briefly the laws against Chinese in California.

4) What are some of the small rituals in my daily life?

5) What does the author mean by saying "Who, I wonder, is going to cook them nice rice?"?

2. [Multiple Choices]

Choose the right answer from the four choices marked A, B, C, and D.

1) The passage is written by a _____.
   A. second-generation American Japanese
   B. fourth-generation American Chinese
   C. third-generation American Chinese
   D. Chinese immigrant

2) In the 1890s, the California law allowed _____.
   A. my great-grandfather to marry Angelia
   B. my great-grandfather to own property in the state
   C. my great-grandfather to become a naturalized citizen
   D. my great-grandfather to work in the United States

3) It can be inferred from para.3 that _____.
   A. the Chinese were all respected in California
   B. the Chinese enjoyed a high social status in the united States
   C. my great-grandfather's sons were not American citizens
   D. the author's great-grandparents basically realized their American Dream

4) The author's attitude toward her sons can be described as _____.
   A. cold   B. doting
   C. loving but strict   D. indulging

5) It can be inferred from the passage that _____.
   A. the author still thinks like a Chinese
   B. the author hates Chinese origin
   C. the author wants her sons to break away from their Chinese origin
   D. the author chose to be an American

Text 3 (Fast Reading)

London: Pollution at its Worst
伦敦：最糟糕的污染

London has been established as a major trading port, which has been the single most important factor in the wealth that the city has accumulated over the centuries. However, another influencing factor in the creation of the wealth the city is renowned for stems from the high degree of manufacturing that, up until the late 20th century, dominated part of the city. And today, it is well known throughout the world as one of the major financial centers, along with Paris, New York and Tokyo. However, it is also well known for being a city that is often covered in fog. Yet while there is truth in this belief, the truth derives from London of years gone by, and does not reflect the London of today.

The city itself is actually divided into east and west, known locally as the East End and the West End. The East End of London has traditionally served as the manufacturing centre of the city, whilst the West End, as is still the case toady, served as the financial centre, housing world famous institutions such as Lloyds of London and the Bank of England. Yet the city actually owes its wealth to the Industrial Revolution that began in England during the 18th century and served to shape the history of both the country itself, and the rest of the world. It was during this time that factories, with the inventions of mass producing goods at affordable prices, were invented. Yet it brought with it a price: pollution, from which London did not escape, and gave rise to the myth that existed—London fog.

London fog, as it is commonly referred to, was, in fact, not fog at all. Instead it was smog—a mixture of fog and smoke, produced by the burning of fossil fuels, such as coal, oil and gas, to produce the necessary to drive the factory machinery. And as the city's industrial sector grew, so did the amount of pollution that filled the surrounding air. In fact, it got so bad at certain times, for example, when there was an absence of wind to disperse the pollution, that on occasions it reached epidemic proportions, sometimes resulting in the deaths of many hundreds of people. The actual number of deaths that resulted from the smog, however, may never be known because whilst the deaths that arose from days when the pollution was at its worst can be counted, slower deaths, over longer periods of time cannot. Deaths from respiratory disorders such as asthma, for example, are not only difficult to assess in number, but it can never be certain that the illness was due to the pollution. It is therefore, more of a guessing game that it is hard, scientific evidence. What is known, however, is that the majority of the deaths occurred in the heavily industrialized East End of London where the factories were gathered. The deaths were made worse by the heavy concentration of people living in the area—ordinary poor workers whose salaries were all commonly so low that they were unable to afford an adequate diet or medication when they fell ill. The West End was reserved for the wealthy factory owners, enjoyed in the luxury of a relatively pollution free environment, as the wind, blowing west to east, drove the smog away from their dwellings and into the back yards of the workers.

Yet it wasn't restricted to air pollution. Chemically laden wastewater, pumped directly in the Thames that runs through the city, literally killed the river of all life with the exception of bacteria which was well adept at surviving in such hostile conditions. The bacteria that thrived on the pollution added problems of its own because the gas given off by the bacteria cause such a pungent smell during warm weather that the House of Parliament, which sits on the banks of Thames, were forced to hang heavy, lime-soaked curtains up at the windows in an attempt to absorb the overwhelming smell whenever the government were in a meeting. The problem became so serious, in fact, that the government were finally forced to take action, and arranged a series of reports to investigate the root cause of the problem, and offer potential solutions. The result was that a series of parliamentary acts were passed during the 18th and 19th centuries, and gradually the city became cleaner. Nevertheless, the serious smog remained. Indeed, even in the 1950s, London smog was so serious at times that cars and buses were forced to have to travel at walking pace, being led by a flag waving guide, to avoid accidents. However, the move away from the use of fossil fuels, to the use of natural gas, which reduced the pollution problem considerably, enabled the city to clean up its act once and for all. And even the Thames, at one time a dead river, began, once again, to teem again all kinds of wildlife, including fish, which are generally very sensitive to pollution.

A second contributing factor to the new, cleaner London was the shift from heavy manufacturing to service industries during the 1970s and the 1980s: a time which saw the enclosure of many factories, and the construction of office blocks. Thus the London of today is clean and relatively smog free. Nevertheless, it is still occasionally plagued with bouts of fog resulting from the country being, in fact, a small island. Yet it is rarely serious enough to cause any great concern. That is not to say, however, that London is a pollution free city. It is not. The pollution today, however, derives from other sources; the worst of these being the pollutant gases produced by overwhelming amount of traffic on London's roads. The centre of London, where most of the traffic converges, is especially vulnerable. And even the subway system and a newly built light railway hardly seem to even make a dent in the seriousness of the problem. In fact, it is often reported that the traffic in London moves so slowly that traveling around London was far quicker in the days of horse drawn carriages, worsening the need for an improved public transport system.

Over the centuries London, this world famous city, has seen many changes. Many decades of serious pollution resulted in government action that failed to fully solve the problem. Indeed, although smog is no longer a major issue, traffic fumes are necessitating the need for further action. Yet it seems that the action will come, not from government intervention, but from the advances in technology, especially computers that allow people to work anywhere, anytime, which is giving rise to new working patterns where people no longer have to gather in big cities in order to carry out their day's work. Thus, the London of tomorrow may well be as clean a city as any you are likely to find anywhere in the world. (1,157 words)

Exercises

1. [True, False, Not Given]

Decide whether the following statements are True, False or Not Given.

T (for True) if the statement agrees with the information given in the passage;

F (for False) if the statement doesn't agree with the information given in the passage;

NG (for Not Given) if the information is not given in the passage.

1) London is often covered in fog.
2) London is actually two cities joined together.
3) The number of deaths caused by the pollution is well known.
4) Poverty was also a major cause of deaths in London.
5) The Thames was so polluted at one point that nothing was able to live there.
6) Government intervention played an important role in making the city less polluted.
7) It is important to improve public transport in Britain.

2. [Blank-Filling]

For questions 1)–3), complete the sentences with the information given in the passage.

1) The fact that _____, has been the single most important factor in the wealth that the city has accumulated over the centuries.
2) During the _____ centuries, a series of parliamentary acts were passed, and gradually the city became cleaner.
3) During the _____, London was shifted from heavy manufacturing to service industries. As a result, many factories were closed and office blocks were constructed.

Unit Three

Text 1 (Intensive Reading)

Background Tips: United Nations Security Council

The United Nations is an international organization whose objective is to maintain peace and friendship among nations in the international arena. When member nations threaten the security of international diplomacy or institute laws or policies in their own countries that are antithetical to the UN's mission, other members can effectively paralyze that country's role in the United Nations.

The Security Council is the most powerful body in the UN. It is responsible for maintaining international peace, and for restoring peace when conflicts arise. Its decisions are binding on all UN members. The Security Council has the power to define what is a threat to security, to determine how the UN should respond, and to enforce its decisions by ordering UN members to take certain actions. For example, the Council may impose economic sanctions, such as halting trade with a country it considers an aggressor.

Live and Let Live—A New Strategy
互不相扰——一种新策略

For a given nation, to live means to pursue its own interests and to realize its rights of survival and developments. To let live refers to respecting the interests and rights of other nations. This simple and clear truth was summed up by our ancestors based on the same and simple fact that we have inhabited, and will continue to inhabit, a planet that is diverse in all aspects.

Superficially, few people find it hard to fathom the truth, or even deny it. In reality, however, there are countless cases that disquiet us. International wars, border skirmishes and racial conflicts, which unfortunately become the fabric of our daily discourse, have provided the evidence that this principle has not been fully accepted and really understood. So, it's still necessary to elaborate on the idea.

No country can really enjoy safety and prosperity without paying attention to others' living rights and conditions. As a matter of fact, the relationship between nations constitutes an important part of the history of human civilization. For those countries that fail to establish normal relations with their neighbors, the problem lies in the fact that they don't quite understand the necessity of letting others live.

How to handle international relations is an art, which is what diplomacy is all about. The highest purpose of diplomacy is to create and maintain a harmonious, at least a harmless, international circumstance in which a nation exists. Here, flexibility is indispensable. As a Malay proverb says, "A diplomat should be yielding and supple as a liana that can be bent but not broken." To yield implies that a nation must acknowledge that its neighboring nations have an equal right to exist and pursue their interests.

Peace is what all of us are seeking. But the way to gain peace is rather sophisticated. Peace requires more knowledge, wisdom and farsightedness than war. It takes all considerate means to nurture a peaceful environment. But it only employs a few random verbal or physical actions to ignite a conflict. Unilateralists cannot understand the absence of respecting others, or, they don't bother to care about others. But they must keep this in mind: unilateralism leads to no peace, and finally will ruin the interests of its advocators and practitioners.

The Chinese have long held that international disputes should be settled by negotiation, while using force should be discouraged. What a war may bring about is only a one-handed, sometimes also a short-term, victory, while peace gives victory and stability to both sides.

Regional or global peace, as we have seen, does not necessarily demand brotherhood, but neighborhood. It doesn't request that every country love its neighbors. All it needs is that countries live together with mutual tolerance, submitting their disputes to a just, fair and peaceful settlement. Yes, common interest sometimes binds countries together, but it also separates them. It is equality, sympathy, mutual tolerance and understanding that unite them, in a realistic yet firm way.

Traditional strategy contains military operations and the life-and-death conceptive pattern. The new strategy we call for in today's world involves a win-win motivation and the doctrine of peaceful coexistence. It is time to introduce this new strategy.

(529 words)

Word List

given	['gɪvən]	adj.	特定的
pursue	[pə'sjuː]	v.	追求
survival	[sə'vaɪvəl]	n.	幸存,生存
inhabit	[ɪn'hæbɪt]	v.	居住
diverse	[daɪ'vɜːs]	adj.	多样的
superficially	['suːpə'fɪʃəlɪ]	adv.	肤浅地,表象地
fathom	['fæðəm]	v.	理解,弄清……的真相
deny	[dɪ'naɪ]	v.	否认
countless	['kaʊntləs]	adj.	数不清的,不计其数的

Unit Three

disquiet	[dɪsˈkwaɪət]	v.	使不安,使忧虑
skirmish	[ˈskɜːmɪʃ]	n.	小规模战斗,小冲突
fabric	[ˈfæbrɪk]	n.	构造,结构
discourse	[ˈdɪskɔːs]	n.	谈话,演讲
evidence	[ˈevɪdəns]	n.	证据
prosperity	[prɒsˈperɪtɪ]	n.	繁荣
diplomacy	[dɪˈpləʊməsɪ]	n.	外交
harmonious	[hɑːˈməʊnɪəs]	adj.	和谐的
circumstance	[ˈsɜːkəmstəns]	n.	环境
flexibility	[ˌfleksɪˈbɪlɪtɪ]	n.	灵活,柔顺
indispensable	[ˌɪndɪˈspensəbl]	adj.	不可缺少的,必需的
diplomat	[ˈdɪpləmæt]	n.	外交官,外交家
yielding	[ˈjiːldɪŋ]	adj.	退让的,畏缩的
supple	[ˈsʌpl]	adj.	柔韧的,灵活的
liana	[lɪˈɑːnə]	n.	藤本植物
sophisticated	[səˈfɪstɪkeɪtɪd]	adj.	复杂的,世故的
farsightedness	[ˈfɑːˈsaitidnɪs]	n.	远见
nurture	[ˈnɜːtʃə]	v.	培养,养育
employ	[ɪmˈplɔɪ]	v.	使用,雇用
random	[ˈrændəm]	adj.	随机的,随意的
ignite	[ɪgˈnaɪt]	v.	点燃,引起(兴趣等)
unilateralist	[juːnɪˈlætərəlɪst]	n.	单方面裁军主义者
advocator	[ˈædvəkeɪt]	n.	支持者,宣扬者
practitioner	[prækˈtɪʃənə]	n.	从事者,实践者
brotherhood	[ˈbrʌðəhʊd]	n.	兄弟关系,手足之情
neighborhood	[ˈneɪbəhʊd]	n.	邻里关系,附近
doctrine	[ˈdɒktrɪn]	n.	教义,信条

Idioms & Expressions

refer to	指的是	sum up	总结
in all aspects	在所有方面	in reality	实际上
elaborate on	对……加以阐述	as a matter of fact	实际上
lie in	存在于	submit ... to ...	使……屈服于……
win-win	双赢		

Exercises

1. [Definitions]

Match the words in the box with their meanings. Write the word that stands for the definition in the appropriate answer space.

pursue	survival	inhabit	diverse	deny
disquiet	prosperity	harmonious	circumstance	indispensable
sophisticated	nurture	random	advocator	ignite

1) _____ : be friendly and helpful to one another.
2) _____ : disturb in mind or make uneasy or cause to be worried or alarmed.
3) _____ : an event or condition connected with what is happening or has happened.
4) _____ : knowledgeable of the world and its ways, so that you are not easily fooled, and having an understanding of people and ideas without simplifying them.
5) _____ : the state of continuing to live or exist.
6) _____ : so important or useful that it is impossible to manage without.
7) _____ : happening or chosen without any definite plan, aim, or pattern.
8) _____ : to continue doing an activity or trying to achieve something over a long period of time.
9) _____ : to live in (a place).
10) _____ : to help a plan, idea, feeling etc to develop.
11) _____ : very different from each other.
12) _____ : a person who pleads for a cause or propounds an idea.
13) _____ : to cause a dangerous, excited or angry situation to begin.
14) _____ : to say that something is not true, or that you do not believe something.
15) _____ : an economic state of growth with rising profits and full employment.

2. [Sample Sentences]

Use the new words you have learned from the box in the following sentence. Change the form where necessary.

1) Johnson vehemently _____ the allegations.
2) The new government ushered in a period of _____ .
3) They are the people from _____ cultures.
4) A lot of small companies are having to fight for _____ .
5) His appointment _____ many board members.
6) _____ readers understood the book's hidden meaning.
7) The woods are _____ by many wild animals.

8) European Union is an ideal that has been _____ since the post-war years.
9) The proposed restrictions have _____ a storm of protest from human rights groups.
10) We looked at a _____ sample of 120 families.
11) She is a passionate _____ of natural childbirth.
12) Mobile phones have become a(n) _____ part of our lives.
13) It's the best result that could be expected under the _____ .
14) Mr. Smith plans to _____ a career in politics.
15) _____ relations with other countries are very important.

3. 【Translation】

A. Translate the following English sentences into Chinese.

1) We asked a random sample of people what they thought.

2) Survival is our first imperative.

3) Students should pursue their own interests, as well as do their school work.

4) The increasing sale of luxury goods is an index of a country's prosperity.

5) The computer is now an indispensable tool in many businesses.

B. Translate the following Chinese sentences into English by using the word in the bracket.

1) 这个学生的兴趣十分广泛。(diverse)

2) 许多农村孩子得不到上学的机会。(deny)

3) 她在大学继续深造。(pursue)

4) 我们希望拥有成功幸福的生活。(prosperity)

5) 天空和大海构成了一幅和谐的画面。(harmonious)

4. 【Writing】

Write an article of 150-200 words in English. Use the ideas given below.

Topic: Some people like similar friends. Others like different friends. Compare the advantages of these two kinds of friends. Which kind of friends do you prefer? Explain why.

Introduction: Do you have many friends? Have you ever noticed their similarities and differences?

Development: Having similar friends may bring you many advantages—easy to get along with—share common feelings—different friends are also a rich treasure—they are like a mirror which can reflect your good and bad points.

Conclusion: Whether they are similar or different friends, sincerity is most important.

Reading Skills：长难句突破法(3)

汉语被称为意合语,也可理解为平行语,即构成一句话的各个部分呈平行排列,没有主次之分,形似竹子结构;英语则不然,是一种形合语,或称层次语,即一句话的各个组成部分有主次之分,呈树形排列。例：

孔乙己**着了慌**,**伸开五指将碟子罩住**,**弯腰下去说道**:"不多了,我已经不多了。"

从汉语结构看,该句的五个动词(划线部分)是平行关系,即 $S+V_1+V_2+V_3+V_4+V_5$,但译成英文时,则必须分出主次,因此可以灵活处理为：

Kong Yiji grew flushed, covering the dish with his hand, **bending** forward from his waist, and **would say**: "There aren't many left, not many at all."

转化为 $S + V_1 +Ving+Ving+ V_4$ 结构,强化了"着了慌"、"说道"两个动作,淡化了"罩住"、"弯腰"两个行为,省掉"伸开",主次分明,重点突出。了解了英汉之间的这种本质差别,对于突破英语长难句是很有帮助的。比如：

Money spent on advertising is money spent as well as any I know of.

首先,要找到该句的主干结构,即主(S)+ 谓(V)+ 宾(O)。根据语法知识,主干是 **Money is money**,两个 **money** 之后的 **spent** 均是过去分词,作 **money** 的后置定语；**I know of** 是 **any** 的定语从句,**as... as...** 构成同级比较结构,**well** 是程度状语,修饰临近的 **spent**。因此,整句可以分解为：

Money (spent //on advertising//) is money (spent as well as any //I know of//).

大意是:广告所投入的钱和我所知道的任何一笔花掉的钱都一样值得。

再看一例：

Claims that eating a diet consisting entirely of organically grown foods prevents or cures or provides other benefits to health have become widely publicized.

这个句子比较复杂,还是首先寻找主干。经过分析,迅速可以梳理出：**Claims have become widely publicized**；**Claims** 之后的 **that** 引导的是其同位语从句,该从句的主语是动名词短语 **eating... grown foods**,谓语是三个并列的动词 **prevents, cures** 和 **provides**,后面的 **other benefits to health** 是 **provides** 的宾语。整句大致可以切分为：

Claims (that eating a diet consisting entirely of organically grown foods // prevents or cures or provides other benefits to health) have become widely publicized.

大意是:完全吃有机食物,就可以防病、治病、促进健康,这种观点已经广为流传。

Unit Three

Text 2 (Extensive Reading)

This is New York
这就是纽约

On any person who desires such strange prizes, New York will bestow the gift of loneliness and the gift of privacy. It is this largess that accounts for the presence within the city's walls of a considerable section of the population; for the residents of Manhattan are to a large extent strangers who have pulled up stakes somewhere and come to town, seeking sanctuary or fulfillment or some greater or lesser success. The capacity to make such dubious gifts is a mysterious quality of New York. It can destroy an individual, or it can fulfill him, depending a good deal on luck. No one should come to New York to live unless he is willing to be lucky.

There are roughly three New Yorks. There is, first, the New York of the man or woman who was born here, who takes the city for granted and accepts its size and its turbulence as natural and inevitable. Second, there is the New York of the commuter—the city that is devoured by locusts each day and spat out each night. Third, there is the New York of the person who was born somewhere else and came to New York in quest of something. Of these three trembling cities the greatest is the last—the city of final destination, the city that is a goal. It is this third city that accounts for New York's unique disposition, its poetical deportment, its dedication to the arts, and its incomparable achievements. Commuters give the city its tidal restlessness, natives give it solidity and continuity, but the settlers give it passion.

A poem compresses much in a small space and adds music, thus heightening its meaning. The city is like poetry: it compresses all life, all races and breeds, into a small island and adds music and the accompaniment of internal engines. The island of Manhattan is without any doubt the greatest human settlement on earth. Manhattan has been compelled to expand skyward because of the absence of any other direction in which to grow. This, more than any other thing, is responsible for its physical majesty. It is to the nation what the white church spire is to the village. At the feet of the tallest and plushiest offices lie the crummiest slums.

The slums are gradually giving way to the lofty housing projects-high in stature, high in purpose, low in rent. There are a couple of dozens of these new developments scattered around; each is a city in itself. Federal money, state money, city money, and private money have flowed into these projects. Banks and insurance companies are in back of them.

To an outlander a stay in New York can be and often is a series of small embarrassments and discomforts and disappointments: not understanding the waiter, not being able to distinguish between a sucker joint and a friendly saloon, riding the wrong the subway, being slapped down by a bus driver for asking an innocent question, enduring sleepless nights when the street noises fill the bedroom.

To a New Yorker the city is both changeless and changing. In many respects it neither looks nor feels the way it did 25 years ago. The elevated railways have been pulled down. An old-timer walking past the Jefferson Market misses the railroad, misses its sound, its spotted shade. Broadway has changed. It used to have a discernible bony structure beneath its loud bright surface; but the signs are so enormous now, the buildings and shops and hotels have largely disappeared under the neon lights and letters.

At certain hours on certain days it is almost impossible to find an empty taxi and there is a great deal of chasing around after them. You grab a handle and open the door, and find that some other citizen is entering from the other side. Doormen blow their whistles for cabs; and some doormen belong to no door at all—merely wonder about through the streets, opening cabs for people as they happen to find them. By comparison with other less hectic days, the city is uncomfortable and inconvenient; but New Yorkers temperamentally do not crave comfort and convenience—if they did they would live elsewhere.

I am, at the moment of writing this essay, living not as a neighborhood man in New York but as a transient, or vagrant, from the country for a few days. Summertime is a good time to reexamine New York and to receive again the gift of privacy, the jewel of loneliness. In summer the city contains (except for tourists) only die-hards and authentic characters. No casual, spotty dwellers are around, only the real article. And the town has a somewhat relaxed air, and one can lie in a sofa, gasping and remembering things.

I've been remembering what it felt like as a young man to live in the same town with giants. When I first arrived in New York, my personal giants were a dozen or so columnists and critics and poets whose names regularly in the papers. I burned with a low steady fever just because I was on the same island with them. New York is always full of young worshipful beginners—young actors, young aspiring poets, painters, reporters, singers—each depending on his own brand of tonic to stay alive, each with his own stable of giants.

(893 words)

Word List

privacy	['praɪvəsɪ]	n.	隐私,独处
largess	['lɑːdʒes]	n.	慷慨,赏赐
considerable	[kən'sɪdərəbəl]	adj.	大量的,很多的
sanctuary	['sæŋktʃuərɪ]	n.	圣所,庇护所
fulfillment	[fʊl'fɪlmənt]	n.	完成,成就
capacity	[kə'pæsɪtɪ]	n.	容量,能力
dubious	['djuːbjəs]	adj.	令人怀疑的

Unit Three

mysterious	[mɪs'tɪərɪəs]	adj.	神秘的
turbulence	['tɜːbjʊləns]	n.	动荡,骚乱
inevitable	[ɪ'nevɪtəbəl]	adj.	不可避免的
commuter	[kə'mjuːtə]	n.	(尤指市郊之间的)乘车上下班者
devour	[dɪ'vaʊə]	v.	吞食,狼吞虎咽
destination	[,destɪ'neɪʃən]	n.	目的地,终点
unique	[juː'niːk]	adj.	独特的,唯一的
disposition	[,dɪspə'zɪʃən]	n.	性情,性格
deportment	[dɪ'pɔːtmənt]	n.	举止,风度
incomparable	[ɪn'kɒmpərəbəl]	adj.	无可比拟的
restlessness	['restlɪsnɪs]	n.	永无休止,焦躁不安
solidity	[sə'lɪdɪtɪ]	n.	团结一致
accompaniment	[ə'kʌmpənɪmənt]	n.	伴随物,伴奏
majesty	['mædʒɪstɪ]	n.	雄伟,壮丽
crummy	['krʌmɪ]	adj.	肮脏的,破旧的
lofty	['lɒftɪ]	adj.	高耸的,崇高的
stature	['stætʃə]	n.	身材,身高
scatter	['skætə]	v.	散落
distinguish	[dɪ'stɪŋgwɪʃ]	v.	辨别,区分
discernible	[dɪ'sɜːnəbl]	adj.	可识别的,看得清的
temperamentally	[,temprə'mentlɪ]	adv.	气质上,性格上
transient	['trænzɪənt]	adj.	转瞬即逝的,暂住的
die-hard	[,daɪ'hɑːd]	n.	顽固分子,死硬派
authentic	[ɔː'θentɪk]	adj.	纯正的,地道的
worshipful	['wɜːʃɪpfʊl]	adj.	崇拜的,充满敬意的
tonic	['tɒnɪk]	n.	补药,有兴奋作用的东西
stable	['steɪbəl]	n.	(有共同目标或利益的)人群

Idioms & Expressions

bestow sth on sb	把某物馈赠给某人		account for	解释,说明
to a large extent	很大程度上		pull up stakes	搬家,迁址
take... for granted	认为……理所当然		in quest of	寻找
without any doubt	毫无疑问		more than any other thing	更加
give way to	让位于		a couple of	两个,几个
dozens of	很多		be in back of	支持
a series of	一系列		slap down	断然拒绝,压制

| in many respects | 在许多方面 | happen to do | 碰巧…… |
| by comparison with | 与……相比 | | |

Exercises

1. [Questions]

Based on the information provided in the text, answer the following questions briefly.

1) What kind of gift will New York give to any person who wants it?

2) What are the three New Yorks?

3) Why New York is compared to a poem?

4) What are emerging in the place of slums?

5) At the moment of writing this essay, what is the author's condition?

2. [Multiple Choices]

Choose the right answer from the four choices marked A, B, C, and D.

1) As New York can destroy an individual or it can fulfill him, depending a good deal on luck, people come to New York prepared to _____.
   A. demonstrate their abilities to do business
   B. try their luck
   C. live a life unknown before
   D. try their best not to be destroyed

2) Three are roughly three New Yorks of which the greatest is the New York of _____.
   A. the men and women who were born in the city
   B. the men and women who come to work in the morning and leave in the evening
   C. the settlers who were born somewhere else and consider the city to be their final destination and their goal
   D. the men and women who are like locusts restlessly embracing the city with the intense excitement of first love

3) According to the author, when a foreigner or a man who has never been in New York pays a short visit to the city, he will find his stay _____.
   A. too short to go to all the places of interest
   B. an exciting experience in his life
   C. very expensive
   D. a series of embarrassments, discomforts and disappointments

4) What is responsible for Manhattan's physical majesty is _____.
   A. Times Square
   B. the skyscrapers
   C. the white church
   D. Hell Gate Bridge

5) Broadway has changed. It used to have a discernible bony structure beneath its loud bright surface, but now _____.
   A. Broadway has taken on a new look with new hotels, shops and office buildings
   B. enormous signs, bright neon lights, large letters keep the buildings out of sight
   C. tall, new buildings stand in the place of old, low, bony structures
   D. the old buildings, shops and hotels have largely disappeared and new ones are under construction

Text 3 (Fast Reading)

Road Rage: A Western Phenomenon?
道路泄愤：西方现象吗？

Have you ever been sitting in a car and expressed anger towards other road users? Have other road users ever expressed anger towards you? If the answer to both these questions is yes then you are one of many who both exhibit, and become victims of, road rage.

Road rage is, in fact, a serious problem in many Western countries. Nevertheless, the vast majority of reported cases of road rage amount to little more than verbal abuse: shouting or swearing at another driver because he did something that upset you. Sometimes, however, such incidences can result in actual physical damage to vehicles, or even people themselves. And in the most extreme cases, killings have occurred. The latter, however, is more common in the United States than it is in most European countries or Australia.

The Psychological Cause for Road Rage

But what is it that causes us to get so angry with other people when we are sitting behind the wheel of our car? Naturally, psychologists have studied the phenomenon. Basically, evidence from research concludes that a car acts as a physical barrier: quite literally a tin box that isolates us from the outside world. We feel separated from the rest of humanity, serving to amplify the feeling of individualism. Moreover, this feeling is due to being isolated. In other words we feel as though we are somehow elevated above other people and that we have ultimate right of way, giving rise to the feeling that I am right, that I, and I alone have ultimate authority. Thus, the idea that we are part of a complex whole is put aside, thrown into the trashcan along with any feeling of social unity.

However, arguments such as this beg the question of why only cars? If isolation from other people is the major issue why don't we feel this way when sitting in our office, or relaxing at home? Yet in truth we do. When in our office or at home we command respect from visitors, insisting that they ask permission to enter, and that they observe the rules that we lay down (no smoking, for example). In other words, when in our own houses, we have the authority. And it is this concept of authority that translates to the feelings of being in control. A feeling that is expanded many times when we are driving a car. In fact the concept of the mobility, which cars provide, brings forth a perceived ability to control speed, direction, time and even the elements (temperature inside of the car), which leads to a feeling of ultimate power and control. And it is when the control over our immediate environment is threatened, or violated in some way by other road users that anger and rage result.

The Different Spatial Concepts in Western and Eastern Cultures

Yet the concept of road rage is more or less restricted to the West. In Eastern countries, although cases of road rage occur, they are usually the exception rather than the rule. And they hardly ever turn to physical acts of violence, let alone killings! Yet why should this be? Are Asians innately more placid? Are they better able to control their emotions? Or is it a cultural difference?

In many Asian countries the concept of personal space is far less pronounced than in most Western countries. Indeed, in countries such as Britain and America, individuals consider their personal space to be in the region of three to six feet, and feel uncomfortable at best, and threatened at worst, when that space is encroached upon by others. In many Asian countries, however, the awareness of personal space is far more restricted, extending to little more than a few inches. Indeed, physical contact between strangers is not only more common in Eastern countries, but also more socially acceptable, whereas Westerners prefer to maintain a greater distance and often will actually go out of their way to avoid body contact if at all possible, giving the impression that they are more aloof. And it is this concept of spatial awareness that is believed to be at the center of road rage.

The Feeling of Oneness vs. the Feeling of Unity

As soon as we sit in a car, the vehicle, in effect, becomes an extension of ourselves. It obeys our every command and takes on the role that our legs would normally play. Thus we find ourselves sitting at the kingdom of a powerful machine that ultimately has one master: the driver. More importantly, however, the feeling of oneness with the vehicle distracts from the feeling of spiritual unity with other people, thereby adding to the feeling of individualism. However, in many Asian countries, where the concept of personal space is restricted to little more than a few inches, and the concept of collectivism is more deeply rooted in people's mind, one's sphere of authority is rarely threatened outside of actual contact. In Western countries people's culturally rooted concept of personal space extends way beyond the physical limitations of the car. Thus, personal space is easily violated, resulting in high incidences of road rage.

Unit Three

Maybe it's time for us here in the West to broaden our concepts of individualism and personal boundaries beyond our current realms of thinking. Indeed, only by waking up to the fact that unity and oneness is a universal law will the world become a much safer and more compassionate place in which to live.

(908 words)

Exercises

1. [True, False, Not Given]

Decide whether the following statements are True, False or Not Given.

T (for True) if the statement agrees with the information given in the passage;

F (for False) if the statement doesn't agree with the information given in the passage;

NG (for Not Given) if the information is not given in the passage.

1) This passage discusses the causes for road rage in America from the cultural and psychological perspectives.
2) Most incidences of road rage are non-violent.
3) Road rage is more common in America than in Britain.
4) Cars separate us from the rest of the society.
5) Cars allow us a greater ability to control our environment.
6) Road rage is more common amongst men than women.
7) Incidences of road rage are less serious in Asia.

2. [Blank-Filling]

For questions 1)–3), complete the sentences with the information given in the passage.

1) In eastern countries, although cases of road rage occur, they are usually _____ rather than _____.
2) In western countries, the idea of personal space is considered to be in the region of _____. In Asian countries, it is only extended to _____.
3) To make the world a much safer and more compassionate place in which to live, the author suggests that Westerners broaden _____.

Unit Four

Text 1 (Intensive Reading)

Background Tips: Martin Luther King

King, Martin Luther, Jr. (1929—1968), American clergyman and Nobel Prize winner, one of the principal leaders of the American civil rights movement and a prominent advocate of nonviolent protest. King's challenges to segregation and racial discrimination in the 1950s and 1960s helped convince many white Americans to support the cause of civil rights in the United States. He emerged as a leader of the American civil rights movement after organizing the famous 1955 bus boycott in Montgomery, Alabama. Throughout his career he pressed for equal treatment and improved circumstances for blacks, organizing nonviolent protests and delivering powerful speeches on the necessity of eradicating institutional racial inequalities. In 1963 King led a peaceful march between the Washington Monument and the Lincoln Memorial, where he delivered his most famous speech, "I Have a Dream." After his assassination in 1968, King became a symbol of protest in the struggle for racial justice.

A Race to Conquer Racism
消除种族歧视的战斗

The United States has a major racial problem on its hand. The only way to solve it is through education. Negroes should know about the contributions that black individuals and groups have made towards building America. This is of vital importance for their self-respect; and it is perhaps even more important for white people to know. For if you believe that a man has no history worth mentioning, it is easy to assume that he has no value as a man.

Many people believe that, since the Negro's achievements do not appear in the history books, he did not have any. Most people are taken aback when they learn that Negroes sailed with Columbus, marched with the Spanish conquerors of South America and fought side by side with white Americans in all their wars.

How, then, did the image of the Negro as a brave fighting man disappear? To justify the evil institution of slavery, slaveholders had to create the myth of the docile, slow-witted Negro, incapable of self-improvement, and even contented with his fortune. Nothing could be further from the truth. The slave fought for his freedom at every chance he got, and there numerous uprisings. Yet the myth of docility persisted.

There are several other areas where the truth has been twisted or concealed. Most people have heard of the Negro, Carver, who invented scores of new uses for the lowly peanut. But whoever heard of Norbert Rilieux, who in 1846 invented a vacuum pan that revolutionized the sugar-refining industry? Or of Elijah MacCoy, who in 1872 invented the drip cup that feeds oil to the moving parts of heavy machinery? How many people know that Negroes are credited with inventing such different items such as ice-cream, potato chips, the gas mask and the first traffic light? Not many.

As for winning the West, the black cowboy and the frontiersman have been almost ignored, though film producers are becoming more aware of their importance. Yet in the typical trail crew of eight men that drove cattle from Texas to Kansas, at least two would have been Negroes. The black troops of the Ninth and Tenth Cavalry formed one-fifth of all the mounted troops assigned to protect the frontier after the Civil War. What difference does it make? You may ask. A lot. The cowboy is the American folk-hero. Youngsters identify with him instantly. The average cowboy film is really a kind of morality play, with good guys and bad guys and right finally triumphing over wrong. You should see the amazement and happiness on black youngsters' faces when they learn that their ancestors really had a part in all that.

(442 words)

Word List

major	['meɪdʒə]	*adj.*	主要的
racial	['reɪʃəl]	*adj.*	种族的
contribution	[ˌkɒntrɪ'bjuːʃən]	*n.*	贡献
assume	[ə'sjuːm]	*v.*	假定,认为
conqueror	['kɒŋkərə]	*n.*	征服者
justify	['dʒʌstɪfaɪ]	*v.*	合理解释,证明
evil	['iːvəl]	*adj.*	罪恶的,邪恶的
institution	[ˌɪnstɪ'tjuːʃən]	*n.*	机构,制度
slaveholder	['sleɪvˌhəʊldə]	*n.*	奴隶主
myth	[mɪθ]	*n.*	神话
docile	['dəʊsaɪl]	*adj.*	听话的,易管教的
uprising	['ʌpˌraɪzɪŋ]	*n.*	起义,暴动
docility	[dəʊ'sɪlɪtɪ]	*n.*	顺从,乖顺
persist	[pə'sɪst]	*v.*	坚持,持续
twist	[twɪst]	*v.*	扭曲
conceal	[kən'siːl]	*v.*	隐藏,隐瞒

revolutionize	[ˌrevəˈluːʃənaɪz]	v.	使革命化,改革
frontiersman	[frʌnˈtɪəzmən]	n.	边远地区的居民
amazement	[əˈmeɪzmənt]	n.	惊奇,吃惊

Idioms & Expressions

side by side	肩并肩	be incapable of	无法……
be contented with	对……满意	hear of	听说
scores of	许多,大量	be credited with	具有……
as for	关于	be aware of	意识到
triumph over	战胜,胜过		

Exercises

1. [Definitions]

Match the words in the box with their meanings. Write the word that stands for the definition in the appropriate answer space.

major	contribution	vital	assume	achievement
justify	evil	docile	numerous	persist
conceal	revolutionize	amazement	typical	triumph

1) _____ : something important that you succeed in doing by your own efforts.
2) _____ : show to be reasonable or provide adequate ground for.
3) _____ : tending to cause great harm.
4) _____ : prevent from being seen or discovered.
5) _____ : to completely change the way people do something or think about something.
6) _____ : a feeling of great surprise.
7) _____ : having the usual features or qualities of a particular group or thing.
8) _____ : amounting to a large indefinite number.
9) _____ : to think that something is true, although you do not have definite proof.
10) _____ : extremely important and necessary for something to succeed or exist.
11) _____ : to continue to do something, although this is difficult, or other people oppose it; continue to exist.
12) _____ : having very serious or worrying results.

Unit Four

13) _____ : to gain a victory or success after a difficult struggle.
14) _____ : willing to be taught or led or supervised or directed.
15) _____ : something that you give or do in order to help something be successful.

2. [Sample Sentences]

Use the new words you have learned from the box in the following sentence. Change the form where necessary.

1) Slavery has always been condemned as _____.
2) The Earth is only one of the _____ planets in the universe.
3) The cold weather will _____ for the rest of the week.
4) This advertisement is a(n) _____ example of their marketing strategy.
5) They have a big dog, but it is really friendly and _____.
6) To everyone's _____, he was enrolled by Harvard.
7) There is a _____ problem with parking in London.
8) A woman, especially if she has the misfortune of knowing anything, shall _____ it as well as she can.
9) New technology is going to _____ everything we do.
10) The policeman was _____ in shooting the criminal in self-defense.
11) It seems reasonable to _____ that the book was written in the 17th century.
12) Einstein was awarded the Nobel Prize for his _____ to Quantum Theory.
13) In the end, good shall _____ over evil.
14) As we reached the peak of the mountain, we felt a sense of _____.
15) These measures are _____ to national security.

3. [Translation]

A. Translate the following English sentences into Chinese.

1) Nothing can justify your cheating on an exam.

2) The book gives, as it were, a picture of the evil old society.

3) His great achievement is to make all the players into a united team.

4) I think we can safely assume that interest rates will go up again soon.

5) The school sees its job as preparing students to make a contribution to society.

B. Translate the following Chinese sentences into English by using the word in the bracket.

1) 日常锻炼对于身体健康很重要。(vital)

2) 努力和成就总是相辅相承的。(achievement)

3) 尽管经济困难,她还是坚持学业。(persist)

4) 我们总是掩饰不住对他人成功的忌妒。(conceal)

5) 计算机的运用彻底改变了办公室工作。(revolutionize)

4.【Writing】

Write an article of 150–200 words in English. Use the ideas given below.

Title: Equality

Introduction: I am a sports fan—my favorite sport—it has become part of my life.

Development: My favorite sport is applicable—it is well-accepted among the public.

Conclusion: Doing sports can improve our physical well-being—doing sports is a good distraction from dull routine life—doing sports is a good way of making new friends.

Reading Skills：便捷阅读法(4)

在阅读过程中,为了提高速度和效率,以下原则也是有必要注意的:

1) 同位语、定语部分一般略读;
2) 从句内容一般略读;
3) 转折词后的部分细读;
4) 主语和谓语中间有双逗号、破折号间隔,间隔内容略读;
5) 冒号前后是从抽象到具体的过程,后面进一步说明前面内容;
6) 分号前后是并列关系,包括结构并列和语义并列。

另外,阅读文章后面的题目设置一般遵循五大原则:

1) 题目顺序一般与段落顺序相符
2) 语言简化

相对而言,正确选项的语言难度一般低于原文,某选项里原文中的词汇出现的越多,对的几率越小。

3) 正话反说;

出题者为了增加解题难度,会采用一些手段迷惑读者,正话反说就是其中之一。如原文说:A 导致了 B,则题目中则说 B 是由 A 引起的。

4) 常规词汇非常规含义

如前所述，阅读中最常使用的方法就是熟词生义，这在词汇学习过程中尤其要加以注意。

5) 题干与正选避免使用相同的修饰语

题目设置中还有一种方法称为关键词替换，即在选项中用一个难度值较低的词汇取代原文中的词汇；因此，选项中关键词、尤其是难词与原文中一样的一般不是正确答案。

Text 2（Extensive Reading）

Going to School—Why?
为什么要上学？

Let me tell you one of the earliest sufferings in my career as a teacher. It was January of 1956 and I was fresh out of graduate school starting my first semester at a university. A tall, thin boy came into my class, sat down, folded his arms, and looked at me as if to say: "All right, damn you, teach me something." One week later I started *Jane Eyre*. A few days later he came into my office with his hands on his hips. "Look," he said, "I came here to be an engineer. Why do I have to read this stuff?" He pointed to the book which was lying on the desk.

Though I was a total newcomer, I could have told this boy that he had enrolled, not in a technical training school, but in a university, and that in a university students enroll for both training and education. I tried to put it this way. "For the rest of my life," I said, "your days are going to average out to about twenty-four hours. For eight of these hours, more or less, you will be asleep, and I suppose you need neither education nor training to get through that third of your life."

"Then for about eight hours of each working day you will, I hope, be usefully employed. Suppose you have gone through engineering school, or law school, or whatever, during those eight hours you will be using your professional skills. You will see to it during this third of your life that the bull doesn't jump the fence, or that your client doesn't go to the electric chair as a result of your incompetence. They involve skills every man must respect, and they can all bring you good basic satisfactions. Along with everything else, they will probably be what provides food for your table, supports your wife, and rears your children. They will be your income, and may it always be sufficient."

"But having finished the day's work, what do you do with those other eight hours— with the other third of your life? Let's say you go home to your family. What sort of family are you raising? Will the children ever be exposed to a profound idea at home? We all think ourselves as citizens of great civilization. Civilizations can exist, however, only as long as they remain intellectually alive. Will you be head of a family that maintains some basic contact with the great continuity of civilized intellect? Or is your family life going to be merely beer on ice? Will there be a book in the house? Will there be a painting? Will your family be able to speak English and to talk about an idea? Will the kids ever get to hear Mozart?"

That is about what I said, but this boy was not interested. "Look," he said, "you professors raise your kids your way; I take care of my own. Me, I'm out to make money."

"I hope you make a lot of it," I told him. "Because you are going to be badly in need of something to do when you're not signing checks."

Twenty years later, I am still teaching, and I am here to tell you that the business of the college is not only to train you, but to put you in touch with what the best human minds have thought. If you have no time for Shakespeare, for a basic look at philosophy, for the fine arts, for that lesson of man's development we call history—then you have no business being in college. You are on your way to being the mechanized savage, the push-button savage.

No one becomes a human being unaided. There is not time enough in a single lifetime to invent for oneself everything one needs to know in order to be a civilized human.

Any of you who managed to stay awake through part of a high school course in physics knows more about physics than did many of the great scientists of the past. You know more because they left you what they knew. The first course in any science is essentially a history course. You have to begin learning what the past learned for you.

This is true of the techniques of mankind. It is also true of mankind's spiritual resources. Most of these resources, both technical and spiritual, are stored in books. When you have read a book, you have added to your human experience. Read Homer and your mind includes a piece of Homer's mind. Through books you can acquire at least fragments of the mind and experience of Virgil, Dante, Shakespeare—the list is endless. For a great book is necessarily a gift; it offers you a life you have no time to live yourself, and it takes you into a world you have no time to travel in literal time. A civilized mind is one that contains many such lives and many such worlds. If you are too much in a hurry, or too proud of your own limitations, to accept as a gift to your humanity some pieces of the minds of Aristotle or Einstein, you are neither a developed human nor a useful citizen of a civilization.

I say that a university has no real existence and no real purpose except as it succeeds in putting you in touch, both as specialists and as humans, with those human minds your human mind needs to include.

(916 words)

Unit Four

Word List

semester	[sɪˈmestə]	n.		学期
damn	[dæm]	v.		诅咒,骂
stuff	[stʌf]	n.		素材,题材,内容
newcomer	[ˈnjuːkʌmə]	n.		新人,初来乍到者
put	[pʊt]	v.		表达,表述
bull	[bʊl]	n.		公牛
client	[ˈklaɪənt]	n.		(律师的)当事人,(医生的)患者
incompetence	[ɪnˈkɒmpɪtəns]	n.		无能,不称职
involve	[ɪnˈvɒlv]	v.		涉及,包含
rear	[rɪə]	v.		抚育,抚养
profound	[prəˈfaʊnd]	adj.		深刻的,深奥的
civilization	[ˌsɪvəlaɪˈzeɪʃən]	n.		文明
intellect	[ˈɪntɪlekt]	n.		智力,思维能力
continuity	[ˌkɒntɪˈnjuːɪtɪ]	n.		持续,连续性
savage	[ˈsævɪdʒ]	n.		野人,野蛮人
unaided	[ʌnˈeɪdɪd]	adj.		无人帮助的
essentially	[ɪˈsenʃəlɪ]	adv.		本质上,根本上
spiritual	[ˈspɪrɪtʃʊəl]	adj.		精神的
resource	[rɪˈzɔːs]	n.		资源
acquire	[əˈkwaɪə]	v.		获得,获取
fragment	[ˈfræɡmənt]	n.		碎片,片段,部分
literal	[ˈlɪtərəl]	adj.		文字的,直译的,实际的
humanity	[hjuːˈmænɪtɪ]	n.		人性,人类
specialist	[ˈspeʃəlɪst]	n.		专家,专业人员

Idioms & Expressions

more or less	或多或少	see to it that...	务必
along with	以及,连同	do with	处理
be exposed to	接触,接受	in need of	需要
in touch with	与……联系	add to	增加
in a hurry	匆忙	be proud of	以……为豪

Exercises

1. [Questions]

Based on the information provided in the text, answer the following questions briefly.

1) What do we learn about the author from the text?

2) How did the tall, thin boy behave in the author's literature class?

3) According to the author what is the basic difference between a technical training and a university?

4) What does one have to do in order to be a civilized human being?

5) What is your idea of college education after reading the text?

2. [Multiple Choices]

Choose the right answer from the four choices marked A, B, C, and D.

1) The boy questioned the author in class because _____.
   A. he wanted to be independent
   B. he did not like the stuff taught in class
   C. he thought the teacher was not qualified
   D. he wanted to challenge the teacher's authority

2) The author used the example of the electric chair (para.3) to show that _____.
   A. the student should concentrate on his studies
   B. the student would be put in the electric chair if he failed
   C. the electric chair could be used as a teaching instrument
   D. the student should keep away from the electric chair

3) The author mentioned "the mechanized savage" (para.7) in order to express the idea that _____.
   A. With social advance, more and more robots will appear
   B. Without a profound knowledge of earlier civilization, we would be illiterate.
   C. Without knowledge, there would be savages everywhere.
   D. Equipped with knowledge, we can conquer savages.

4) By saying "The first course in any science is essentially a history course", the author means _____.
   A. history is the most important course
   B. history can actually take the place of science .

C. students should at first learn the achievements of earlier times

D. science used to be taught in the form of history

5) The author said that a university had no real existence and no real purpose unless it _____.

A. had wide connections with other universities

B. had sufficient enrollments and finance

C. possessed well-qualified teaching staff

D. enabled learners to deeply understand some noble minds

Text 3 (Fast Reading)

The Calendar
日 历

What day is today? What day of the month is it? And what month of the year? To answer questions like these we look at a calendar.

The story of our calendar dates back to the dawn of civilization. Probably the first way of keeping time was to count days. Our early ancestors counted days by the time between each sunrise and sundown, as some primitive peoples still do. A day as we take it is day-time and night-time together, but for a long, long time people did not think of days like we do.

Almost as soon as people began counting "days", they must have noticed the changes in the moon. The moon was full. Then it got smaller and smaller until it disappeared altogether. Then it grew night by night to a full moon again. From full moon to full moon was a good measure of time. But it was still too short a period for men to base a calendar on.

In time, men saw that there were seasons which followed one another in regular order. In ancient Egypt, for example, the season when the Nile flooded the land was followed by the season when crops were planted and cared for. Then came the season of harvest. This cycle of seasons became the year.

Yet for a long time no one tried to fit days and months and years together. When they did, they ran into trouble. Days do not fit evenly into months, since the time from full moon to full moon is about 29 1/2 days. And days do not fit evenly into years, since the actual journey of the earth round the sun takes 365 days, 5 hours, 49 minutes and 46 seconds. And months do not fit evenly into years either, since the moon travels round the earth between 12 and 13 times in a year.

The priests of ancient Babylon worked out a calendar which had 29 days in some months and 30 in others. Their year normally had 12 months in it. But it was several days too short. Soon the months had slipped out of place in the seasons. To keep the months from slipping too far out of place, the priests put an extra month in the years every few years. It was a calendar quite similar to the Chinese lunar calendar.

The early Greeks had a calendar much like the Babylonians'. So did the early Romans. But by the time Julius Caesar became the ruler of the Roam Empire, the calendar had been very badly mixed up. Caesar decided to throw out the old calendar and start all over again. He sought the advice of the astronomer Sosigenes, who suggested that the true length of the year be adopted as 365 1/4 days. Caesar then decreed that the year should consist of 365 days, but every fourth year an extra day should be inserted at the end of February to make up for the quarter days that were lost.

To get his new calendar started in line with the seasons, Caesar moved New Year's Day from March 1 to January 1, and so January became the first month of the year. But the old numerical names of the months were unchanged. So the ninth month is called September, although the word means seventh. Also, the names of the tenth, eleventh, and twelfth months, October, November, and December, come from the Latin for eighth, ninth and tenth.

Caesar's astronomers chose to divide the year into 12 months of about the same length. This gave five 31-day months and seven 30-day months. The Romans thought that odd numbers were lucky and they took a day from a 30-day month—from February—to get an extra 31-day month.

It was just like Caesar to change the name of one month to honor himself. This month, of course, was given 31 days. This is our month of July (after Julius). When Augustus Octavian became emperor after Caesar's death, he also named a month for himself-August.

Caesar's plan of leap years was followed for about 1,600 years. But by that time, an error of about 10 days had again piled up. The trouble was that a year is not quite the 365 1/4 days that Sosigenes recommended.

In 1582 Pope Gregory XIII ordered that 10 days be dropped from the calendar. He also asked someone to work out a better rule for leap years to prevent the piling up of error in future. We still follow this clever rule. It is: If a year's number can be divided by 4, it won't be a leap year if it can be further divided by 100. Again, even it can be divided by 100, it remains a leap year if it can be divided by 400. Thus the year A.D. 2000 will be a leap year, but the year 2100 will not, nor was 1900.

This Gregorian-calendar year, remarkably accurate as it is, is about 26 seconds too long. The error amounts to about one day in 3,000 years.

All Catholic countries adopted the Gregorian Calendar immediately, but the Greek Church and most Protestant nations refused to recognized it. It was not until nearly 200 years later that England found it necessary to drop 11 days from the calendar to bring it in line. This was established by *Act of Parliament* in 1752, but many people thought they were losing 11 days out of their lives. There were great gatherings at which people often cried, "Give us back our 11 days!"

(924 words)

Unit Four

Exercises

1. [True, False, Not Given]

Decide whether the following statements are True, False or Not Given.

T (for True) if the statement agrees with the information given in the passage;

F (for False) if the statement doesn't agree with the information given in the passage;

NG (for Not Given) if the information is not given in the passage.

1) Probably the first way of keeping time was to count numbers.
2) As soon as people began counting days, they must have noticed the changes in the moon.
3) In ancient Egypt, the flooding season followed the planting season.
4) The time from full moon to full moon is about 29 days.
5) The priests of ancient Babylon worked out a calendar of 29 days in a month.
6) In 1682 Pope Gregory XIII ordered that 10 days be dropped from the calendar.
7) Asians also adopted the Gregorian-calendar year.

2. [Blank-Filling]

For questions 1)–3), complete the sentences with the information given in the passage.

1) The early _____ had a calendar much like the Babylonians'.
2) To get his new calendar started in line with the seasons, Caesar moved New Year's Day from _____ to January 1.
3) All _____ countries adopted the Gregorian Calendar immediately, but the Greek Church and most _____ nations refused to recognized it

Unit Five

Text 1 (Intensive Reading)

Background Tips: Olympic Games

Olympic Games (modern), international sports competition, held every four years at a different site, in which athletes from different nations compete against each other in a variety of sports. There are two types of Olympics, the Summer Olympics and the Winter Olympics. Through 1992 they were held in the same year, but beginning in 1994 they were rescheduled so that they are held in alternate even-numbered years. For example, the Winter Olympics were held in 2006 and the Summer Olympics in 2008. The Winter Olympics will next be held in 2010, and the Summer Olympics will next occurr in 2012.

The modern Olympic Games began in Athens, Greece, in 1896, two years after French educator and thinker Pierre de Coubertin proposed that the Olympic Games of ancient Greece be revived to promote a more peaceful world. The program for the 1896 Games, including only summer events (the Winter Olympics were not established until 1924), included about 300 athletes from fewer than 15 countries competing in 43 events in nine different sports. In contrast, the program over 100 years later for the 2008 Summer Olympics in Beijing, China, included more than 11,468 athletes from more than 200 countries competing in 302 events in 28 different sports.

A Nation of Sports
体育国度

  In many parts of the world, there are four seasons: spring, summer, fall and winter. In the U.S., there are only three: football, basketball and baseball. That's not completely true, but almost. In every season, Americans have a ball. If you want to know what season it is, just look at what people are playing. For many Americans, sports do not just occupy the sidelines. They take center court.

  Besides "the big three" sports, Americans play a variety of other sports. In warm weather, people enjoy water sports. Lovers of surfing, sailing and scuba diving flock to the ocean. Swimmers and water skiers also revel in the wet stuff. Fishermen try their luck in ponds, lakes and rivers. In winter sportsmen delight in freezing fun. From the first snowfall, skiers hit the slopes. Frozen ponds and ice rinks become playgrounds for skating and hockey. People play indoor sports whatever the weather. Racquetball, weightlifting and bowling are year-round activities.

For many people in the U.S., sports are not just for fun. They're almost a religion. Thousands of sports fans buy expensive tickets to watch their favorite teams and athletes play in person. Other fans watch the games at home, glued to their TV sets. The most devoted sports buffs never miss a game. Many a wife becomes a "sports widow" during her husband's favorite season. America's devotion to athletics has created a new class of wealthy people: professional athletes. Sports stars often receive million-dollar salaries. Some even make big money appearing in advertisements for soft drinks, shoes and even toiletries.

Not all Americans worship sports, but athletics are an important part of their culture. Throughout their school life, Americans learn to play many sports. All students take physical education classes in school. Some try out for the school teams, while others join intramural sports leagues. Athletic events at universities attract scores of fans and benefit the whole community. Many people also enjoy non-competitive activities like hiking, biking, horse-back riding, camping or hunting. To communicate with American sports nuts, it helps if you can talk sports.

Sports in America represent the international heritage of the people who play. Many sports were imported from other countries. European immigrants brought tennis, golf, bowling and boxing to America. Football and baseball came from other Old World games. Only basketball has a truly American origin. Even today some formerly "foreign" sports like soccer are gaining American fans. In 1994 the U.S. hosted the World Cup for the first time ever.

Not only do Americans import sports, but they export sports forever, as well. Satellites broadcast games to sports fans around the globe. The World Series, the U.S. professional baseball championship, has begun to live up to its name. The names of American superstars like basketball great Michael Jordan have become household words the world over. Who knows? sports seasons may even change world weather patterns.

(478 words)

Word List

fall	[fɔːl]	n.	(美)秋天
baseball	['beɪsbɔːl]	n.	棒球
occupy	['ɒkjʊpaɪ]	v.	占据,占领
sideline	['saɪdlaɪn]	n.	(足球、网球等球场的)边线
surfing	['sɜːfɪŋ]	n.	冲浪
sailing	['seɪlɪŋ]	n.	航海
freezing	['friːzɪŋ]	adj.	冰冷的

rink	[rɪŋk]	n.	溜冰场
hockey	['hɒkɪ]	n.	曲棍球
weightlifting	['weɪtˌlɪftɪŋ]	n.	举重
bowling	['bəʊlɪŋ]	n.	保龄球
widow	['wɪdəʊ]	n.	寡妇
athletics	[æθ'letɪks]	n.	体育运动,竞技
advertisement	[əd'vɜːtɪsmənt]	n.	广告
toiletry	['tɔɪlɪtrɪ]	n.	化妆品
worship	['wɜːʃɪp]	v.	崇拜,仰慕
intramural	[ˌɪntrə'mjʊərəl]	adj.	学校内部的,单位内部的
hiking	['haɪkɪŋ]	n.	远足
camping	['kæmpɪŋ]	n.	野营
heritage	['herɪtɪdʒ]	n.	传统
immigrant	['ɪmɪgrənt]	n.	移民
origin	['ɒrɪdʒɪn]	n.	起源,根源
host	[həʊst]	v.	主办,主持
broadcast	['brɔːdkɑːst]	v.	广播,播报
championship	['tʃæmpɪənʃɪp]	n.	锦标赛

Idioms & Expressions

take center court	占据主要位置
a variety of	许多,各种各样
flock to	涌向……
scuba diving	戴水肺的潜水,斯库巴潜水
revel in	以……为乐
delight in	以……为乐
many a	许多(后接单数谓语动词)
physical education	体育课
not only... but... as well	不仅……而且……
live up to	不辜负,达到

Unit Five

Exercises

1. [Definitions]

Match the words in the box with their meanings. Write the word that stands for the definition in the appropriate answer space.

occupy	variety	flock	revel	freezing
advertisement	worship	represent	devoted	immigrant
origin	host	broadcast	household	pattern

1) _____ : giving someone or something a lot of love and attention.
2) _____ : to officially speak or take action for another person or group of people.
3) _____ : someone who enters another country to live there permanently.
4) _____ : an event that is a beginning; a first part or stage of subsequent events.
5) _____ : to show respect and love for a god, especially by praying in a religious building.
6) _____ : to send out radio or television programmes.
7) _____ : a social unit living together.
8) _____ : to fill, use, or exist in (a place or a time).
9) _____ : the regular way in which something happens, develops, or is done.
10) _____ : to provide the place and everything that is needed for an organized event.
11) _____ : below the temperature at which water turns to ice.
12) _____ : celebrate noisily, often indulging in drinking; engage in uproarious festivities.
13) _____ : a picture, set of words, or a short film, which is intended to persuade people to buy a product or use a service, or that gives information about a job that is available, an event that is going to happen, etc.
14) _____ : move as a crowd or in a group.
15) _____ : a lot of things of the same type that are different from each other in some way.

2. [Sample Sentences]

Use the new words you have learned from the box in the following sentence. Change the form where necessary.

1) They put a(n) _____ in *The Morning News*, offering a high salary for the right person.
2) In the west, Jesus Christ is _____ by the majority of people.
3) The chairman's speech will be _____ nationwide.

4) The child shows a normal _____ of development.
5) Britain _____ the World Cup in 1966.
6) Immigrants rarely return to their country of _____.
7) McDonald's has become a _____ word.
8) Soccer player Beckham has many _____ fans.
9) He _____ in his new-found fame.
10) A large couch _____ most of the space in the living room.
11) It's _____ in this house. Can't I turn on the heating?
12) The girls come from a _____ of different backgrounds.
13) In the summer, tourists _____ to the museums and art galleries.
14) California has many _____ from other states.
15) Brown areas _____ deserts on the map.

3. [Translation]

A. Translate the following English sentences into Chinese.

1) This treatment represents a significant advance in the field of cancer research.

2) This country has assimilated immigrants from many countries.

3) How does he occupy himself now that he's retired?

4) Coca Cola is a household name around the world.

5) School authorities should pay close attention to the changing patterns of behaviour among students.

B. Translate the following Chinese sentences into English by using the word in the bracket.

1) 哪个国家将主办下届奥运会？(host)

2) 她是一位贤妻良母。(devoted)

3) 阅读占去了我大部分的闲暇时间。(occupy)

4) 这位女演员陶醉于传媒对她的吹捧。(revel)

5) 社会动荡是经济问题引起的。(origin)

Unit Five

4. 【Writing】

Write an article of 150–200 words in English. Use the ideas given below.

Title: My Favorite Sport
Introduction: I am a sports fan—my favorite sport—it has become part of my life.
Development: My favorite sport is applicable—it is well-accepted among the public.
Conclusion: Doing sports can improve our physical well-being—doing sports is a good distraction from dull routine life—doing sports is a good way of making new friends.

Reading Skills：解题思路(5)

一般而论,阅读文章的题目类型可大致分为6类,即:主旨题、态度题、例子题、细节题、词汇题、推理题。接着就是题干寻词,即寻找问题中的关键词,这些关键词通常可以设定为:首字母大写的名词、人名、地名、机构、引号内容等。然后将这些关键词做一简单叠加,得出的相关意思一般就是文章的主要内容。最后,利用这些关键词回文定位,再对照每个问题的四个选项,就可得出正确答案。

主旨题的正确选项特点是:概括性强、且通常不含过分肯定或绝对意义的词,如 **all, no one, only, absolutely, entirely** 等。

态度题的正确选项是比较有限度、有保留的词语,如 **partially correct, critical, skeptical, approve, disapprove** 等。而具有过于中性、攻击、热情等特点的词语一般排除,如 **indifferent, neutral, condemn, absolutely, fervent** 等。

例子题的应对策略是:例子本身可迅速扫过,不需细读。考题答案往往在例子前后总结性的话里。

推理判断题应对的方法是:注意那些话中有话的间接表达句、含义深刻或结构复杂的句子、文章或段落的开头或结尾处。

此外,文章中数字频繁出处、转折处、引用内容、谚语、比喻处、长难句处要多加留心,往往是出题重点。

Text 2 (Extensive Reading)

Parents—A Soul Harbor
父母——心灵的港湾

As our country heads into the fourth week of recovery from the tragic events of September 11, it's more important than ever to understand how people respond to the chronic stress that comes in the wake of trauma. Everyone will experience some kind of stress reaction, and for each of us the healing process will be unique. Shock, grief, sadness, fear, anger, and emotional numbness are among the initial reactions that for some may now be abating but for others may persist. For survivors, victims' families, and rescue workers, stress reactions may be particularly severe. We need to appreciate that this trauma is like none seen before in the United States. Not only do we have the horrifying images of what happened played and replayed on television, but we also have the continuing worry that there may be more conflict ahead. All of this adds to a critical public-health challenge for our country. While much is being done to combat terrorism, there are some immediate steps Americans can take to get through this stressful period, which can also serve to strengthen relationships, families and communities.

Parents especially need to be cautious at this time. Children's unmistakable signs of stress in the first days—clinging fears, sleep problems—may now give way to symptoms that are trickier to interpret. Children of different ages will understand and react differently to what has happened. As a result of chronic stress, some kids might become even more withdrawn, irritable, or reluctant to leave home, while others may react with headaches, stomachaches, or uncustomary disobedience such as neglecting chores, ignoring homework, or acting out at school. Indeed, this is a time to stay in close contact with teachers and officials, who are often among the first to spot signs emotional distress.

There are many things that parents can do to help their children through these difficult times, and those actions will be more effective when parents make some basic resolutions of their own. First, parents need to recognize and deal with their own emotional reactions in order to more effectively help children with their feelings. Parents have the difficult task of striking the balance between sharing their own feelings with their children and at the same time not transferring their own anxiety to them. One of the best things parents can do for their children in the weeks and months ahead is to take steps to promote their physical activity, and seeking support from friends, family, and colleagues who can listen and empathize. For some adults and children whose symptoms are interfering with work, school, or relationships, consulting with a mental health professional will be an important source of help.

Just as a distressed parent may be a source of anxiety for children, an optimistic parent can instill a sense of security. Spend time with your child and provide reassurance. Physical presence demonstrates connection and consistency of people in the child's life. Provide ongoing opportunities for children to talk. Structure is very important now. For example, it's important to maintain the household schedule as closely as possible. Parents who take their kids to the park at a certain time should continue to do so; meals should take place as usual.

When parents do talk to their children about recent events, they should focus not on the horror but on what's being done to protect them. Let children know that people in authority—including the president, Congress, local police, and their teachers—are doing everything possible. Explain that people from all over the country—and even from other nations—are offering their services. And let them know especially that their home and school are safe, and that ensuring their security is your main job.

Finally—and this may be very difficult for parents who are understandably upset and concerned—it is crucial now to convey the message that it's OK to enjoy life—and even to have fun. It doesn't diminish the loss or the scope of the tragedy to point out that much of what was important to their well-being before—family, friends, school, community life—is unchanged and that terrorist attacks are rare aberrations in America. Also, remember that in coping with challenges and tragedy, we can become stronger and more resilient as people, families, and as a nation.

(715 words)

Word List

chronic	['krɒnɪk]	adj.	慢性的
stress	[stres]	n.	压力
trauma	['trɔːmə]	n.	精神创伤
grief	[griːf]	n.	悲伤,痛苦
numbness	[nʌmnɪs]	n.	麻木
initial	[ɪ'nɪʃəl]	adj.	起初的,开始的
abate	[ə'beɪt]	v.	减弱,减轻
severe	[sɪ'vɪə]	adj.	严重的
horrifying	['hɒrɪfaɪŋ]	adj.	令人恐怖的
combat	['kɒmbæt]	v.	与……抗争,对抗
terrorism	['terərɪzəm]	n.	恐怖主义
cautious	['kɔːʃəs]	adj.	谨慎的,小心的
unmistakable	[ˌʌnmɪ'steɪkəbəl]	adj.	明白无误的
symptom	['sɪmptəm]	n.	症状
interpret	[ɪn'tɜːprɪt]	v.	解释,说明
withdrawn	[wɪð'drɔːn]	adj.	孤僻的,内向的
irritable	['ɪrɪtəbəl]	adj.	易怒的,暴躁的
disobedience	[ˌdɪsə'biːdɪəns]	n.	不顺从,违抗
optimistic	[ˌɒptɪmɪstɪk]	adj.	乐观的
instill	[ɪn'stɪl]	v.	灌输
reassurance	[ˌriːə'ʃʊərəns]	n.	安慰,保证
household	['haʊshəʊld]	n.	家庭
crucial	['kruːʃəl]	adj.	关键的,重要的
diminish	[dɪ'mɪnɪʃ]	v.	减少,降低
aberration	[ˌæbə'reɪʃən]	n.	差错,偏离
resilient	[rɪ'zɪlɪənt]	adj.	迅速复原的

Idioms & Expressions

respond to	对……作出回应	in the wake of	随着
be reluctant to do	不乐意做……	act out	（用行动来）发泄
in close contact with	与……保持密切联系	interfere with	干涉……
sense of security	安全感	in authority	当权
cope with	处理……		

Exercises

1. [Questions]

Based on the information provided in the text, answer the following questions briefly.

1) After the September 11 tragedy, what seems more important?

2) What adds to a critical public-health challenge for the U.S.A.?

3) What is the first advice for parents mentioned in the passage?

4) What is expected of an optimistic parent?

5) What is the final and most difficult advice for parents?

2. [Multiple Choices]

Choose the right answer from the four choices marked A, B, C, and D.

1) The main idea of the passage is _____.

   A. long live America

   B. we are living in a changing world in a changing time

   C. live your life and hug your children

   D. you may choose not to see it, but you may not choose to know it

2) According to the passage, the one which is NOT the symptom of emotional distress is _____.

   A. ignoring homework

   B. neglecting chores

   C. acting out school

   D. back pain

3) It can be inferred from the 4th paragraph that _____.

   A. Americans should live normal life

   B. Americans should live a cautious life

   C. Americans should live a war-time life

   D. Americans should live a menaced life

4) The author's attitude toward children is _____.

   A. strict and expecting

   B. kind and loving

   C. ambivalent

   D. disinterested

5) It can be concluded from the passage that _____.

   A. children should be isolated from the outside world

   B. children should play more computer games

   C. children should learn the importance of self-reliance

   D. it is of vital importance that parents control their own emotions properly

Text 3 (Fast Reading)

The "Mommy Track"
"妈妈的未来"

For many thousands of years, in cultures across the globe, women have traditionally been seen to be subservient to men. Thus, they have not, over the centuries, been awarded the same social privileges of rank, title and earning capacity. The technical revolution, however, has brought about significant changes in working practices that are resulting in the re-definition of women's role in society and the workplace: the so-called "mommy track".

Traditional Ideas about Genders

Differences in gender have traditionally been so deeply rooted in social thinking that boys and girls have been treated differently, even from the moment of birth. Indeed, psychologists have shown that new born babies, if they are dressed in blue (a traditional colour for male babies) have been described by adults as strong and handsome, and when they cried people would say they were showing their frustrations in the only way they were able. In contrast, however, if the baby was dressed in pink (a traditional colour for female babies) they were described as pretty and delicate. And when they cried people would say they were displaying their feminine emotions.

Yet this social phenomenon existed regardless of the true sex of the baby. For example, if a male baby was dressed in pink he would still be described as having feminine traits, and displaying feminine emotions so long as the people believed the (boy) child was actually a girl. Thus, the scene was set for the remainder of the child's life, when, traditionally, schools argued that boys were better at math and girls better at art subjects. And in adulthood, there would be jobs for men, involving positions of authority and responsibility, which it has traditionally assumed women were too emotionally weak to undertake. Thus, they found themselves relegated to positions either as a mother and housewife, or in the caring professions such as nursing or teaching. Yet it seems these attitudes may be changing.

New Gender Roles in the New Age

The rapid, and as yet uncapped development in technology, especially computer technology, is leading to a whole new way of working, and a revised thinking in the roles played by both men and women in modern societies, intensified by a shortage of skilled professionals and an aging population. Furthermore, the latter half of the last century witnessed a rapid growth in service industries that rose from 56% to 69% between 1960 and 1985 in America and from 33% to 55% during the same period in Europe. This, coupled with the integration of computers in virtually every aspect of work, from farming to telecommunications, has given rise to what is often termed the information age. That is an age where information and knowledge replaces traditional manufacturing techniques that are more often than not, at least in part, undertaken by machines, making their human counterparts redundant and making it easier, argues Charles Handy, "...for women to do satisfying jobs".

What this also means, however, is that organizations now require well-educated, creative and talented people. Traditional industries, on the other hand, simply needed people who were competent at doing whatever it was the job demanded of them. Yet the demands of work have changed significantly from a "can-do" environment to one where people are expected to cooperate with colleagues, solve problems, and make decisions, whilst computers have revolutionized the way in which data is collected, stored, and retrieved. And electronic communication such as e-mail and video conferencing enables people to communicate effectively over distance and even time, negating the need for people to be gathered in one building. In short, people are now able to work from home.

The new practices have also opened up a gateway for women, who may have other commitments such as child care, to return to work. Indeed, as more and more business is conducted on a global scale where different time zones have to be considered, work is demanding a great deal more flexibility in terms of working time. Thus the days of the traditional 9:00 to 5:00 office job are rapidly disappearing. And this type of work, as it happens, is often ideally suited to women who may have other commitments, such as child care, to consider along with their work commitments.

New "Mommy track": Pros and Cons

Even so, employers have yet to fully realize, and accept, the valuable role that woman can, and do play in modern working environments. Indeed, as Felice Schwartz (1989) argues: "the mommy track enables a company to keep many talented career-and-family women who otherwise would leave because of family demands." And this is an essential consideration for any company because the cost of employing and training new people far exceeds the cost of retaining their present personnel, especially when those people hold key positions within the company. Others, however, argue that the responsibility for child care, and other such roles traditionally reserved for women, should be borne by both parties, that is to say both the husband and the wife equally, and should not be shouldered by the woman alone. This, however, may cause more problems than it would intend to solve, as most of the working population would demand greater flexibility in their working hours, rather than, as it is at present, around half the working population.

Change is a natural process in any society, and work patterns are in no way isolated from those changes. Yet along with changes such as the types of work people do, and the re-structuring of working hours, comes a change in attitudes. Attitudes, however, are far more resistant to change than are more tangible or visible changes. Nevertheless, the changes are happening, and no doubt will continue to happen, changing forever the traditional roles played out by men and women in the workplace and society at large.   (960 words)

Exercises

1. [True, False, Not Given]

Decide whether the following statements are True, False or Not Given.

T (for True) if the statement agrees with the information given in the passage;

F (for False) if the statement doesn't agree with the information given in the passage;

NG (for Not Given) if the information is not given in the passage.

1) Psychologists have shown that the way babies are treated depends on their sex.
2) Boys are better at math and science while girls are better at art subjects.
3) The information age has led to higher unemployment for men.
4) Modern work practices have led to a "can-do" environment.
5) Employing new staff is often very expensive for companies.
6) According to the author, shared child responsibility would not be very beneficial.
7) People's attitudes to work are quickly changing.

2. 【Blank-Filling】

For questions 1)–3), complete the sentences with the information given in the passage.

1) "Mommy track" in this article means the re-definition of women's role in society and the workplace caused by _____.

2) Between 1960 and 1985 in Europe service industry grew from _____.

3) Modern work demands have changed from a "can-do" environment to one where people are expected to _____.

 # Unit Six

Text 1 (Intensive Reading)

> **Background Tips: Inclusion Education**
> Inclusion education refers to the practice of educating students with special needs in regular classes for all or nearly all of the day instead of in special education classes. Advocates of regular inclusion and full inclusion believe that students with special needs "belong" to the regular classroom. Students with and without special needs can learn from each other. No one is deficit.

An Open-classroom System
开 放 的 教 室

I began teaching at the James School twenty-two years ago when I was twenty-six. In those days, the place was very different. But times change, and of course educational theory changes too. Methods and materials change. Even the building looks different. Let me show you what I mean.

Here, look around. I like this room. I love the light. Twenty years ago, it was a lot less pleasant. We had fewer windows, for example. We have all desks in a row. Since everything was fastened to the floor, a student sat in the same place all day long. Oh! We had to be very strict! Now, students move all over the room. They go to different areas for different subjects and they write at these movable tables. The students are more active, thus they are less restless and more attentive. At least that's the basic theory.

We use an open-classroom system here at the James. Each student makes a work contract with his teacher. Basically, he agrees to do a certain amount of work on a certain project. He hands the work in when he gets it done. He works at his own speed and plans his own time. If he is particularly interested in one subject—math, for instance—he can study that subject more thoroughly than the others. But he must also complete his contract in arts or reading or social science. Freedom within a well-planned system: that's what we are trying to offer.

You can see some of the advantages of an open classroom. Julie does beautiful work with her hands, and she's as good in math as the best students. But Julie has a learning problem in reading. She is still far behind the other students. But we're working hard with her, and she's making good progress at her own level. More important, she is continuing to work and grow with students of her own age. But twenty years ago we put special students like Julie in lower classes, sometimes in separate schools. What a waste!

Nowadays, we are trying to extend our classroom beyond the walls of the school building. This month we're doing a project with the local police. The kids are learning about policemen's lives by reading the police reports, riding in police cars, and even walking with them when they are on duty. They're learning that the problems of the police are the problems of the whole city. They are investigating their own attitudes about policemen, and writing down their own feelings. The students are learning by living. I guess the policemen are learning, too.

I feel excited about the new system, which is not perfect, though. But excitement is what learning is all about. You cannot be an exciting teacher unless you excite yourself. (463 words)

Word List

theory	[ˈθɪərɪ]	n.	理论
method	[ˈmeθəd]	n.	方法，办法
fasten	[ˈfɑːsən]	v.	拴紧，使固定，系
separate	[ˈsepəreɪt]	adj.	单独的，不同的
strict	[strɪkt]	adj.	严格的，精确的
movable	[ˈmuːvəbl]	adj.	可动的，不定的
restless	[ˈrestlɪs]	adj.	不安宁的，焦虑的
attentive	[əˈtentɪv]	adj.	注意的，留意的
contract	[ˈkɒntrækt]	n.	合约
thoroughly	[ˈθʌrəlɪ]	adv.	彻底地
social	[ˈsəʊʃəl]	adj.	社会的
extend	[ɪkˈstend]	v.	扩充，延伸，扩展
beyond	[bɪˈjɒnd]	prep.	超出，越过
investigate	[ɪnˈvestɪgeɪt]	v.	调查，研究
attitude	[ˈætɪtjuːd]	n.	态度，看法
excitement	[ɪkˈsaɪtmənt]	n.	激动，兴奋

Idioms & Expressions

be fastened to	固定于
make good progress at...	在……方面取得很大进步
on duty	在上班，在值班

Unit Six

Exercises

1. [Definitions]

Match the words in the box with their meanings. Write the word that stands for the definition in the appropriate answer space.

restless	thoroughly	extend	beyond	attitude
movable	separate	strict	fasten	contract
attentive	excitement	theory	social	basic

1) _____ : able to be moved and not fixed in one place or position.
2) _____ : the opinions and feelings that you usually have about something.
3) _____ : outside the range or limits of something or someone.
4) _____ : expecting people to obey rules or to do what you say.
5) _____ : an idea or set of ideas that is intended to explain something about life or the world, especially an idea that has not yet been proved to be true.
6) _____ : the feeling of being excited.
7) _____ : listening to or watching someone carefully because you are interested.
8) _____ : to make something affect more people, situations, areas etc than before.
9) _____ : to be attached to something firmly.
10) _____ : to divide or split into different parts.
11) _____ : completely.
12) _____ : an official agreement between two or more people, stating what each will do.
13) _____ : forming the most important or most necessary part of something.
14) _____ : relating to human society and its organization, or the quality of people's lives.
15) _____ : unwilling to keep still or stay where you are, especially because you are nervous or bored.

2. [Sample Sentences]

Use the new words and phrases you have learned from the box in the following sentence. Change the form where necessary.

1) The news caused great _____ among scientists.
2) Expensive luxuries that are _____ the reach of ordinary people.
3) As soon as they found out I was a doctor their whole _____ changed.
4) Audiences like those actors and actresses who are _____ to their show.
5) I'm taking a course on political _____ .

65

6) This company is very _____ about punctuality.

7) Management have agreed to _____ the deadline.

8) The rope is _____ to a tree.

9) The lighthouse is _____ from the land by a wide channel.

10) Tyler has agreed a seven-year _____ with a Hollywood studio.

11) She sat feeling _____ miserable.

12) Poor families unable to meet their _____ needs.

13) The financial crisis provokes serious _____ problems.

14) The children had been indoors all day, and were getting _____.

15) There is a teddy bear with _____ arms and legs.

3. [Translation]

A. Translate the following English sentences into Chinese.

1) The students are more active, thus they are less restless and more attentive.

2) If he is particularly interested in one subject—math, for instance—he can study that subject more thoroughly than the others.

3) Nowadays, we are trying to extend our classroom beyond the walls of the school building.

4) They are investigating their own attitudes about policemen, and writing down their own feelings.

5) You cannot be an exciting teacher unless you excite yourself.

B. Translate the following Chinese sentences into English by using the word in the bracket.

1) 船只在汹涌的大海中缓慢前进。(make progress)

2) 那工作他只干了一个月就厌倦了,决定不干了。(restless)

3) 我们马上就要在盖特威克(Gatwick)机场着陆,请大家系好座位上的安全带。(fasten)

4) 这个词有三种不同的意思。(separate)

5) 通货膨胀已经超过了 8%。(go beyond)

4. 【Writing】

Some people feel that in order to improve the quality of our education, we should encourage high school students to evaluate and criticize their teachers. Other feels it will cause the loss of respect and discipline in the classroom. To what extent do you agree or disagree? Please write a 120–150 words essay to state your opinion.

Reading Skills: 精炼生动的俚语

如同中文中成语的作用一般,英语中的俚语往往能以简练、生动、形象的方式表达复杂的涵义。辨析,并在日常的英语阅读中积累俚语是体味英美文化和提高阅读水平的一个重点。

在阅读中,识别俚语是第一步,通常俚语以简单而形象的名词构成。很常见的是动物型俚语,例如在英语中 wolf 经常带有贬义, a lone wolf 指 a solitary person, a cry wolf 意为 a person usually gives a wrong alarm。猫通常带有神秘色彩,比如说 Do not let the cat out of the bag,意思是 Do not give away the secret。蝴蝶则通常拿来形容人的心情起伏不定。比如说 I have been waiting for the test result with butterflies in my stomach,意思是 I have been waiting for the test result nervously。

还有一种经常在阅读出现的俚语是由两个发音相似的或者是首字母相同的叠词组成。比如 bumpy-pumpy（崎岖不平的）, wishy-washy（淡然无味的）, rest and recreation（休息）, thick and thin（艰难险阻）。

积累了许多俚语,但在阅读中还常会遇到生词,这就需要动用想象力和英美文化常识来辨别了。比如 Life is sometimes just a bowl of cherries. Strawberry（草莓）, Blueberry（蓝莓）, Raspberry（蔓越莓）, Blackberry（黑莓、桑葚）等词都享有一个词根 'berry'。所以读者根据自己在吃新鲜美味水果时的感受便可猜出 a bowl of cherries 的意思为 delightful。

Text 2 (Extensive Reading)

A Handful of History
扑克——手中的历史

The next time you do a card trick—remember this. You're playing with history. The playing cards we use today are much like those having been used for hundreds of years. The most interesting things are the suits and face cards. A suit of a playing card is not a thing to be worn. It means Hearts, Spades, Diamonds or Clubs. The figures are placed on each card with the number or value of the card. The face cards are the Jacks, Queens, Kings, and, of course, the Jokers.

What do you think the suits stand for? Let's take the Hearts first. When you say that an athlete has a lot of heart, what do you mean? You mean that he is brave. So, you see, the King of Hearts is a Brave King.

Look at the design of the Spade on a card. The word spade comes from the Italian word, which means sword. With a little imagination, you can see the handle and the blade. Of course, the blade has been made much shorter on the card.

The Diamond and Club designs also have interesting stories. The Diamond design is one that you probably know already. It stands for the expensive gems that you and I have seen in jewelry stores. At first it stood for the rich traders who found and sold such gems. The Club looks a little like a three-leaf clover design. It has the lowest rank of the suits. It is like a captain, and the Heart is like a general. The Spade means the regular farmers or peasants.

Now you see how some suits of playing cards have more value or power than others. The face cards are usually powerful in any card game. The King is one of the strongest. There are four different Kings, and each one stands for a real person. The King of Hearts first meant Charlemagne. He lived about 800 years after the birth of Christ. He was one of the most powerful kings in Europe after Julius Caesar of Rome. Julius Caesar, by the way, is the king of Diamonds.

We must go further back in history to find out the names of the two other kings. The young Alexander the Great of Macedonia is the King of Clubs and King David is the King of Spades. David is the person who killed the giant Goliath. When someone talks about David and Goliath, he means that a smaller or weaker person is trying to fight a very large and strong enemy. David beat Goliath and became a king. He probably never thought that he would have a place in playing cards.

We must go back to the Bible and the times of David again to find two of our queens. Rachel was a famous woman in the Bible. She is the Queen of Diamonds.

Remember that the Heart stands for bravery. A very brave woman is the Queen of Hearts. That was Judith, who killed an enemy general.

When Alexander the great was a general, one of the important women goddesses was Athena. She stood for wisdom. Athena is the Queen of Spades.

Queen Elizabeth I of England is thought to be the Queen of Clubs. She ruled England when America was mostly a wilderness.

The Jacks are sometimes called Knaves. A knave is usually a person who gets into trouble. But the playing cards stand for famous knights in history. These men made themselves famous for their courage and bravery, but they were not kings.

The Joker of the card deck is the one that doesn't always fit. He is sometimes used as an extra card. He sometimes becomes more powerful than any other card. He does not stand for any one person like some of the other cards. But I think that you can see what his name means.

Unit Six

So, you see that you can hold some history in your hands. History from King David to Queen Elizabeth is all on the front of playing cards.

(674 words)

Word List

trick	[trɪk]	n.	诡计,欺诈,恶作剧
suit	[sjuːt]	n.	套装,诉讼,请求
heart	[hɑːt]	n.	心,要点,红桃(扑克牌)
spade	[speɪd]	n.	铲子,黑桃(扑克牌)
diamond	[ˈdaɪəmənd]	n.	钻石,方块(扑克牌)
club	[klʌb]	n.	俱乐部,梅花(扑克牌)
figure	[ˈfɪɡə]	n.	图形,数字,形状
brave	[breɪv]	adj.	勇敢的
imagination	[ɪˌmædʒɪˈneɪʃən]	n.	想象,想象力
handle	[ˈhændl]	v.	处理,操作
gem	[dʒem]	n.	宝石
clover	[ˈkləʊvə]	n.	四叶草,幸运草
design	[dɪˈzaɪn]	n.	设计,图样
captain	[ˈkæptɪn]	n.	船长
general	[ˈdʒenərəl]	n.	将军
value	[ˈvæljuː]	n.	价值,重要性
giant	[ˈdʒaɪənt]	n.	巨人
enemy	[ˈenəmɪ]	n.	敌人
beat	[biːt]	v.	打,打败
wisdom	[ˈwɪzdəm]	n.	智慧
wilderness	[ˈwɪldənɪs]	n.	荒野,荒地
knight	[naɪt]	n.	骑士,武士
courage	[ˈkʌrɪdʒ]	n.	勇气

Idioms & Expressions

a handful of	一把;少量		stand for	代表
find out	找出,查明,发现			

Exercises

1. [Cloze]

The sentences below are from the text you have just read. Please fill in the same words as in the text.

Queen Elizabeth I of England is thought _____ be the Queen of Clubs. She ruled England _____ America was mostly a wilderness.

The Jacks are sometimes called Knaves. A knave is usually a person _____ gets into trouble. But the playing cards stand _____ famous knights in history. These men made _____ famous for their courage and bravery, _____ they were not kings.

The Joker of the card deck is the one _____ doesn't always fit. He is sometimes used _____ an extra card.

2. [Multiple Choices]

Choose the right answer from the four choices marked A, B, and C.

1) The most interesting things of the playing cards are _____.
   A. the suits and face cards
   B. those cards used hundreds of years ago
   C. the Jacks and the Joker

2) The word "Heart" means _____.
   A. bravery   B. love   C. hate

3) Which of the three has the lowest rank of suits?
   A. the Diamond   B. the Spade   C. the Club

4) Which of the following is the most powerful king?
   A. Alexander   B. Charlemagne   C. King David

5) The Joker is _____.
   A. a person who makes you love
   B. a game that makes love
   C. a person who make you sad

Text 3 (Fast Reading)

Food Politics
食物政治

Two of the top buzzwords in the food world are "local" and "organic." The popularity of both movements is on the rise, but is one better than the other? We went to the experts to find out.

Lindsay Coulter, Nature Conservation Outreach Coordinator says, "The best and perhaps most obvious choice would be to look for organic food that is produced locally. By supporting organic farmers, you are not only reducing your personal exposure to pesticides, herbicides, hormones and genetically modified organisms, you are also supporting organic farming principles. Certification depends on maintaining standards that protect the health of our land, air, water, and wildlife."

Leslie Huffman, Apple Specialist, Ontario Ministry of Agriculture, Food and Rural Affairs remarks: "The choice between locally grown or organic produce depends on the consumer's priorities. In general, locally grown food is the best choice. Purchasing locally grown food will minimize the environmental impact of transportation needed to import produce, and will support the local growers and the local economy. Local growers offer the freshest, highest-quality produce."

Serena Strulovitch, professional dietitian states: "There are health benefits to both buying locally grown food and organic food. Organic foods offer the health benefit of not having any pesticides. Locally grown food is normally picked (at a riper stage) since it does not need to go through the long shipping process, so it often contains more nutrients. Since buying organic foods often means that items travel far distances and this equals high oil dependency and pollution, there is a benefit to buying locally grown food."

Growth hormones in cows, pesticides on produce and antibiotics in poultry—these are among the reasons many Americans are turning to organic foods. In fact, sales of organics have surged more than 20 percent each year in the past decade. According to the Food Marketing Institute, more than half of Americans now buy organic food at least once a month.

Whether organic chicken or pesticide-free lettuce represents "healthier" alternatives has long been a subject for debate.

Proponents, such as Katherine DiMatteo, executive director of the Organic Trade Association, cite the fact that organics are grown under strict standards of purity based on the elimination of toxic agricultural chemicals.

DiMatteo says even the soil is better: "The soil that organic is grown in is healthier. This comes from the fact that the soil has nutrient value. Healthy soil, healthy plants."

But any suggestion that organic food is somehow superior doesn't sit well with Alex Avery, director of research at The Hudson Institute Center for Global Food Issues.

"Organic foods have never been shown to be healthier, more nutritious or safer than conventional foods," said Avery, "despite dozens of scientific studies. There is no weight that organic is better or healthier for you."

Food safety experts say organic or not, consumers have to observe the same rules if they want to avoid getting sick. Thoroughly wash—even scrub—all produce. And, if the skin won't come clean, peel it off.

Organic livestock may have had the run of the farm and eaten pesticide-free grain, but that doesn't mean they won't come to slaughter loaded with bacteria. Just like conventional chickens, organic birds can harbor salmonella, E. coli and campylobacter. These can cause anything from a mild intestinal illness to a life-threatening infection. To avoid that, organic chickens (or any organic meat) should be handled the same as a regular product—observing cleanliness rules in the kitchen and making sure they are cooked to the proper temperature: 180 degrees for poultry, 160 degrees for beef.

If, in fact, organics have nothing much to offer beyond a higher price—they often cost more than conventional items—why bother with them at all? Taste is one reason. Some insist that organic products are more flavorful than other foods.

DiMatteo said there are broader reasons to go organic: "Environmental pollution does have an impact on the health of humans. We can definitely see a connection between chemical pest control and the potential for disease."

Plus, those who fear bio-engineered foods may be able to put their minds at ease by buying organic—not that there's necessarily anything to fear in the first place say proponents of genetically modified foods. However, the Organic Trade Association supports a moratorium on genetically modified foods, known in the trade as GMOs.

The OTA fears that interspecies movement of DNA might one day lead to unwarranted effects on the environment and/or human health. But that is far from the intent.

"Food (might) be modified to provide enriched vitamins, nutrients, improve food quality, make food last longer and eventually decrease the cost of food," said plant biotechnologist Sivramiah Shantharam, with the International Food Policy Research Institute.

Some examples of bioengineering: increasing the protein content of potatoes, making oils healthier and increasing nutrient levels in rice. Shantharam says the benefits don't end with food: "In China, cotton fields are sown with seeds that are genetically implanted with a bacterium that is toxic to bollworms, the larval stage of boll weevils. Without these seeds, the crop would be wiped out."

Organic producers have waged a vigorous fight to keep bio-engineered foods from being included in the government's new organic standards. Some GMOs were included the first time the government proposed those standards, in 1997. They were withdrawn after criticism they included non-organic components—such as food irradiation and the use of sewage sludge fertilizer.

Until the USDA announced its standards, "certified organic" labels meant a food had been recognized as such under a particular program or law. For example, the California Organic Foods Act has been in place since 1990.

"Sometimes it will be certified by a private program and sometimes by a state program," said DiMatteo.

But no matter how the product is labeled, Avery said the message should be clear: "The label does not imply organic food is healthier, safer or better for you in any way. It's purely a marketing label."

(994 words)

Exercises

1. [Questions]

Based on the information provided in the text, answer the following questions briefly.

1) What is organic food? Is it popular in China? Why/Why not?
2) What is local food? Is local-produced food welcomed in your area? Do people support it? How often do you buy it? Why/Why not?
3) Do experts suggest to wash food thoroughly no matter it is organic or not? Why?
4) Why does the organic chicken should be handled the same as the regular product?
5) Is there any scientific proof that organic food is healthier? Why are the proponents crazy about it?
6) What is GMO food? Why does organic food eater fight for banning it?

2. [Blank-Filling]

For questions 1)–4), complete the sentences with the information given in the passage.

1) Organic food is more expensive than the regular. _____ is one reason. Some people believe that organic products are more _____ than other foods.
2) Food might be modified to provide enriched _____ and _____, improve food quality, make food last longer, and eventually decrease the cost of food.
3) Organic producers have been fighting to keep _____ foods from being included in the government's new organic standards.
4) Certified organic labels meant a food had been recognized as such under a _____ or _____.

Unit Seven

Text 1 (Intensive Reading)

> **Background Tips: Best Living Standard in Canada**
> In size, Canada is the second largest country on earth. Its scenery of mountains, oceans, forests and prairies is spectacular. It has lively and rich culture, with many world famous actors, pop stars and writers. In annual "quality of life" surveys produced by the United Nation each year Canada regularly is rated as having the best standard of living in the world because of its health care, education, clean environment, social welfare, and so on.

What's in a Name?
名字的内涵？

While the vast regions of North America were long populated by Aboriginal peoples—the native Indians—with rich cultures and highly developed societies, Canada as a concept and a country is a very recent phenomenon. European contact with the landmass that would one day become Canada is thought to have begun with the arrival of Norsemen (Vikings) in the 11th century who came from the northern European regions and explored Canada's far north—but they did not stay. Later, the French and the British compete for territory and trading centers in Canada. Throughout the 18th century there were battles fought between the various Indian tribes and the French and British entrepreneurs. American history also affected Canada's history: following the American war of Independence, many of those who had remained loyal to the British monarchy left the newly republican America to settle the north of the border. So in 1867, Canada was born when Quebec, Ontario, New Brunswick and Nova Scotia all joined together. As time passed, other provinces and territories also joined.

What does the word "Canada" mean? Its actual derivation is uncertain, but many explanations exist. These stories about the very word "Canada" are indications of the diverse cultural backgrounds of the country. Some say that it comes from the Spanish for "nothing here", which might well have been the comments of the Spanish explorers who, looking for a passage to Asia, encountered this large, wild, forested, apparently unpopulated islands off the west coast of the country. (In fact, it was explorers who mistook Canada for India that began calling Aboriginal peoples "Indians").

Unit Seven

Others suggest the name of Canada comes from one or more of the languages spoken by the First Nations (a term now used to describe original Canadians). In Cree, it means "clean land"; in Mohawk, "castle"; to the Iroquois, ka-na-ka meant "village".

Place names can tell us a lot about the history of Canada. We find English rulers and nobles celebrated as in the provincial capitals of Halifax and Victoria. There are also, of course, French names especially in Quebec (Montreal is the translation of "Mount Royal"). Other names are vivid reflections of the adventures of early explorers—you can wonder about how Medicine Hat and Moosejaw, both cities in Alberta, got their names. At Sioux (pronounced "Sue") Lookout in Ontario, you can imagine early settlers keeping watch for native Indians. Others, like Great Bear Lake and Buffalo Narrows, suggest the dangerous forms of wildlife that still roam Canada.

(417 words)

Word List

vast	[vɑːst]	adj.	广阔的, 巨大的
aboriginal	[ˌæbəˈrɪdʒɪnəl]	adj.	原始的, 土著的
concept	[ˈkɒnsept]	n.	概念, 观念
phenomenon	[fɪˈnɒmɪnən]	n.	现象
contact	[ˈkɒntækt]	v.	接触, 联系
explore	[ɪkˈsplɔː]	v.	探险, 探究
territory	[ˈterɪtərɪ]	n.	领土, 版图, 领域
throughout	[θruː(ː)ˈaʊt]	prep.	遍及, 贯穿
entrepreneur	[ˌɒntrəprəˈnɜː]	n.	企业家
independence	[ˌɪndɪˈpendəns]	n.	独立, 自主, 自立
monarchy	[ˈmɒnəkɪ]	n.	君主政体, 君主国
derivation	[ˌderɪˈveɪʃən]	n.	来历
exist	[ɪɡˈzɪst]	v.	存在
diverse	[daɪˈvɜːs]	adj.	不同的, 多种多样的
encounter	[ɪnˈkaʊntə]	n.	意外的相见, 遭遇
		v.	遇到, 偶然碰到, 遭遇
apparently	[əˈpærəntlɪ]	adv.	显然, 似乎
celebrate	[ˈselɪbreɪt]	v.	庆祝, 祝贺, 颂扬
explorer	[ɪkˈsplɔːrə]	n.	探测者
settler	[ˈsetlə]	n.	移居者
roam	[rəʊm]	v.	漫游, 闲逛, 徘徊

Idioms & Expressions

compete for...	争夺……，为……而竞争	remain loyal to...	始终忠实于……
keep watch for	留心(注意，看守)		

Exercises

1. [Definitions]

Match the words in the box with their meanings. Write the word that stands for the definition in the appropriate answer space.

encounter	phenomenon	aboriginal	monarchy	throughout
territory	contact	concept	independence	vast
exist	diverse	apparently	roam	settler

1) _____: someone who goes to live in a country or area where not many people like them have lived before, and that is a long way from any towns or cities.

2) _____: relating to the people or animals that have existed in a place or country from the earliest times.

3) _____: to meet someone without planning to.

4) _____: to happen or be present in a particular situation or place.

5) _____: an idea of how something is, or how something should be done.

6) _____: political freedom from control by the government of another country.

7) _____: land that is owned or controlled by a particular country, ruler, or military force.

8) _____: to write to or telephone someone.

9) _____: extremely large.

10) _____: something that happens or exists in society, science, or nature, especially something that is studied because it is difficult to understand.

11) _____: very different from each other.

12) _____: according to the way someone looks or a situation appears, although you cannot be sure.

13) _____: during all of a particular period, from the beginning to the end.

14) _____: to walk or travel, usually for a long time, with no clear purpose or direction.

15) _____: the system in which a country is ruled by a king or queen.

Unit Seven

2. [Sample Sentences]

Use the new words and phrases you have learned from the box in the following sentence. Change the form where necessary.

1) I first _____ him when studying at Cambridge.
2) _____ people are the first nation on the land of America.
3) European _____ have negotiated with native people about the land issue.
4) The custom of arranged marriages still _____ in many countries.
5) The plane was flying over enemy _____ .
6) Nigeria gained _____ from Britain in 1960.
7) It's very simple, once you grasp the _____ .
8) The refugees come across the border in _____ numbers.
9) Please do not hesitate to _____ me if you have any queries.
10) Language is a social and cultural _____ .
11) Mary likes subjects as _____ as pop music and archaeology.
12) She turned to face him, and he saw her anger had _____ gone.
13) The _____ of the emperor has been abolished after the war.
14) Chickens and geese _____ freely in the back yard.
15) We are open every weekend _____ the year.

3. [Translation]

A. Translate the following English sentences into Chinese.

1) Canada as a concept and a country is a very recent phenomenon.

2) Later, the French and the British compete for territory and trading centers in Canada.

3) Its actual derivation is uncertain, but many explanations exist.

4) These stories about the very word "Canada" are indications of the diverse cultural backgrounds of the country.

5) Others, like Great Bear Lake and Buffalo Narrows, suggest the dangerous forms of wildlife that still roam Canada.

B. Translate the following Chinese sentences into English by using the word in the bracket.

1) 雪整整下了一夜。(throughout)

2) 他们是些有着不同文化背景的人。(diverse)

3) 我在罗马邂逅了一位老朋友。(encounter)

4) 我无法理解如此抽象的概念。(concept)

5) 专家们正在勘察这个岛的各个部分。(explore)

4. 【Writing】

Some people spend their entire lives in one place. Others move a number of times throughout their lives, looking for a better job, house, community, or even climate. Which do you prefer: staying in one place or moving in search of another place? Write a 120–150 words essay, and you may refer to the following structure:

Introduction: Some spend life in one place—others choose to search around.
Development: I prefer... the reasons are...
Conclusion: Although I choose to... I understand another way.

Reading Skills: 辨别"信号"词

与中文表达方式中以"意"表形不同，英语文章需要大量的连结词，也就是信号词来起到承上启下的作用，即以"形"表意。

英语阅读中的信号词往往就像路标引路一样指引读者顺利把握文章提前设定的思路。所以理解什么样的词是信号词与其所发挥的作用十分关键。

信号词可以在任何句与句之间、段落之间找到。根据其作用，可以将其总结为以下几类：

1. 举例型(Illustration)：**for example, for instance, such as, as, like**

例如：People wear gowns at some serious ceremonies, like at marriages and graduations. 在阅读此句时，大家对 **ceremony** 这个词可能有些模糊，但之后由信号词"**like**"所引出的"**marriages**"(婚礼)and"**graduations**"(毕业典礼)中可以明白"**ceremony**"是表示正式场合、典礼。

2. 转折型(Conversion)：**but, however, on the contrast, instead, yet, although**

例如：Although he is intelligent,... 之后读者应该马上提高敏感度，后面所说的肯定是跟"**he is intelligent**"相反的论调，比如并不努力、成绩并不突出等。

3. 因果型(Cause and Effect)：

Cause: because, for, since, the reason is that
Effect: thus, accordingly, consequently, therefore

例如：Some countries increase the expense on the national defense. 接下来这个论点的原因(**cause**)作者是有责任向读者阐述清楚的，所以读者在熟知作者的心理和手法后，在阅读中往往可以更快更清晰地把握要点。

4. 递进型（Sequence）：**moreover, besides, furthermore, in addition**

例如：A couple of decades ago, women took the responsibilities of household, baby-caring, and cooking. Moreover,... 接下来读者便应该根据递进信号词的指示得知妇女还需要承担更多的责任。

Text 2 (Extensive Reading)

Oral and Non-material Cultural Heritage
口头与非物质文化遗产

Beijing Opera is the quintessence of China. As the largest Chinese opera form, it is extolled as "Oriental Opera". Having a history of 160 years, it has created many "firsts" in Chinese dramas: the abundance of repertoires, the number of artists, opera troupes, and spectators.

Beijing Opera is developed from absorbing many other dramatic forms, mostly from the local drama "Huiban" which was popular in South China during the 18th century. It is a scenic art integrating music, performance, literature, aria, and face-painting. Certain rules are set up and regulations are standardized during many artists' long practice on stage. Different from regional plays, it is stricter on the variety of the workmanship. The combination of virtual and reality—a special technique of expression, keeps it largely free from the restriction of time and space on stage performance. Beijing Opera has had many interesting names since it came into being, such as Jinghuang, Daxi, Pingju, Jingxi.

Beijing Opera presents dramatic plays and figures mainly by infusing four artistic methods: singing, dialogue, dancing and martial arts. Singing is utilized to intensify the appeal of the art by all kinds of tones. Dialogue is the complement of singing which is full of musical and rhythm sensation. Dancing refers to the body movements requiring high performing skills. Martial art is the combination and transformation of traditional Chinese combat exercises with dances.

The followings are the main roles in Beijing Opera performance:

Sheng: It's a common name of male characters and composed of Lao Sheng and Xiao Sheng. Lao Sheng refers to the middle-aged man with a beard who acts as the decency figure; for example, Zhugeliang in "Empty City Scheme". Xiao Sheng means young man without a beard. Zhangsheng in "The Story of the West Room" is a representative of Xiao Sheng.

Dan: The general name for female characters in Beijing Opera can be divided into Zhengdan, Huadan, Laodan, Wudan. Zhengdan is also called "Qingyi", who mainly plays the part of the strong-minded middle-aged woman who behaves elegantly. Huadan refers to little girls who often live in the bottom of society. Laodan refers to the senior woman and Wudan indicates the female who is good at fighting.

Jing: Painted face often refers to male characters with unique appearance or personality, such as Baozheng and Caocao. Besides, Chou is a comic role or righteous person. The actor's nose is painted by a piece of white powder, making him or her easily recognizable.

Lianpu is formed through dramatic artists' long-term practice and their understanding and judgment of the roles in plays. It is the colorful dressing on actors' faces. By using transformative and exaggerated figures, professional spectators would easily tell the characteristic of a role. In this way, it is called "the picture of hearts". There are certain formats of the facial painting in the aspect of color, type and shape. Usually, eyes, foreheads and cheeks are painted like wings of butterflies, swallows and bats.

Colors of Lianpu are varied with each representing a characteristic. For example, red symbolizes loyalty, such as Guanyu, a great general during Three Kingdoms Period (220—280). Black signifies honesty and frankness, such as Lord Bao, a righteous official during Northern Song Dynasty (960—1127), or abruptness and impertinence, such as Likui, an important figure in the famous Chinese ancient novel *All Men Are Brothers*. White stands for cattiness and cunning, with Caocao as its representative, a famous politician in the late Eastern Han Dynasty (25—220).

Qimo is a general designation for all kinds of stage properties and simple settings used in Beijing Opera performances. It comes from the real life experience. For example, an actor can practice the scene of galloping the horse simply by using a horsewhip without riding a real horse on stage. A bridge is made up of two chairs standing on each side of a table. Storms are realized by performers dancing with umbrellas. The imaginary performance skills largely bring to performers the freedom to express more life scenes.

There are many famous masters who are good at performing Beijing Opera. Among them, the Four Famous Dans—Mei Lanfang, Cheng Yanqiu, Shang Xiaoyun and Xun Huisheng—are most well-known at home and abroad. They are experts in performing the role of Dan and each has his own artistic feature. Their wonderful performances are still appreciated by many audiences. For example, "Farewell My Concubine" by Mei Lanfang, "Injustice to Dou'e" by Cheng Yanqiu, "Lady Zhaojun Going beyond the Great Wall" by Shang Xiaoyun and "Matchmaker" by Xun Huisheng.

Beijing Opera contains the soul of Chinese national culture. Its unique charm inspires ethos of Chinese people. There is no doubt that it is really the treasure of Chinese culture.

(785 words)

Unit Seven

Word List

quintessence	[kwɪn'tesəns]	n.	精粹，典型
extol	[ɪk'stəʊl]	v.	颂杨，称赞
repertoire	['repətwɑː]	n.	(准备演出的)节目，保留剧目
integrate	['ɪntɪgreɪt]	v.	综合
strict	[strɪkt]	adj.	严格的，精确的
workmanship	['wɜːkmənʃɪp]	n.	手艺，技巧
combination	[ˌkɒmbɪ'neɪʃn]	n.	结合，联合
virtual	['vɜːtʃuəl]	adj.	虚拟的
present	['prezənt]	v.	赠送，提出，呈现
infuse	[ɪn'fjuːz]	v.	注入，鼓舞
rhythm	['rɪðəm]	n.	节奏，韵律
transformation	[ˌtrænsfə'meɪʃn]	n.	变形，变质
combat	['kɒmbæt]	n.	争斗，战斗
decency	['diːsənsɪ]	n.	得体，礼貌
scheme	[skiːm]	n.	方案，计划，阴谋
senior	['siːnɪə]	adj.	年长的，高级的，资历深的
indicate	['ɪndɪkeɪt]	n.	指示，表明
unique	[juː'niːk]	adj.	独一无二的
comic	['kɒmɪk]	adj.	滑稽的，有趣的，喜剧的
exaggerate	[ɪg'zædʒəreɪt]	v.	夸张，扩大
spectator	[spek'teɪtə;'spekteɪtə]	n.	观众
symbolize	['sɪmbəlaɪz]	v.	象征，用记号表现
cattiness	['kætɪnɪs]	n.	如猫的性格，阴险
cunning	['kʌnɪŋ]	adj.	狡猾的，巧妙的，可爱的
politician	[ˌpɒlɪ'tɪʃən]	n.	政治家，政客
property	['prɒpətɪ]	n.	财产，性质
setting	['setɪŋ]	n.	周围，环境
largely	['lɑːdʒlɪ]	adv.	大部分，主要地
master	['mɑːstə]	n.	主人，大师
feature	['fiːtʃə]	n.	特点，特色，特性
appreciate	[ə'priːʃɪeɪt]	v.	欣赏，感激，赏识
matchmaker	['mætʃmeɪkə]	n.	媒人，安排比赛的人
treasure	['treʒə]	n.	宝物，财富

Idioms & Expressions

set up	建立	martial arts	武术
refer to	引用,指的是	bring to	使恢复知觉
no doubt	无疑		

Exercises

1. 【Questions】

Based on the information provided in the text, answer the following questions briefly.

1) What names have Beijing Opera been called in history?

2) In what way does Beijing Opera present the drama and interpret the figure?

3) Comments on the four roles in Beijing Opera performance.

4) What does the color White of the Lianpu stand for in Beijing Opera? Who is the main representative of this usage of color?

5) The four Beijing Opera masters: Mei Lanfang, Cheng Yanqiu, Shang Xiaoyun and Xun Huisheng are well known at home and abroad. Can you list the appreciated performance for each of them?

2. 【Blank-Filling】

For questions 1)–5), complete the sentences with the information given in the passage.

1) Qimo, as the settings used in Beijing Opera performance, comes from the _____.

2) Having a history of 160 years, Beijing Opera has absorbed many dramatic forms, mostly from the local drama _____.

3) _____ is the combination and transformation of traditional Chinese combat exercises with dances.

4) Zhengdan, also called "Qingyi", plays strong-minded and middle-aged woman, while Huadan refers to young girls who live in the _____ of society.

5) Colors of Lianpu can represent various characteristics, and Black suggests _____ and _____.

Unit Seven

Text 3 (Fast Reading)

Baseball
棒球的故事

Baseball may still be the great American game, even though many other countries are deeply involved with the game. It is very popular, for instance, in Japan, in Cuba, and in the Dominican Republic. In America, many children (not only boys these days) still play informal, "sadlot" baseball in their neighborhoods. Small towns and cities still maintain organized Little League or (for older children) Base Ruth baseball teams. In many cities, young adults organize informal "softball" leagues, and universities still maintain varsity baseball teams. Finally, professional baseball is still "big business".

Earlier, before television and air travel, professional baseball was confined to a few cities mostly, but not exclusively, on the east coast. Baseball parks were located near the urban centers and were small compared to football fields. Even today, the largest baseball stadium is the home field of the California Angels, Anaheim Stadium, which holds almost 65,000 spectators, while older Fenway Park, the home of the Boston Red Sox, holds only 34,000 fans. The activity involved in baseball is not as intense as that in other sports, hence games can be played one day after another, and even two games on one day—a double-header. Baseball used to be played only in the daytime, but after World War II, parks began to install massive lighting systems, and night baseball increased in popularity.

The less intense activity on the playing field also means that spectators can watch the game in a more relaxed and lazy way, an ideal way to fritter away a hot summer afternoon. Beer and soft drinks are available in addition to such snacks as peanuts, popcorn and Crackerjacks (popped corn covered with a crisp coating of dried molasses). Fans will undoubtedly eat at least one of the American sausages called a Frankfurter (Hot Dog, Frank, Red Hot), with pickles, onions, relish and slathered with mustard or ketchup.

Before World War II, there were two major leagues, or groupings, of baseball teams, the older National League and the American League. A third professional grouping, located in the South and attended almost entirely by African Americans, was the Negro League, a reflection of the segregation policies prevalent then even in Northern cities. Players usually were identified over long periods of time with one team. As a result, there was much fan loyalty not only to the team but also to individual players. Fans could quote the performance records of their favorite players, readjusting the figures every day after reviewing the newspapers accounts of the previous day's game. Children(especially boys) would collect Baseball Cards, 2×3 inch cards having a posed picture of a player on one side, and information about him on the other. These cards were only available in packages of chewing gum marketed particularly for children. (Later these cards were sold separately from the chewing gum. Early cards are collectors items, and command high prices in the souvenir business.)

This was the period of hero worship, the era of the Lone Eagle, Lindbergh, who conquered the Atlantic Ocean. Perhaps, as industrialization spread through America, people felt they were losing control of their lives, and that they were becoming buried and lost in a mass, faceless society. To return to some mythical past, where woodsmen and cowboys supposedly conquered nature and wild savages through personal effort and courage, was one way to preserve the notion of individual triumph. And in the present, sports heroes could also serve to remind Americans that talented individuals can succeed through hard work.

The radio announcers broadcasting descriptions of the games, and newspaper columnists (who frequently were masters of the short colloquial essay or story) writing about the games, exaggerated the exploits on the field and idealized the personal lives of players, thus actually creating many of the colorful heroes of this time. Sportswriter Westbrook Pegler became later in life a conservative political columnist, and sports radio announcer Ronald Reagan also became involved in politics later in his life.

After world War II, great changes in the game took place. First, there was demolition of the color barrier, starting slowly with the hiring of the superb athlete, African-American Jackie Robinson, by Brooklyn Dodgers manager Branch Rickey. At first, Robinson was booed whenever he appeared on the field. But several of his respected teammates showed their solidarity with him. Then a few other teams hired African-Americans who had demonstrated their abilities with the Negro Baseball League. Still there were problems with segregated transportation facilities and with segregated dining and housing regulations in some cities. Gradually all teams have become integrated. The courage and determination of Jackie Robinson (and Branch Rickey) will never be forgotten.

Improved transportation led to the wider distribution of teams; cities that formerly had two teams lost one to cities that had no local baseball team. Television too brought in increasing revenues, and players began to negotiate for higher salaries. Players themselves began to be traded to other teams almost as easily as children trade the players' cards. Even then there were not enough baseball teams to locate in every city that wanted one, so a modest number of new teams were created. This necessitated a longer playing season, which in turn led to the desirability of covered stadiums, especially in the far northern pat of the country.

The baseball season now begins with Spring Training in February at places such as Florida and Arizona, where the weather is mild at that time of year. The regular season begins at the beginning of April, and ends in October. The World (sic) Series between the leading teams in their respective leagues takes place in the latter part of October, when it is frequently uncomfortably cold for the players. This best four out of seven games determines the annual World's (sic) Champions, and marks the end of the baseball season. The World Series is an occasion for neighbors and co-workers to engage in some minor wagering on the outcome of the games. Betting on baseball games has always been present, even leading once to a scandal of players affecting the outcome of a game on direction by big money gamblers (The "Black Sox" scandal of 1919). Yet until recently the amount of money wagered had been relatively small. Now, gambling on sporting events such as baseball (and football and basketball, too) represents a sizable amount of money, as more and more Americans wager larger and larger amounts on these events.

　　Major league baseball stadiums have gotten larger and larger in recent times. The price of tickets has also risen considerably. Thus, more and more Americans are turning to minor league baseball played in some of the smaller cities around America. The minor league teams are supported by the major league owners as a place where new players can gain experience and improve their skills. Frequently a young player is called up to play major league, and sometimes a player in the majors who is not performing well may be sent down to the minors.　　　　　　　　　　　　　　　　　　　　　　　　　　　　　(1,170 words)

1. 【Questions】

Based on the information provided in the text, answer the following questions briefly.

1) Why do you think a lot of people love sports? In what way do sports reflect a country's culture?
2) Compared to football and basketball, baseball can be watched in a more relaxed and lazy way. Why?
3) Baseball is a very popular sport in the U.S. Is it popular in China? Why/Why not?
4) What type of sports are Chinese athletes good at? Why?
5) Comment on the role of media in Sport competition. Do you like to watch a match via television at home or would you prefer to watch in the stadium?

2. 【Blank-Filling】

For questions 1)–5), complete the sentences with the information given in the passage.

1) _____ may still be the great American game, even though it is also popular in other countries.
2) _____ is an occasion for neighbors and co-workers to engage in some minor wagering on the outcome of the games.
3) Before television and air travel, professional baseball was confined to a few cities mostly on the _____.
4) After world War Ⅱ, great changes, such as hiring the super sport star _____, in the baseball game took place.
5) _____ may still be the great American game, even though it is also popular in other countries.

Unit Eight

Text 1 (Intensive Reading)

Background Tips: The United States Constitution
The American Constitution was adopted on September 17, 1787, by the Constitutional Convention in Philadelphia, Pennsylvania, and later approved by conventions in each U.S. state in the name of "The People"; it has since been amended twenty-seven times, the first ten amendments being known as the Bill of Rights. The Articles of Confederation and Perpetual Union was actually the first constitution of the United States of America. The U.S. Constitution replaced the Articles of Confederation as the governing document for the United States after being approved by nine states. The Constitution has a central place in United States law and political culture.

American Constitution
美国宪法的由来

In the course of the Convention, the delegates designed a new form of government for the United States. The plan for the government was written in very simple language in a document called the Constitution of the United States. The Constitution set up a federal system with a strong central government. A federal system is one in which power is shared between a central authority and its constituent parts, with some rights reserved to each. The Constitution also called for the election of a national leader or president. It provided that federal laws would be made only by a Congress made up of representatives elected by the people. It also provided for a national court system headed by a Supreme Court.

In writing the Constitution, the delegated had to deal with two main fears shared by most Americans.

One fear was that one person or group, including the majority, might become too powerful or be able to seize control of the country and create a tyranny. To guard against this possibility, the delegates set up a government consisting of three parts, the executive, the legislative and the judicial. Each branch has powers that the others do not have and each branch has a way of counteracting and limiting any wrongful action by another branch.

Another fear was that the new central government might weaken or take away the power of the state governments to run their own affairs. To deal with this the Constitution specified exactly what power the central government had and which power was reserved for the states. The states were allowed to run their own governments as they wished, provided that their governments were republican.

The Constitution opens with a statement, called a Preamble, which make it clear that the government is set up by "We, the People" and its purpose is to "promote the general welfare and secure the blessing of liberty to ourselves and our posterity."

Before the new government could become a reality, a majority of the citizens in 9 of the 13 states would have to approve it. Those in favor of the adoption of the Constitution argued long and hard in speeches and writing. They finally prevailed, but the states made it clear that one more change would have to be made as soon as the new government was established.

Representatives of various states noted that the Constitution did not have any words guaranteeing the freedoms or basic rights and privileges of citizens. Though the Convention delegates did not think it necessary to include such explicit guarantees, many people felt that they needed further written protection against tyranny. So, a "Bill of Rights" was added to the Constitution in 1791.

(450 words)

Word List

constitution	[ˌkɒnstɪˈtjuːʃən]	n.	宪法
delegate	[ˈdelɪgeɪt]	n.	代表
federal	[ˈfedərəl]	adj.	联邦的
authority	[ɔːˈθɒrɪtɪ]	n.	权力，当局
reserved	[rɪˈzɜːvd]	adj.	保留的，缄默的
main	[meɪn]	adj.	主要的
tyranny	[ˈtɪrənɪ]	n.	压治统治，暴政
guard	[gɑːd]	v.	保卫，看守
executive	[ɪgˈzekjutɪv]	adj.	行政的
legislative	[ˈledʒɪslətɪv]	adj.	立法的，有立法权的
judicial	[dʒuːˈdɪʃəl]	adj.	法庭的，公正的，审判上的
counteract	[ˌkauntəˈrækt]	v.	抵消，中和
exactly	[ɪgˈzæktlɪ]	adv.	恰好地，精确地
provided	[prəˈvaɪdɪd]	conj.	假如，若是
statement	[ˈsteɪtmənt]	n.	声明，陈述
liberty	[ˈlɪbətɪ]	n.	自由
posterity	[pɒˈsterɪtɪ]	n.	后代
majority	[məˈdʒɒrɪtɪ]	n.	多数，大多数
adoption	[əˈdɒpʃən]	n.	采用，采纳，收养
guarantee	[ˌgærənˈtiː]	v.	保证，担保

privilege	['prɪvɪlɪdʒ]		n.	特权，特别恩典
explicit	[ɪk'splɪsɪt]		adj.	明确的，详述的

Idioms & Expressions

set up	建立	deal with	处理
make up	组成	in favor of	赞成，支持
consist of	组成		

Exercises

1. [Definitions]

Match the words in the box with their meanings. Write the word that stands for the definition in the appropriate answer space.

privilege	exactly	attend	counteract	explicit
statement	liberty	guard	consisted of	guarantee
main	majority	adopt	provided	legislative

1) _____: used to emphasize that a number, amount, or piece of information is or should be completely correct in every detail.

2) _____: concerned with making laws.

3) _____: cruel and unfair government.

4) _____: most of the people or things in a group.

5) _____: a special advantage that is given only to one person or group of people.

6) _____: to reduce or prevent the bad effect of something, by doing something that has the opposite effect.

7) _____: to be formed from two or more things or people.

8) _____: something you say or write, especially publicly or officially, to let people know your intentions or opinions, or to record facts.

9) _____: to promise to do something or to promise that something will happen.

10) _____: the act of starting to use a particular plan, method, way of speaking etc.

11) _____: bigger or more important than all other things, ideas etc of the same kind.

12) _____: the freedom and the right to do whatever you want without asking permission or being afraid of authority.

13) _____: to protect a person, place, or object by staying near them and watching them.

14) _____: used to say that something will only be possible if something else happens

or is done.

15) _____: expressed in a way that is very clear and direct.

2. [Sample Sentences]

Use the new words and phrases you have learned from the box in the following sentence. Change the form where necessary.

1) The new assemblies will have no _____ power.
2) The figures may not be _____ right, but they're close enough.
3) He had no special _____ and was treated just like every other prisoner.
4) The _____ of students find it quite hard to live on the amount of money they get.
5) Around 350 delegates _____ the conference.
6) They gave him drugs to _____ his withdrawal symptoms.
7) The Prime Minister's recent _____ on Europe aroused rage among people.
8) The buffet _____ several different Indian dishes.
9) If you send the application form in straight away, I can _____ you an interview.
10) Fighting for _____ and equality is still demonstrated by the poor.
11) What do you consider to be the _____ problem?
12) We should _____ the consumers' suggestion.
13) The contrast could not have been made more _____.
14) He can come with us, _____ he pays for his own meals.
15) There is no one to _____ these isolated farms against attack.

3. [Translation]

A. Translate the following English sentences into Chinese.

1) The plan for the government was written in very simple language in a document called the Constitution of the United States.

2) The Constitution also called for the election of a national leader or president.

3) In writing the Constitution, the delegates had to deal with two main fears shared by most Americans.

4) One fear was that one person or group, including the majority, might become too powerful or be able to seize control of the country and create a tyranny.

5) Those in favor of the adoption of the Constitution argued long and hard in speeches and writing.

B. Translate the following Chinese sentences into English.

1) 联合王国由大不列颠和北爱尔兰组成。(consist of)

2) 公众舆论正在强烈支持减税。(in favor of)

3) 只要情况允许,我们下周将举行会议。(provided)

4) 蔚蓝的天空不一定保证天气持续晴朗。(guarantee)

5) 我想我们应该制定出一项行动计划来应对这种情况。(deal with)

4.【Writing】

A foreign friend you know is planning to move to the community where you live. What do you think this person would like and dislike about living in your community? Why? Use specific reasons and details to develop your essay. Please write an essay from 120–150 words.

Reading Skills: 同义词线索

在阅读中遇到生词时,很多读者都习惯于停下来向各类词典求助,这种习惯大大影响了阅读速度和整体阅读效果。依靠同义词寻找上下文线索往往可以帮助读者理解语境和具体词汇。在一句话或一段话中常会有某个熟悉的词汇帮助读者了解生僻词。例如:

Even as a child Thomas Edison had a very inquisitive mind; at the age of three he performed his first experiment out of curiosity.

刚看到 **inquisitive** 我们或许并不解其意,但是读完整个句子便可发现 **curiosity** 和 **inquisitive** 意思相近。所以 **curiosity** 在此便是 **inquisitive** 的线索同义词,只不过词性不同而已。

类似的同义词线索很多,虽然在精读时字典作为工具书极为重要,但读者若想避免生词影响全文理解,或者改掉经常停止阅读查阅工具书的习惯,则可利用线索同义词对生词进行猜测来帮助提高阅读效果。从以下几组例子中可更进一步体会出同义词线索的作用:

1. You must <u>bathe</u> the wound with clean water, and after you <u>wash</u> it, put some medicine on it and bandage it carefully. "bathe" 和 "wash" 是一对同义词。

2. He holds a <u>cynical</u> attitude after years of frustration. He was always in low spirits because of this <u>negativeness</u>. "cynical" 和 "negativeness" 同义。

3. The punishment seems very <u>harsh</u> for such a tiny joke. I cannot see any point in such a <u>strictness</u>. "harsh" 和 "strict" 同义。

Unit Eight

Text 2 (Extensive Reading)

Mister Imagination
想象先生

There were very few places in the world that Jules Verne, the writer, did not visit. He went round the world a hundred times or more. Once he did it in eighty days, unheard of in the nineteenth century. He voyaged sixty thousand miles under the sea, toured around the moon, exploded the center of the earth, and chatted with natives in Australia.

Jules Verne, the man, was a stay-at-home. He was more likely to be tired from writing than from traveling. He did make a few visits to Europe and North Africa. And he made one six-week tour of New York State. But that was all. He spent less than one of his seventy-seven years really traveling. Yet he was the world's most extraordinary tourist.

His books are crowded with hunting and fishing expeditions. Jules actually went hunting only once. Then he raised his gun and shot off the guard's hat!

He never held a test tube in his hand. But he was an inspiration to the scientist in the laboratory. Long before radio was invented, he had TV working in his books. His name for it was photo-telephoto. He had helicopters fifty years before the Wright brothers flew their first plane at Kitty Hawk. In fact, there were few wonders of the twentieth century that this man of the nineteenth century did not foresee. In his stories you can read about neon lights, moving sidewalks, air-conditioners, sky-scrapers, guided missiles, tanks, electrically operated submarines, and air-planes.

Many people took his ideas seriously. One reason was that he wrote about these wonderful things in such exact details. Learned men would argue with him. Experts in mathematics would spend weeks checking his figures. When his book about going to the moon was published, five hundred persons volunteered for the next expedition.

He inspired many famous people. Admiral Richard E. Byrd, returning from his flight across the North Pole, said that Jules Verne had been his guide. Simon Lake, father of the modern submarine, wrote in the first sentence of his autobiography: "Jules Verne was the director general of my life." He started many other men thinking. Among them were the inventor of the helicopter and creator of the telegraph.

Verne's first book was *Five weeks in a Balloon*. Fifteen publishers looked at it, and fifteen sent it back. In a rage, Jules flung it into the fire. His wife rescued it and made him promise he would try once more. So he tucked the slightly burned manuscript under his arm. He went to show it to one last publisher, a man named Pierre Hetzel, Jules waited nervously while the man read the book through. Finally, Hetzel said he would publish it if Jules would rewrite it in the form of a novel.

In two weeks Jules had done so. *Five weeks in a Balloon* became a best seller. It was translated into every great language. At the age of thirty-four, Jules Verne was famous.

Verne signed a contract with Hetzel. He promised to produce two novels a year. This he did. In his forty-year career he was actually to write more than one hundred books!

Perhaps the best known of all his books is *Around the World in Eighty Days*. It first appeared as a serial in a Paris newspaper. Its hero had made a bet that he could circle the globe in eighty days, and his progress aroused great interest.

In every country of Europe people made bets on whether the imaginary Mr. Fogg would arrive in London in time to win his bet. Verne kept the popular interest alive. His hero rescued a widow from death and fell in love with her. He was attacked by Indians while crossing the American plains. Arriving in New York, he saw the ship that was to take him to England disappearing over the horizon without him.

All the big steamship companies offered Verne large sums of money if he would put Fogg on one of their ships: The author refused. Instead, he had Fogg rent a ship. As the world held its breath, Fogg reached London with only minutes to spare.

Many of Verne's other books were set in the future. In these stories, people made diamonds and developed a kind of automobile-ship-helicopter-plane. They received news flashes on televisions, worked in giant skyscrapers, and rode to work on high-ways much like the ones we ride today. It is hard to believe that the books were written nearly one hundred years ago.

Jules Verne had lived to see many of his fancies come true. But this had not surprised him, for he had once said: "What one man can imagine, another man can do." (783 words)

Word List

voyage	['vɔɪ-ɪdʒ]	n.	航行,旅程
explode	[ɪk'spləʊd]	v.	爆炸,爆发
native	['neɪtɪv]	adj.	本国的,本土的
stay-at-home		n.	不爱出门的人
extraordinary	[ɪk'strɔːdɪnərɪ]	adj.	非常的,特别的
expedition	[ˌekspɪ'dɪʃən]	n.	远征,探险队
inspiration	[ˌɪnspɪ'reɪʃən]	n.	灵感
foresee	[fɔː'siː]	v.	预见,预知
neon light		n.	霓虹灯
detail	['diːteɪl, dɪ'teɪl]	n.	细节
autobiography	[ˌɔːtəbaɪ'ɒɡrəfɪ]	n.	自传
helicopter	['helɪkɒptə]	n.	直升机
rage	[reɪdʒ]	n.	愤怒,情绪激动

Unit Eight

fling	[flɪŋ]	v.	投,猛冲,嘲笑	
tuck	[tʌk]	v.	打摺,卷起	
slightly	['slaɪtlɪ]	adv.	轻微地	
manuscript	['mænjʊskrɪpt]	n.	手稿,原稿	
serial	['sɪərɪəl]	adj.	连续的,一连串的	
bet	[bet]	v.	打赌	
circle	['sɜːkəl]	v.	包围,盘旋,环绕	
attack	[ə'tæk]	v.	攻击,动手	
spare	[speə]	v.	节约,剩下	
flash	[flæʃ]	n.	闪光,闪现,一瞬间	

Idioms & Expressions

be crowded with	充满	in details	详细地
make a bet	打赌		

Exercises

【Cloze】

Directions: These sentences are from the text you have just read. Please fill in the words as in the text.

_____1)_____ every country of Europe people made bets on _____2)_____ the imaginary Mr. Fogg would arrive in London _____3)_____ time _____4)_____ win his bet. Verne kept the popular interest alive. His hero rescued a widow _____5)_____ death and fell in love _____6)_____ her. He was attacked _____7)_____ Indians _____8)_____ crossing the American plains. Arriving in New York, he saw the ship that was _____9)_____ take him to England disappearing _____10)_____ the horizon.

Text 3 (Fast Reading)

The Truth about Cats and Dogs
有关猫与狗的真理

Every February, the Westminster Kennel Club holds its yearly dog show in New York City. Westminster has been awarding prizes to special show dogs for one hundred and thirty-three years. Dogs are judged against a description of the perfect dog for each kind or breed. Then one is chosen as "Best in Show".

The Westminster Kennel Club was the first member of the pure breed dog registry group, The American Kennel Club. The AKC recognizes dog breeds in the United States. Every year, it develops a list of the most popular breeds. The same breed has won that honor for the past eighteen years—the Labrador retriever. The club's Web site describes Labs as gentle, intelligent and family friendly. Yet not all Labs are the same.

American writer John Grogan discovered this after he and his wife adopted a Labrador retriever they named Marley.

The dog caused Mister Grogan a lot of trouble, but also provided many stories for his newspaper articles. Later, he wrote a best-selling book, *Marley and Me: Life and Love with the World's Worst Dog*. Marley was happy and fun-loving. But he was also extremely large and difficult to control. He ate anything that he found around the house, including plastic, clothing and jewelry. He was expelled from dog training school. And he had an abnormal fear of loud noises, especially thunderstorms. Unfortunately, the Grogans lived in Florida where many of these storms develop. Marley would attack the furniture, walls and doors until his feet bled if he was left alone in the house during a storm.

John Grogan, his wife Jenny and their three children all loved Marley even though the dog almost destroyed their home a number of times. John Grogan wrote that he briefly considered the possibility that his dog could be trained to be a show champion. But he soon realized that this was not to be.

The American Pet Products Association carries out a National Pet Owners Study every two years. The latest one shows that in 2008, seventy-one million homes in the United States included a pet. That is sixty-two percent of all the homes in America. The study also showed that Americans owned more than seventy-seven million dogs and more than ninety-three million cats.

The association's market research shows that, during 2008, Americans spent more than forty-three billion dollars on pets, pet products and pet medical care. And it expects that number to increase to forty-five billion dollars by the end of this year, even with the current economic downturn.

Unit Eight

However, the economic downturn is creating problems for some pet owners. The Humane Society says that more people are leaving pets at animal shelters. This is because they have lost their homes and can no longer care for their animals. The group provides money for shelters and rescue organizations to help them care for homeless dogs and cats.

Humane Society official Nancy Peterson says groups are also helping pet owners pay for pet food. And they are placing animals in temporary homes until their owners can take them back.

The central part of the United States suffered its own economic crisis in the 1980s. The price of farm land dropped and banks no longer provided the credit farmers needed. Unemployment reduced the population. The number of people in the small town of Spencer, Iowa, for example, dropped from eleven thousand to eight thousand in just a few years.

The Spencer public library worked to help people in the town find jobs. It created a list of jobs and offered books on job skills and training. It also set up a computer so people could research job openings and write applications.

One cold January morning in 1988 library workers found a small, almost frozen kitten in the book drop. A book drop is the small metal door in the wall of the building where people can return books when the library is closed. No one knows who put the kitten there or why. But it turned out to be lucky for both the kitten and the town.

The library held a contest to name the cat. The winning name was Dewey Readmore Books. Library officials agreed to permit him to live in the building. Dewey loved to keep people company while they chose books or used the library computer. Soon, Dewey's presence began attracting families and school groups to the library.

The local newspaper wrote about the new library cat. His story spread across the nation. Dewey began receiving letters from people in other countries. And a film crew from Japan arrived to include him in a movie about cats.

Head librarian Vicki Myron was Dewey's main caretaker. Last year, she published the best-selling book *Dewey: The Small-Town Library Cat Who Touched the World*. Here she gives readers an idea of how much the cat meant to her town.

"How much of an impact can an animal have? How many lives can one cat touch? How is it possible for an abandoned kitten to transform a small library into a meeting place and tourist attraction, inspire a classic American town, bring together an entire region and eventually become famous around the world? You can't even begin to answer those questions until you hear the story of Dewey Readmore Books, the beloved library cat of Spencer, Iowa."

Pets are important in American homes, and that includes the White House. President Obama has promised his two daughters a dog.

When it arrives, the new family member will join a long list of pets that have lived in the White House. Some presidents kept rather unusual animals. For example, President Benjamin Harrison's son had a pet goat. President Calvin Coolidge had raccoons.

President Theodore Roosevelt's family had a pony, a sheep, a bird, guinea pigs, dogs, cats, rats and a snake. President John Kennedy's daughter Caroline had a pony named Macaroni. The Kennedys also had hamsters, dogs, birds, and cats.

Many presidents seem to have taken the advice of President Harry Truman who said: "If you want a friend in Washington, get a dog."

Perhaps the most famous presidential dog was President Franklin Roosevelt's Scottish terrier, Fala. Mister Roosevelt took him just about everywhere. In 1943 Fala appeared in a short movie about life in Washington during World War II. A statue of Fala is part of the Franklin Delano Roosevelt Memorial in Washington, D.C. (1,072 words)

Exercises

1. [True, False, Not Given]

1) The winner in the dog show will be awarded as the best dog in the country.
2) Marley, in John Grogan's writing, is as gentle and friendly as the ordinary Labrador retriever is.
3) The National Pet Owner Study shows that by 2008, Americans owned more than seventy-seven million dogs and more than ninety-three million cats.
4) Financial downturn has created problems for some pet owners, so that they have lost their homes and had to put pets at animal shelters.
5) Those temporary homes promise that pets owners can take their pets back.

2. [Blank-filling]

Fill in the blanks according to what you have read in the text.

1) In Spencer public library, the officials agreed to _____ Dewey, the lucky cat, to live in the building.
2) Dewey liked to keep people around _____ while they chose books. His _____ began attracting families and school groups to the library.
3) The caretaker of Dewey, Myron, published a book remarked Dewey's impact on the town. She thought to what extent it is possible for an _____ kitten _____ a small into a meeting place and tourist attraction, _____ a classic American town, _____ an entire region and eventually become famous around the world?
4) Some presidents kept rather _____ animals. For example, President Benjamin Harrison's son had a pet goat. President Calvin Coolidge had raccoons.
5) Perhaps the most famous _____ dog was President Franklin Roosevelt's Scottish terrier, Fala.

Unit Nine

Text 1 (Intensive Reading)

Background Tips: Advertising or Flattering?

Advertising is a form of communication that typically attempts to persuade potential customers to purchase or to consume more of a particular brand of product or service. Many advertisements are designed to generate increased consumption of those products and services through the creation and reinvention of the "brand image". For these purposes, advertisements sometimes embed their persuasive message with factual information.

"For skin like peaches and cream"
"如桃子和奶油般的皮肤"

Whenever advertisers want you to stop thinking about the product and to start thinking about something bigger, better, or more attractive than the product, they use that very popular word "like". The word "like" is the advertiser's equivalent of the magician's use of misdirection. "Like" gets you to ignore the product and concentrate on the claim the advertiser is making about it. "For skin like peaches and cream" claims the ad for a skin cream. What is this ad really claiming? It doesn't say this cream will give you peaches-and-cream skin. There is no verb in this claim, so it doesn't even mention using the product. How is skin ever like "peaches and cream"? Remember, ads must be read exactly according to the dictionary definition of words. This ad is making absolutely no promise for this skin cream. If you think this cream will give you soft, smooth, and youthful-looking skin, you are the one who had read the meaning into the ad.

The wine that claims "It's like taking trip to France" wants you to think about a romantic evening in Paris as you walk along the street after a wonderful meal in an intimate café. Of course, you don't really believe that a wine can take you to France, but the goal of the ad is to get you to think pleasant, romantic thoughts about France and not about how the wine tastes or how expensive it may be. That little word "like" has taken you away from crushed grapes into a world of your own imaginative making. Who knows, maybe the next time you buy wine, you'll think those pleasant thought when you see this brand of wine, and you'll buy it.

How about the most famous "like" claim of all, "Winston tastes good like a cigarette should"? Ignoring the grammatical error here, you might want to know what this claim is saying. Whether a cigarette tastes good or bad is a subjective judgment because what tastes good to one person may well taste horrible to another. There are many people who say that all cigarettes taste terrible, other people who say only some cigarettes taste all right and still others who say all cigarettes taste good.

(377 words)

Word List

advertiser	[ˈædvətaɪzə]	n.	广告者,广告客户
attractive	[əˈtræktɪv]	adj.	有吸引力的,引起注意的
equivalent	[ɪˈkwɪvələnt]	n.	相等物
magician	[məˈdʒɪʃən]	n.	魔术师
misdirection	[ˌmɪsdɪˈrekʃən]	n.	指导错误
ignore	[ɪgˈnɔː]	v.	不顾,忽视
concentrate	[ˈkɒnsəntreɪt]	v.	集中,专心,浓缩
mention	[ˈmenʃən]	v.	提到,谈到
absolutely	[ˈæbsəluːtlɪ]	adv.	绝对地,完全地
promise	[ˈprɒmɪs]	n.	诺言,约定
smooth	[smuːð]	adj.	平稳的,流畅的,安祥的
romantic	[rəʊˈmæntɪk]	adj.	浪漫的
intimate	[ˈɪntɪmɪt]	adj.	亲密的,私人的
crush	[krʌʃ]	v.	压破,压碎
pleasant	[ˈplezənt]	adj.	令人愉快的,舒适的
claim	[kleɪm]	n.	要求
subjective	[səbˈdʒektɪv]	adj.	主观的
judgment	[ˈdʒʌdʒmənt]	n.	判断
horrible	[ˈhɒrɪbl]	adj.	可怕的,令人讨厌的
cigarette	[ˌsɪgəˈret]	n.	香烟

Exercises

1. [Definitions]

Match the words in the box with their meanings. Write the word that stands for the definition in the appropriate answer space.

attractive	absolutely	promise	intimate	claim	equivalent
mention	ignore	horrible	pleasant	subjective	smooth
advertiser	judgment				

98

Unit Nine

1) _____ : statement that you will definitely do or provide something or that something will definitely happen.
2) _____ : to talk or write about something or someone, usually quickly and without saying very much or giving details.
3) _____ : to deliberately pay no attention to something that you have been told or that you know about.
4) _____ : completely and in every way.
5) _____ : having qualities that make you want to accept something or be involved in it.
6) _____ : a person or company that advertises something.
7) _____ : to state that something is true, even though it has not been proved.
8) _____ : a statement, report, attitude etc that is influenced by personal opinion and can therefore be unfair.
9) _____ : having the same value, purpose, job etc as a person or thing of a different kind.
10) _____ : an opinion that you form, especially after thinking carefully about something.
11) _____ : enjoyable or attractive and making you feel happy.
12) _____ : private and friendly so that you feel comfortable.
13) _____ : to press something in order to break it into very small pieces or into a powder.
14) _____ : a surface has no rough parts, lumps, or holes, especially in a way that is pleasant and attractive to touch.
15) _____ : very bad about things you see, taste, or smell, or about the weather.

2. [Sample Sentences]

Use the new words and phrases you have learned from the box in the following sentence. Change the form where necessary.

1) You can't _____ the fact that many criminals never go to prison.
2) Some of the problems were _____ in his report.
3) She made a _____ to visit them once a month.
4) Television _____ can exploit a captive audience.
5) Ice cream looks _____ to the children.
6) This cake is _____ delicious.
7) The product _____ "to make you thin without dieting".
8) A dime is _____ to ten pennies.
9) As a critic, he is far too _____ .
10) It's too soon to make a _____ about what the outcome will be.
11) Can you please help the chef to _____ two cloves of garlic?
12) The collection has been moved from its _____ setting to the British Museum.

13) We spent many hours in a _____ conversation.
14) Her skin felt _____ and cool.
15) My first attempt at a chocolate cake tasted _____.

3.【Translation】

A. Translate the following English sentences into Chinese.

1) The new government has promised a smooth transition of power.

2) Doctors are aiming to concentrate more on prevention than cure.

3) He made his reasons for resigning absolutely clear.

4) "Like" gets you to ignore the product and concentrate on the claim the advertiser is making about it.

5) Whether a cigarette tastes good or bad is a subjective judgment because what tastes good to one person may well taste horrible to another.

B. Translate the following Chinese sentences into English by using the word in the bracket.

1) 那样调换他的工作等于是解雇了他。(equivalent)

2) 我累了就无法集中精力工作。(concentrate on)

3) 依我看,我们应该接受他们的道歉。(judgment)

4) 她一拒绝,我的希望就全都破灭了。(crush)

5) 她把桌布上的皱褶弄平。(smooth)

4.【Writing】

There are many advertisements directed at children, such as snacks, toys and other goods. Parents argue that children are under pressure. Advertisers claim that the advertisements provide useful information. How do you see this phenomenon? Please write a 120–150 words argument.

Unit Nine

Reading Skills: 反义词线索

获得同义词线索猜词义这种技巧之后，读者在阅读过程中能很快通过上下文提供的线索或生词本身的结构特点推断出词义来，从而提高阅读速度和阅读能力。有时作者运用对比的手法来表现事物之间的差异。在进行对比的过程中，作者必然会用一些互为对应、互为反义的词语，使不同事物的特点更为突出。通过上下文的逻辑关系，从对两种事物或现象进行对比的描述中，读者可以根据其中一个熟悉的词推断出另一个生词的词义来。

另外，在表示这种对比关系时，作者通常会用一些信号词来表明另一个词语与前面的词语互为反义。这些信号词无疑为读者理解和猜测生词词义提供了非常好的线索。常用来表示对应关系和提供相反信息的信号词有：

But, yet, however, while, whereas, otherwise, in spite of, despite, even though, although, though, unlike, instead(of), rather than, nevertheless, nonetheless, on the other hand, still, none the less, by contrast, on the contrary, in the end, compared to

例如：Professor Erica's attitude showed his concern. The students' attitudes, on the other hand, were very casual. 以 on the other hand 为线索，可以看出 "casual" 是 "concern" 的反义词，也就是 indifferent 的意思。

例如：It is better to be reflective about problems than to be thoughtless. 以 "better...than..." 为线索，可以看出 "reflective" 同 "thoughtless" 反义，即为 thoughtful 的意思。

Text 2 (Extensive Reading)

Life in Death
生死消长

The painter was known for his ability to put life on canvas like no other artist of his time. His skills in the use of colors was so great that some who viewed the paintings he created said that they were more true to life than life itself.

He, indeed, was a skilled artist. When he painted fruit, it seemed as if you could take it from the picture and eat it. When he put a field of spring flowers on canvas, you could view the scene in the painting and imagine yourself walking in that field, feeling a gentle breeze canoeing the fragrance of the flowers. And when he put a face on his canvas with his brush, it looked like a person of flesh arid blood with life arid breath.

One day this skilled artist met a beautiful woman who immediately became the object of his affections. As he observed her and spoke with her, he admired her more and more. He showered her with kindness and words of praise until she consented to be his wife.

Not long after they were married, however, the beautiful woman found out that she was more the object of his artistic interest than of his affections. When he admired her classic beauty, it was as though he were standing in front of a work of art rather than in front of a human being to whom he had pledged his love and promised his life. And soon he expressed his great desire to put her rare beauty on canvas.

"Please sit for me in the studio," he pleaded, "and I will immortalize your beauty. The work will be my masterpiece!"

She was humble and obedient as well as flattered by his words, so she said, "Yes, my love. I will be happy to pose for you.

So the beautiful, young wife of the artist sat patiently for hours in his painting room, not complaining. Day after day she sat obediently, smiling as she posed, because she loved him and because she hoped that he would see her love in her smile and obedience.

She sometimes wanted to call out to him, "Please love me and want me as a person rather than as an object!" But instead, she spoke nothing but words which pleased him.

Once, as she lay sleepless in bed at night, she planned to say to him the next day, "My dear husband, I am jealous of your mistress!" She thought that surely he would answer in surprise. "Mistress? I have no one but you!" And then she would say, "Your mistress is your art!" However, somehow she was never courageous enough to say any of the words, so she continued to sit for him patiently, hour after hour, day after day, week after week. Her love for him gave her the patience, for she knew how much pleasure he took in this task.

The artist was a passionate, wild, and moody man who became so involved in his work that he saw only what he wanted to see. He did not, or could not, see, as she smiled on, that she was becoming weak and dispirited. He did not, or could not, see that though the flesh tones were fresh and beautiful on his canvas, the color was leaving the face of his lovely model.

At length, as the labor drew nearer to its conclusion, the painter became wilder in his passion for his work. He only rarely turned his eyes from the canvas to look at his wife, though she continued to sit patiently for him. If he had looked at her more often and more carefully, he would have noticed that the tints which he so skillfully spread on the canvas were drawn from her cheeks and the smile was taken from her lips.

Finally, after weeks passed, he surveyed his work for the finishing touches. A brush needed to he touched lightly to the mouth, and a tint needed to be added carefully to the eye.

Since the woman knew that he had almost completed the task, her spirits were revived for a moment. Then, when the brush was given and the tint placed, the painter stood back, overjoyed at what he had placed on the canvas with tile skill of his hand and mind!

As he stood there gazing at his beautiful work of art, he cried with a loud voice, "This is indeed life itself!" Then he turned to his beloved and saw that she was dead! (757 words)

Unit Nine

Word List

skilled	[skɪld]	*adj.*	有技能的,熟练的
canvas	['kænvəs]	*n.*	帆布
breeze	[briːz]	*n.*	微风,轻而易举的事
canoe	[kə'nuː]	*n.*	独木舟,轻舟
		v.	乘独木舟
fragrance	['freɪgrəns]	*n.*	香味
immediately	[ɪ'miːdɪətlɪ]	*adv.*	立即
affection	[ə'fekʃən]	*n.*	慈爱,爱,感情
shower	['ʃaʊə]	*v.*	淋浴,淋湿,下骤雨
consent	[kən'sent]	*v.*	同意,承诺
pledge	[pledʒ]	*v.*	保证,誓言
obedient	[ə'biːdɪənt]	*adj.*	服从的,顺从的
flatter	['flætə]	*v.*	过份夸赞,奉承,阿谀
instead	[ɪn'sted]	*adv.*	代替,顶替
jealous	['dʒeləs]	*adj.*	妒忌的
somehow	['sʌmhaʊ]	*adv.*	不知怎么地
rarely	['reəlɪ]	*adv.*	很少,难得
tint	[tɪnt]	*n.*	色彩,痕迹
touch	[tʌtʃ]	*n.*	色彩,触觉
lightly	['laɪtlɪ]	*adv.*	轻轻地,不费力地
beloved	[bɪ'lʌvɪd]	*adj.*	心爱的

Idioms & Expressions

as if	仿佛,好像	call out	召集,大声叫喊
at length	终于		

Exercises

[Cloze]

These sentences are from the text you have just read. Please fill in the same words as in the text.

The artist was a passionate, wild, and moody man ___1)___ became so involved in his work ___2)___ he saw only ___3)___ he wanted to see. He did not, ___4)___ could not, see, 5) _____ she smiled on, that she was becoming weak 6) _____ unhappy. He did not, 7) _____ could not, see that 8) _____ the flesh tones were fresh and beautiful 9) _____ his canvas, the color was leaving the face 10) _____ his lovely model.

Text 3 (Fast Reading)

Abraham Lincoln
亚伯拉罕·林肯

Abraham Lincoln is the only president in American history to lead a nation divided by civil war.

At the heart of the issues that divided the South from the North was slavery. Southern states withdrew from the Union because they saw a threat to their way of life. Their agricultural economy depended on the labor of slaves originally brought from Africa. The states thought the federal government would free the slaves.

South Carolina was the first to leave. It did so shortly after Lincoln's election in November of 1860. Six other states followed by the time he took office in March of 1861. In his inaugural speech, Lincoln begged southern states not to leave the Union. "We are not enemies, but friends. We must not be enemies. Though passion may have strained, it must not break our bonds of affection."

Abraham Lincoln did not receive a majority of the popular vote in the eighteen sixty election. But he won enough electoral votes to become president.

Lincoln fought to keep the Union together. He led a civil war in which more than six hundred thousand Americans were killed. And, in leading that war, he took the first steps that would destroy the institution of slavery.

Most whites did not consider blacks—or negroes, as they called them—to be their equal. Lincoln was no different. But he believed that slavery was wrong.

Yet he thought that slavery would die out naturally over time—and that outsiders should not force southerners to end slavery. He explained his position many times in speeches, debates and letters, including this one written in eighteen fifty-eight:

I have made it equally plain that I think the negro is included in the word "men" used in the Declaration of Independence.

I believe the declaration that "all men are created equal" is the great fundamental principle upon which our free institutions rest; that negro slavery is violative of that principle; but that, by our frame of government, that principle has not been made one of legal obligation; that by our frame of government, the states which have slavery are to retain it, or surrender it at their own pleasure; and that all others—individuals, free states and national government—are constitutionally bound to leave them alone about it.

But Lincoln changed his mind. Some historians think the death of his eleven-year-old son Willie had an influence. The president and his wife, Mary Todd Lincoln, had four children, all sons. Three got sick and died. Only one lived past the age of eighteen.

Lincoln never joined a church, but he believed in a supreme being who created every person with a purpose in life. After his son's death, Lincoln decided that one of his purposes was to be an emancipator—to begin the process of freeing the slaves. A few months later, he wrote the Emancipation Proclamation.

Many people think the Emancipation Proclamation freed the slaves. It did not. It only declared slaves in the Confederacy to be free. In other words, only slaves in the southern states that did not recognize Lincoln as president.

Historians say that by writing the Emancipation Proclamation, Lincoln established a moral purpose for the war. No longer was the purpose simply to bring the southern states back into the Union. Now his declaration made freeing the slaves a long-term goal of the conflict.

It put the Confederate states in the position of fighting for slavery—even though most of the soldiers were too poor to own slaves. And it increased the military strength of the Union by making it possible for free blacks to serve in the northern army.

Abraham Lincoln was born into a poor family in Kentucky. He grew up in Indiana and later moved to Illinois. He loved to learn. He was a self-taught lawyer who served for eight years as an Illinois state representative.

But he also suffered from depression all his life. Doctors at that time called it melancholia. He wrote letters about killing himself and saying that he was the "most miserable man alive."

Lincoln was a tall man with a long face, long arms and large hands. Political opponents called him names like "gorilla." Many said he was unqualified to be president because of his limited experience in national government. Lincoln had served only two years in Congress before his election to the White House.

Yet Abraham Lincoln is often called America's greatest president. He is remembered as the man who saved the Union and re-invented it at the same time.

By including blacks, Lincoln expanded "the borders of freedom," says historian Tom Schwartz. Lincoln himself said his purpose was to provide "an open field and a fair chance in life." He succeeded in beginning that process, though black Americans did not gain full civil rights until the nineteen sixties.

Abraham Lincoln was the first presidential candidate of the modern Republican Party. He included political opponents in his cabinet, which is unusual. Doris Kearns Goodwin wrote about this in her two thousand five book "Team of Rivals: The Political Genius of Abraham Lincoln."

On April fourteenth, eighty sixty-five, Southern sympathizer and actor John Wilkes Booth shot Lincoln in Ford's Theatre. It happened five days after the South surrendered and the Civil War ended.

Not surprisingly, America's sixteenth president is a hero of another former Illinois lawmaker. Barack Obama has spoken repeatedly of Lincoln's influence in making it possible for the country to have its first African-American president. (920 words)

Exercises

1. [True, False, Not Given]

1) In American history, Abraham Lincoln is the only president who has lead a country divided by civil war.
2) Abraham Lincoln received the support from the majority of the vote to become president in the 1860 election
3) Abraham Lincoln thinks blacks are as equal as white men.
4) Abraham Lincoln did not join any church, nor did he have any belief.
5) According to the passage, Abraham Lincoln has enemies both in the white and back.

2. [Blank-filling]

Please fill in the following blanks according what you have read in the text.

1) Most white men did not consider blacks, or _____ to be their equal.
2) After his son's death, Lincoln's purpose was to become an _____, to begin the process of freeing the slaves.
3) Abraham Lincoln is often called America's greatest president. He is remembered as the man who saved the Union and _____ it at the same time.
4) Abraham Lincoln was a _____ lawyer who served for eight years as an Illinois state representative.
5) On April 14th, 1864, Lincoln was shot in Ford's theatre. It happened five days after the South _____ and the Civil War _____.

 # Unit Ten

Text 1 (Intensive Reading)

Background Tips: Too Much TV can Make Teens Depressed

Researchers have found out that the more exposed to media, the more likely kids will get depression. There are several possible ways by which media exposure could boost the risk of depression. The time spent watching TV or using other electronic media may replace time spent socializing, participating in sports or engaging in intellectual activities—all of which may protect against depression. Watching TV at night may disrupt sleep, which is important for normal brain and emotional development. In addition, messages transmitted through the media may reinforce aggression and other risky behaviors, interfere with identity development or inspire fear and anxiety.

Teenagers, Television and Depression
青少年、电视和抑郁症

A new study suggests that the more teenagers watch television, the more likely they are to develop depression as young adults. But the extent to which TV may or may not be to blame is a question that the study leaves unanswered.

The researchers used a national long-term survey of adolescent health to investigate the relationship between media use and depression. They based their findings on more than four thousand adolescents who were not depressed when the survey began in 1995.

As part of the survey, the young people were asked how many hours of television or videos they watched daily. They were also asked how often they played computer games and listened to the radio.

Media use totaled an average of five and one-half hours a day. More than two hours of that was spent watching TV.

Seven years later, in 2002, more than seven percent of the young people had signs of depression. The average age at that time was twenty-one.

Brian Primack at the University of Pittsburgh medical school was the lead author of the new study. He says every extra hour of television meant an eight percent increase in the chances of developing signs of depression.

The researchers say they did not find any such relationship with the use of other media such as movies, video games or radio. But the study did find that young men were more likely than young women to develop depression given the same amount of media use.

Doctor Primack says the study did not explore if watching TV causes depression. But one possibility, he says, is that it may take time away from activities that could help prevent depression, like sports and socializing. It might also interfere with sleep, he says, and that could have an influence.

In December, the journal *Social Indicators Research* published a study of activities that help lead to happy lives. Sociologists from the University of Maryland found that people who describe themselves as happy spend less time watching television than unhappy people. The study found that happy people are more likely to be socially active, to read, to attend religious services and to vote.

(358 words)

Word List

suggest	[sə'dʒest]	v.	建议,提出
depression	[dɪ'preʃən]	n.	沮丧,萧条
extent	[ɪk'stent]	n.	范围,程度
blame	[bleɪm]	v.	责备
adolescent	[ˌædə'lesənt]	adj.	青春期的,青少年的
investigate	[ɪn'vestɡeɪt]	v.	调查,研究
total	['təʊtl]	v.	总计,共计
sign	[saɪn]	n.	符号,迹象
given	['ɡɪvən]	prep.	考虑到
amount	[ə'maʊnt]	n.	数量,总额
cause	[kɔːz]	v.	导致
socialize	['səʊʃəlaɪz]	v.	使……社会化,交际
interfere	[ˌɪntə'fɪə]	v.	妨碍,冲突,干涉
influence	['ɪnfluəns]	n.	影响力,感化力
journal	['dʒɜːnl]	n.	日记,杂志
publish	['pʌblɪʃ]	v.	出版,发行
attend	[ə'tend]	v.	参加,照看
religious	[rɪ'lɪdʒəs]	adj.	宗教的
service	['sɜːvɪs]	n.	仪式
vote	[vəʊt]	v.	投票,选举

Unit Ten

Idioms & Expressions

the more ..., the more	越……越……	an average of	平均有(跟数词)
interfere with	妨碍,干扰		

Exercises

1. [Definitions]

Match the words in the box with their meanings. Write the word that stands for the definition in the appropriate answer space.

depression	investigate	suggest	sign	vote
Journal service	extent	adolescent	given	socialize cause
attend		interfere	total	

1) _____ : used to say how true something is or how great an effect or change is.
2) _____ : taking something into account.
3) _____ : to make someone think that a particular thing is true.
4) _____ : a young person, usually between the ages of 12 and 18, who is developing into an adult.
5) _____ : to try to find out the truth about or the cause of something such as a crime, accident, or scientific problem.
6) _____ : a feeling of sadness that makes you think there is no hope for the future.
7) _____ : a formal religious ceremony, especially in church.
8) _____ : to spend time with other people in a friendly way.
9) _____ : to deliberately get involved in a situation where you are not wanted or needed.
10) _____ : to go to an event such as a meeting or a class.
11) _____ : to make something happen, especially something bad.
12) _____ : an event, fact etc that shows that something is happening or that something is true or exists.
13) _____ : to show by marking a paper, raising your hand etc. which person you want to elect or whether you support a particular plan.
14) _____ : to reach a particular total.
15) _____ : a serious magazine produced for professional people or those with a particular interest.

2. 【Sample Sentences】

Use the new words and phrases you have learned from the box in the following sentence. Change the form where necessary.

1) Trends in spending and investment _____ a gradual economic recovery.
2) Lucy's mood was one of deep _____.
3) We all to some _____ remember the good times and forget the bad.
4) If you describe an adult as _____, you mean that they are silly and childish.
5) The study _____ the impact of violent TV programming on children.
6) _____ the circumstances, you've done really well.
7) The fire _____ £15,000 worth of damage.
8) People don't _____ with their neighbors as much as they used to.
9) Anxiety can _____ with children's performance at school.
10) Please let us know if you are unable to _____.
11) The _____ was held in the chapel.
12) The people of Ulster had finally been given a chance to _____ on the issue.
13) Crying is seen as a _____ of weakness.
14) The group had losses _____ $3 million this year.
15) If you want to apply for that teaching job, you need three papers published on the Canadian Educational _____.

3. 【Translation】

A. Translate the following English sentences into Chinese.

1) The more I thought about it, the less I liked the idea.

2) I was amazed at the extent of his knowledge.

3) His pale face suggests bad health.

4) He tries not to let (his) business interfere with his home life.

5) I'm afraid that the performance was not a total success.

B. Translate the following Chinese sentences into English.

1) 研究者对全国的青少年健康状况做了调查。(adolescent, survey)

2) 听音乐对她起了一种镇静的作用。(influence)

3) 铁路对一定数量的行李免费运送。(amount)

4) 新的研究表明,青少年看电视越多,越可能引发抑郁症。(the more... the more)

5) 我在一定程度上同意你的意见。(extent)

4.【Writing】

Do you agree or disagree with the following statement? Attending a live performance (for example, a play, concert, or sporting event) is more enjoyable than watching the same event on television. Please write a 120-150 essay to state your point of view.

Reading Skills：略过无关紧要之词

如同讲话一样,在阅读中也会发现作者有一些无关紧要的话语可以忽略。如果略过这些话语,往往可以又快又准地把握文章意图和句子意思,也可以节省大量的时间。例如：**After a long day study, I was exhausted and totally worn out.** 在这句话中,"I was exhausted" 足够表明作者想表达的筋疲力竭的感觉,"and totally worn out" 只是作者想做进一步说明,是重复的话,也是我们可以略去不看的话语。从以下例子中可以进一步看出一般是哪些词语可以匆匆扫过而不必去做细致的分析：

1. The boy experimented and tied out new methods.
2. The ladder is seven meters in height.
3. I asked the student to repeat again what she had said.
4. I usually wake up at 7 a.m. in the morning.
5. The cause of the accident was on account of rain.

以上五句话中划横线的部分均为英文写作中为了保证平行或者逻辑结构所添加的话语,如果深谙此规律和原则,在阅读时读者便会自然而然地跳过此类词和短语,更有效地提高阅读效率。

Text 2 (Extensive Reading)

Conquer Yellow Fever
战胜黄热病

"Yellow fever!" Fear gripped anyone who heard the words. Yellow fever epidemics broke out in the 1700s in Italy, France, Spain, and England. 300,000 people are believed to have died from yellow fever in Spain during the 19th century. French soldiers were attacked by yellow fever during the 1802 Haitian Revolution; more than half of the army perished from the disease.

For two hundred yeas learned men had tried to find a way to prevent this sickness. Year after year thousands of people died of it. But no one really knew how it started, or what to do about it.

Except one man—Dr. Carlos Finlay. In 1881 he declared that yellow fever was carried by a mosquito. No one believed him until his theory was proved by a brave little group of doctors and soldiers about twenty years later.

In 1900, soon after the Spanish-American War, many American soldiers still stationed in Cuba were ill with yellow fever. So a group of army doctors, headed by Walter Reed was sent to Cuba to see what could be done. The doctors visited sick soldiers in hospitals. They went into Cuban homes to check food and water, and to see how the people lived. But they could not understand why some people got yellow fever while others, living in the same house with them, did not.

Walter Reed and his helpers went to see Carlos Finlay and listened to him. Finlay explained, "A mosquito that bites a person with yellow fever drinks the blood of the person. Then it flies over to a healthy person and bites him. In this way it carries yellow fever from the sick person to the well person. Nobody catches yellow fever by touching a person who has it, or by wearing this person's clothes."

How could Walter Reed prove this theory? He decided there was only one way: they could let fever-carrying mosquitoes bite well people.

Two of the doctors and many soldiers offered to undergo such a trial. They knew that there was no medicine to cure yellow fever, and half of the yellow-fever patients did not recover. But they were willing to die in order to save the lives of others.

A camp was set up far away from any town. Two little houses were built, with good screen on all the doors and windows so that no mosquitoes could possibly get in. The doors and windows of one house were shut tight.

Into this house stepped three brave volunteers. For twenty days and nights they lived and slept there, wearing clothes from yellow-fever patients. Then they came out. Not one of them got yellow fever! Walter Reed sent in other volunteers to do the same thing. And again not one of them got sick.

Now Walter Reed was ready for the next part of the test. The second little house was clean. It had one room divided into two with screen from floor to ceiling. Four men, two on each side of the room, slept here for two weeks. They stayed perfectly well and healthy.

Walter Reed removed the two men from one side of the room. Then he set free on that side fifteen mosquitoes that had bitten yellow-fever patients. John J. Moran went into that space filled with infected mosquitoes. He had just taken a bath. The bedding and his pajamas were freshly washed. But waiting for him were the fifteen mosquitoes. They pounced upon and bit him at once.

No mosquitoes were allowed to get into the other side of the room. The two young men

Unit Ten

there stayed well, but Moran came down with a bad case of yellow fever.

In all, thirteen men were bitten by mosquitoes infected with yellow-fever virus. Ten of them came down with the disease. Luckily they all got well. So it was proved beyond any doubt that a certain kind of mosquito is the carrier of yellow fewer, and that the disease can be best controlled by taking measures to destroy mosquitoes.

Now people know what to do to prevent yellow fever. But let us never forget those brave men who, by risking their lives to find out how the fearful disease to spread, did a great service to the world.

(712 words)

Word List

conquer	[ˈkɒŋkə]	v.	克服,征服,战胜
grip	[ɡrɪp]	v.	抓紧,抱住
declare	[dɪˈkleə]	v.	宣布,声明
mosquito	[məˈskiːtəʊ]	n.	蚊子
check	[tʃek]	v.	检查,核对
bite	[baɪt]	v.	咬
prove	[pruːv]	v.	证明,显示
undergo	[ˌʌndəˈɡəʊ]	v.	遭受,经历,忍受
trial	[ˈtraɪəl]	n.	尝试,努力,试验
cure	[kjʊə]	v.	治疗,治愈
volunteer	[ˌvɒlənˈtɪə]	n.	志愿者
divide	[dɪˈvaɪd]	v.	除,分割,划分,隔开
infect	[ɪnˈfekt]	v.	传染,感染
pajamas	[pəˈdʒɑːməz]	n.	睡衣,宽长裤
pounce	[paʊns]	v.	猛扑,突然袭击
risky	[ˈrɪski]	adj.	危险的,冒险的
carrier	[ˈkærɪə]	n.	携带者,媒介
fearful	[ˈfɪəful]	adj.	可怕的,担心的
service	[ˈsɜːvɪs]	n.	服务

Idioms & Expressions

set up	建立		at once	立刻,马上
come down	下来(倒下,下垂)		take measures	采取措施
beyond any doubt	无疑			

Exercises

1. 【Comprehension】

Choose the best answer to each of the following question.

1) People were sacred at the words "yellow fever" because _____.
   A. the disease had killed thousands of people
   B. no one knew what to do about the disease
   C. Both A and B

2) Walter Reed carried experiments with healthy people bitten by mosquitoes carrying yellow fever, for it was _____.
   A. the only way to find out the symptoms of the disease
   B. the only way to cure the disease
   C. the only way to prove Dr. Finlay's theory

3) Many volunteers offered to be bitten by infected mosquitoes because _____.
   A. they knew there was no danger
   B. They intended to be heroes
   C. They were ready to die to save the lives of other people

4) John Moran became very ill with yellow fever because _____.
   A. he had just taken a bath
   B. he had been bitten by the infected mosquitoes
   C. He didn't take good care of himself

5) According to the author, yellow fever can be prevented by _____.
   A. controlling the disease
   B. destroying the yellow fever virus
   C. wiping out the fever-carrying mosquitoes

2. 【Vocabulary】

The synonyms can always give you the hints. Please find the word that best fits the meaning below.

1) return to the usual state of health _____
2) cheerfully ready _____
3) persons who offer to do something without payment or reward _____
4) took away from a place _____
5) recently _____

Unit Ten

Text 3 (Fast Reading)

The Story of "John Henry"
"约翰·亨利"的故事

Traditionally, an American story called a "tall tale." A tall tale is a story about a person who is larger than life. The descriptions in the story are exaggerated—much greater than in real life. After a hard day's work, people gathered to tell each other stories.

Each group of workers had its own tall tale hero. An African-American man named John Henry was the hero of former slaves and the people who built the railroads. He was known for his strength.

Confirming details of John Henry's life is not possible. That is because no one knows for sure if he really lived. This is one of the things that makes his story interesting. However, John Henry is based, in part, on real events. Many people say he represents the spirit of growth in America during this period.

The night when John Henry was born was dark and cloudy. Then, lightening lit up the night sky. John Henry's birth was a big event. John Henry was the most powerful looking baby people had ever seen. He had thick arms, wide shoulders and strong muscles. John Henry started growing when he was one day old. He continued growing until he was the strongest man who ever lived.

John Henry grew up in a world that did not let children stay children for long. One day, he was sitting on his father's knee. The boy picked up a small piece of steel and a workman's tool, a hammer. He looked at the two objects, then said, "A hammer will be the death of me."

Before John Henry was six years old, he was carrying stones for workers building a nearby railroad. By the age of ten, he worked from early in the morning until night. Often, he would stop and listen to the sound of a train far away. He told his family, "I am going to be a steel-driver some day."

Steel-drivers helped create pathways for the railroad lines. These laborers had the job of cutting holes in rock. They did this by hitting thick steel drills, or spikes.

By the time John Henry was a young man, he was one of the best steel-drivers in the country. He could work for hours without missing a beat.

John Henry was almost two meters tall. He weighed more than ninety kilograms. He had a beautiful deep voice, and played an instrument called a banjo. John Henry married another steel-driver, a woman named Polly Ann. They had a son.

John Henry went to work as a steel-driver for the Chesapeake and Ohio Railroad, or

C-and-O. The company asked him to lead workers on a project to extend the railroad into the Allegheny Mountains. The workers made good progress on the project until they started working near Big Bend Mountain in West Virginia.

The company's owners said the mountain was too big to build a railroad around it. So the workers were told they had to force their drills through it. This meant creating a tunnel more than one and one-half kilometers long.

The project required about one thousand laborers and lasted three years. Pay was low and the work was difficult. The workers had to breathe thick black smoke and dust. Hundreds of men became sick. Many died.

John Henry was the strongest and fastest man involved in the project. He used a hammer that weighed more than six kilograms. Some people say he was able to cut a path of three to six meters a day.

That July was the hottest month ever in West Virginia. Many workers became tired and weak in the heat. John Henry was concerned about that his friends might lose their jobs. So, he picked up their hammers and began doing their work.

One week, he did his own work and that of several other steel-drivers. He worked day and night, rarely stopping to eat. The men thanked John Henry for his help. He just smiled and said, "A man ain't nothing but a man. He has just got to do his best."

The extreme heat continued for weeks. One day, a salesman came to the work area with a new drilling machine powered by steam. He said it could drill holes faster than twelve men working together. The railroad company planned to buy the machine if it worked as well as the salesman said.

The supervisor of the workers dismissed the salesman's claims. He said, "I have the best steel-driver in the country. His name is John Henry, and he can beat more than twenty men working together." The salesman disputed the statements. He said the company could have the machine without cost if John Henry was faster.

The supervisor called to John Henry. He said, "This man does not believe that you can drill faster. How about a race?"

John Henry looked at the machine and saw images of the future. He saw machines taking the place of America's best laborers. He saw himself and his friends unemployed and standing by a road, asking for food. He saw men losing their families and their rights as human beings.

John Henry told the supervisor he would never let the machine take his job. His friends all cheered. However, John Henry's wife Polly Ann was not happy.

John Henry lifted his son into the air. He told his wife, "A man ain't nothing but a man. But, a man always has to do his best. Tomorrow, I will take my hammer and drive that steel faster than any machine."

On the day of the big event, many people came to Big Bend Mountain to watch. The competition began. John Henry kissed his hammer and started working. At first, the steam-powered drill worked two times faster than he did. Then, he started working with a hammer in each hand. He worked faster and faster. In the mountain, the heat and dust were so thick that most men would have had trouble breathing. The crowd shouted as clouds of dust came from inside the mountain.

Polly Ann and her son cheered when the machine was pulled from the tunnel. It had broken down. Polly Ann urged John Henry to come out. But he kept working, faster and faster. He dug deep into the darkness, hitting the steel so hard that his body began to fail him. He became weak, and his heart burst.

John Henry fell to the ground. There was a terrible silence. Polly Ann did not move because she knew what happened. John Henry's blood spilled over the ground. But he still held one of the hammers.

"I beat them," he said. His wife cried out, "Don't go, John Henry." "Bring me a cool drink of water," he said. Then he took his last breath.

(1,132 words)

Exercises

1. [True, False, Not Given]

1) The tall tale is only popular among workers.
2) According to the story, John Henry was the strongest looking baby people had ever seen.
3) In the story, workers were asked to drill a tunnel through the mountain.
4) In the story, John Henry was the only one who has done a lot of work.
5) According to the passage, John Henry was protecting the rights of laborers which would be taken by the machines.

2. [Blank-Filling]

For questions 1)–5), complete the sentences with the information given in the passage.

1) A tall tale is an incredible story in which the description is _____, which is much greater than in real life.
2) What makes John Henry's story interesting is the lack of confirming _____ of him.
3) When John Henry was a young man, he was one of the best steel-drivers in the country. He could work for a long time without missing a _____.
4) The project lasted three years; the workers had to breathe thick black smoke and dust, thus hundreds of them became _____, and many _____.
5) After helping other workers, John Henry would just show his smile, and say "A man ain't nothing but a man. He has just got to _____."

Unit Eleven

Text 1 (Intensive Reading)

Background Tips: Confucius

Confucius (551—479 B.C.), Chinese philosopher and teacher. Confucius was a dedicated educator, having accepted a total of 3000 students in his life, of whom seventy-two were outstanding scholars. Eventually he and his students emerged as an independent school of thought—the Confucius School which exerted a tremendous impact on China. In order not to forget his teachings, Confucius's students wrote down all his dialogues with them. Later they set about collecting and editing what Confucius had said on other questions. The most famous one is 'the Analects'.

The Personal Qualities of a Teacher
教 师 的 个 性

What personal qualities should a teacher have? Probably no two people would write exactly similar lists, but I think the following would be generally accepted.

First, a teacher should be pleasantly live and attractive. This does not rule out people who are not good-looking or even ugly, because many such have great personal charm. But it does rule out such types as over-excitable, dull, cold-mannered, or any with other undesirable qualities.

Secondly, it is not only desirable but essential for the teacher to have real capacity for sympathy—a capacity to understand the minds and feelings of other people. Closely related with this is the capacity to be tolerant—not indeed, of what is wrong, but of weakness of human nature which induces people, and especially children, to make mistakes.

I find it essential for a teacher to be a bit of an actor. That is part of the technique of teaching, which demands that every now and then a teacher should put on an act to make his lesson interesting and vivid. Children, especially young children live in a world that is rather larger than life.

A teacher must be capable of great patience. This, I may say, is largely a matter of self-training. We are none of us like that. Teaching makes great demands on nervous energy and one should be able to take in his stride countless small irritations that adults dealing with children have to endure.

Finally, I think a teacher should have the kind of mind which always wants to go on learning. Teaching is a job at which one will never be perfect; there is always something more to learn about it. there are three main subjects of study: the subject or subjects which the teacher is teaching; the methods by which they can best be taught to the pupils in the classes he is teaching; and by far the most important—the children, young people or adults to whom they are to be taught. The two main principles of British education today are that education is education of the whole person and that it is best acquired through full and active cooperation between two persons, the teacher and the learner.

(365 words)

Word List

live	[laɪv]	*adj.*	活的,生动的,精力充沛的
excitable	[ɪkˈsaɪtəbəl]	*adj.*	易激动的,易怒的
charm	[tʃɑːm]	*n.*	魅力,诱惑力
dull	[dʌl]	*adj.*	迟钝的,呆滞的
desirable	[dɪˈzaɪərəbəl]	*adj.*	值得做的;值得渴望的
capacity	[kəˈpæsɪtɪ]	*n.*	能力
sympathy	[ˈsɪmpəθɪ]	*n.*	同情心
tolerant	[ˈtɒlərənt]	*adj.*	容忍的,宽容的
induce	[ɪnˈdjuːs]	*v.*	引诱;诱惑
technique	[tekˈniːk]	*n.*	技术,技巧,技能
vivid	[ˈvɪvɪd]	*adj.*	生动的,逼真的,鲜艳的
patience	[ˈpeɪʃəns]	*n.*	耐心,容忍
irritation	[ˌɪrɪˈteɪʃən]	*n.*	激怒,恼怒
principle	[ˈprɪnsɪpl]	*n.*	原则,原理
acquire	[əˈkwaɪə]	*v.*	获得,取得
cooperation	[kəʊˌɒpəˈreɪʃən]	*n.*	合作,协作

Idioms & Expressions

rule out	把……排除在外;排除……的可能性
put on an act	装腔作势;炫耀;夸夸其谈
take in one's stride	轻易地解决(困难),毫不费力地做

Exercises

1. [Definitions]

Match the words in the box with their meanings. Write the word that stands for the definition in the appropriate answer space.

live	excitable	charm	dull	desirable	capacity
sympathy	tolerant	induce	technique	vivid	patience
irritation	principle	acquire	cooperation		

1) _____: to obtain something by buying it or being given it.
2) _____: the feeling of being annoyed about something, especially something that happens repeatedly or for a long time.
3) _____: the ability to continue waiting or doing something for a long time without becoming angry or anxious.
4) _____: worth seeking or doing as advantageous, beneficial, or wise.
5) _____: a special quality someone or something has making people like them, feel attracted to them, or be easily influenced by them.
6) _____: used to describe memories, dreams, descriptions etc which are so clear that they seem real.
7) _____: to persuade someone to do something, especially something that does not seem wise.
8) _____: to work with someone to achieve something that you both want.
9) _____: not dead or artificial.
10) _____: the feeling of being sorry for someone who is in a bad situation.
11) _____: not interesting or exciting.
12) _____: a special way of doing something.
13) _____: the basic idea that a plan or system is based on.
14) _____: allowing people to do, say, or believe what they want without criticizing or punishing them.
15) _____: someone's ability to do something.
16) _____: becoming excited too easily.

2. [Sample Sentences]

Use the new words and phrases you have learned from the box in the following sentence. Change the form where necessary.

1) The _____ meeting made me feel sleepy.
2) The _____ driver blew his horn at the slow truck.

3) His cello _____ is unique.
4) We were so excited to see real _____ elephants.
5) I have a lot of _____ for her; she had to bring up the children on her own.
6) The college _____ a reputation for very high standards.
7) They agreed to _____ with Brazil on a programme to protect the rain-forests.
8) A puppy is naturally affectionate and _____.
9) I've got _____ memories of that summer.
10) He refused to give me any more money as a matter of _____.
11) You'll just have to be _____ and wait till I'm off the phone.
12) She was _____ of different views.
13) The room had seating _____ for about 80.
14) Ms. Liu is a person of quiet _____ and unfailing good humor.
15) The ability to speak a foreign language is highly _____.

3. [Translation]

A. Translate the following English sentences into Chinese.

1) All work and no play makes Jack a dull Boy; all play and no work makes Jack a mere Boy.

2) Our faults irritate us most when we see them in others.

3) Since we want a peaceful environment, we must cooperate with all of the world's forces for peace.

4) Genius is an infinite capacity for taking pains.

5) Alcohol can induce a loosening of the tongue.

B. Translate the following Chinese sentences into English by using the word in the bracket.

1) 他在竞赛中显示出了精湛的技艺。(technique)

2) 有些植物能耐酷热。(tolerant)

3) 她用自己的魅力来左右人们。(charm)

4) 你的慰问给我带来了莫大的安慰。(sympathy)

5) 想象有时比现实生动得多。(vivid)

4.【Writing】

For this part, you are allowed 30 minutes to write a short essay in honor of teachers on the occasion of Teacher's Day. You should write at least 120 words following the outline given below:

1) 向老师致以节日的祝贺
2) 从一件难忘的事回忆老师的教诲和无私的奉献
3) 我如何回报老师的关爱

Reading Skills: 略读

略读(**Skimming**)是非常快速的阅读。略读时,你的目的是为了获取文章的主旨大意和一些(不是所有的)细节。判断文章的主旨大意是各类英语考试阅读部分的常见题型。为了能快速阅读,你必须略去文章的一些内容。略读是一种非常有用的阅读技巧,它可以使你从阅读的材料中很快地获取信息,抓住文章的主旨大意。学会如何略读可以提高你的阅读效率,帮助你获取阅读考试的高分。

略读和普通阅读的区别

了解略读和普通阅读的区别十分重要。在进行普通阅读时,你读所有的内容,不跳过任何部分。但在略读时,跳过一些内容是必需的。在很多情况下,只要你感觉已经掌握了一个段落的大意,就可以跳过一半或三分之二的内容。

略读和普通阅读的又一个区别是你对文章的理解水平要低一些。在进行普通阅读时,你使用适中的阅读速度,努力理解尽可能多的内容。你通常能理解文章70%或80%的内容。但在略读时,你理解的内容要少,能理解文章50%的内容就达到了略读的平均水平,如果理解60%的内容就高于平均水平了。略读时阅读速度应该是你普通阅读速度的两倍。比如,如果你普通阅读的速度是每分钟读400个单词,那么你略读的速度就能达到每分钟800个单词,甚至更多。

如何进行略读

如何才能快速地略读?哪些内容应该跳过去?下面介绍一些帮助你提高略读速度的方法和步骤。

读最前面的几个段落

如果你在读一篇几千词的提供事实的文章,开始时要读最前面的几个段落,以便识别文章的主题和题材,了解作者的风格和观点。不要跳过任何内容,但要用你最快的速度去读。通常,作者最前面的几段是文章的引言,能使你了解整篇文章的概况。

跳过一些内容

如果你想快速略读,一旦你对文章的概况有了了解,就应该立即开始跳过一些内容。在读第4段或第5段时你可以只读关键句,以获取主旨大意,跳过该段的其他内容。你在读关键句时,也可以对段中的一两个关键词、词组或数字做短暂的停留。

找到主旨大意

在略读时,要努力找出每段的主旨大意和一些事实。你不应指望抓住所有事实,但你可以抓住一些关键事实、名字和数字。

有时,主旨大意并不体现在段落的第一句话,而是在段落的中间或最后。所以,你必须花些时间去找关键句。另外,你可能会碰到没有关键句的段落。换句话说,段落的主旨大意没有用一句话来总结。你必须仔细从一些词组和句子中寻找主旨大意。你也许不得不把整个段都读下来,以便找到主旨大意。但是,如果你把这一段都读了,你就必须对下面几段的内容更加快速地略读,以补回失去的时间。请记住,通常文章最后一段总结全文的内容,所以值得对整段进行通读。

要快速地读

略读时你必须和时间赛跑。必须尽快地读,同时跳过大块的内容。要注意避免对内容或故事过于感兴趣,因为这样可能会使你放慢阅读速度去读一些不必要的细节。记住:略读的目的是为了快速获取作者的主旨大意。

Text 2 (Extensive Reading)

Mammals in the Sea
海洋中的哺乳动物

A dolphin looks more like a fish than certain fish do. It has a smooth, streamlined body. It is an excellent swimmer. As its powerful tail moves up and down, the dolphin seems flash through the water. Like fish, dolphins are completely at home in the water. There they play, feed, sleep, and bear their young. Dolphins live in the sea and can live only in the sea. Yet they are not fish.

If you watch a dolphin, you will see something that shows it is not a fish. A dolphin must come to the surface to breathe. Fish can take oxygen out of the water. Dolphins cannot. Like us, they breathe with lungs and must take their oxygen from the air. And, like us, they are mammals.

Mammals are a large class of animals with backbones. Mammals nurse their young on milk. They are warm-blooded. Almost all mammals bear living young. And most of them have hair. Dogs, cats, horses, cows, pigs, mice, monkeys, and bats are all mammals. We are mammals. So are dolphins and their close relatives, the whales and porpoises.

Dolphins belong to a family that scientists call the Cetacea. The family has two main branches.

One branch is made up of the world's giant whales. The scientific name for them is Mystacoceti, which means "mustache whales." Mustache whales do not have teeth. Rather, they have something like a huge mustache inside their mouths. This is baleen, or whalebone. The big whales strain their food out of the sea through the baleen.

The other main branch of the family is made up of Odontoceti, which means "toothed whales." There is only one giant in this branch of the family—the sperm whale. The other members are small whales, dolphins, and porpoises.

Dolphins and porpoises are very much alike. In fact, they are so much alike that there is only one sure way to tell them apart. That is by the shape of their teeth. Porpoises have spade-shaped teeth. Dolphins have cone-shaped teeth.

Because dolphins and porpoises are alike, many people call all of them porpoises. (A second reason is that there is a large fish also named dolphin.) Other people prefer to use both names—porpoise and dolphin.

There are many kinds of dolphins in the sea. Among the best known is the bottle-nosed dolphin. This dolphin lives along coasts. So it is a familiar dolphin and one that scientists have studied closely.

A bottle-nosed dolphin may be 7 to 11 feet long and weigh 300 to 700 pounds. The easiest way to tell a bottle-nose is by its mouth. When the mouth is closed, a bottle-nose appears to be smiling. This is not a real smile but just a curve of the mouth. The curving mouth gives the dolphin a friendly look. And bottle-noses are friendly.

Like all Cetacea, dolphins are mammals of the sea. Most mammals are land animals. So perhaps it is not surprising to learn that dolphins and their relatives are descended from land animals. Long ago, dolphin ancestors left the land for the sea.

We do not know why this happened. But we do know that it happened 50 to 60 million years ago. At that time the earth was very different from the earth we know today. The land was different. Animals and plants were different. And there were no human being on earth.

Among the animals was a kind that would become the dolphin we know.

No one is sure exactly what kind of animal it was. But there is reason to think it was related to grass-eating animals like the cow. Modern dolphins are fish-eaters. Yet their stomachs are like those of animals that eat plants. The makeup of their blood is also like that of grazing animals.

Nor is anyone sure what this early animals looked like. It may have looked a little like a pig with four short legs, some hair and a head that came out into a snout. Set in the head were two small ears, two eyes, a nose, and a mouth.

The animal's tail was probably like an otter's—thick and strong at the base.

For some reason, this animal was drawn toward the water. It was drawn toward swamps, rivers and the sea, where it searched for food. Perhaps it was driven there by bigger, fiercer animals. We do not know. But dolphin ancestors began to spend more and more time in the water. The result was that the animal began to change.

This does not mean that any one animal changed. It means that the form of the animals changed over a very long time.

The easiest way to understand what happened is to take a different example. Suppose a farmer wants short-legged sheep because they are easier to fence in. He or she selects the seep with the shortest legs and breeds them. Their lambs tend to have short legs. Later the farmer breeds the short-legged lambs and gets more lambs with even shorter legs. This way the farmer can develop a race of short-legged sheep.

In the example, a person did the selecting. But such selecting also takes place in nature. It is called natural selection. It works this way. Among animals of a kind, some do better than others. They are better fitted for life. In time, they come to be the only animals of their kind. The others have died out.

That is what happened with the dolphins. (915 words)

Word List

streamlined	['striːmlaɪnd]	adj./a.	流线型的
oxygen	['ɒksɪdʒən]	n.	氧气
backbone	['bækbəʊn]	n.	脊柱,脊骨
nurse	[nɜːs]	v.	看护,哺乳
porpoise	['pɔːpəs]	n.	海豚
branch	[brɑːntʃ]	n.	分支
giant	['dʒaɪənt]	adj.	巨大的
baleen	[bə'liːn]	n.	鲸须
curve	[kɜːv]	n.	曲线,弧线
descend	[dɪ'send]	v.	下来,下降;系出,出自
makeup	[meɪkʌp]	n.	组成
draw	[drɔː]	v.	撤退,退却
swamp	[swɒmp]	n.	湿地,沼泽

Exercises

1. [Questions]

Based on the information provided in the text, answer the following questions briefly.

1) What is the distinction between a dolphin and a fish?

2) How many branches are there in Cetacea? What are they?

3) Why does the author say a bottle-nose appears to be smiling when the mouth isn't open?

4) Why were dolphins once probably grass eaters?

5) According to "natural selection", what do we learn about dolphin ancestors?

2. [Multiple Choices]

Choose the right answer from the four choices marked A, B, C, and D.

1) Dolphins are animals that live _____.
   A. on land   B in the sea   C. in sea caves   D. in the river

2) Dolphins and porpoises are _____.
   A. mammals   B. fish   C. reptiles   D. worms

3) The easiest way to identify a bottle-nose dolphin is by _____.
   A. its mouth   B. the unusual shape of its body
   C. its larger size   D. its ancestor

4) The dolphin's ancestors became dolphins by _____.
   A. suddenly living in the water one day
   B. growing into dolphins while on land
   C. move from the land to the water
   D. spending more and more time in the water

5) According to the author, natural selection means that _____.
   A. "people breed short-legged sheep."
   B. "all animals die sooner or later."
   C. "nature selects the animals best fitted for life."
   D. "some animals extinguished suddenly"

Text 3 (Fast Reading)

Energy from the Sun
来自太阳的能量

Energy in one form or another does all the work in the world. Where does all this energy come from? Let's find out.

It's a hot summer day, and you, your family, and friends decide to drive to the beach for a cookout.

When you get to the beach, the sand and the rocks are so hot that they hurt your bare feet. You put on sneakers in a hurry. The water is so bright and shining in the sun that you can hardly look at it.

While the charcoal fire is starting to burn in the cookout stove, everyone goes for a swim. The water feels good-warm at the top, but cooler down around your toes.

A little wind is blowing when you come out. The fire isn't quite ready for cooking yet, so you play tag or read.

For lunch there are hot dogs, corn, salad, and rolls, sodas, fruit, and coffee for the adults. By the time the coffee water boils and the corn and hot dogs are cooked, all the bathing suits are dry. So are the towels spread out on the rocks in the sun.

Lunch is good. Just as you are finishing, it starts to rain, so you pack up and run. But nobody minds the rain. It will cool things off.

At the same time you were having fun at the beach, work was being done. Energy from the sun dried the towels. It heated the sand and the rocks, the water, and the air. It even made the rain and the wind. Heat from the sun does small work and big work, all over the earth.

Light energy from the sun was working on the beach too. It supplied the daylight. It lit the earth and made the sand bright and the water sparkling.

The sun also supplied the energy that grew the food you ate.

Plants use light energy from the sun to make food for themselves. The food is a kind of sugar. It is also a kind of energy called chemical energy. Green plants change light energy from the sun into chemical energy.

Plants use some of that energy for everyday living and growing. They store the rest in their leaves and seeds, in fruit, roots, stems, and berries.

The salad and the corn, the rolls, fruit, and coffee all came from plants. You and all animals depend on plants for food.

The charcoal you used for cooking began as a plant too. Once, that charcoal was a living tree that used sunlight to make food and then stored part of the food it made. The energy in this stored food remained, even after the tree died. You used that energy when you burned the charcoal.

The gasoline you used for driving to the beach began with energy from the sun too. It was made from oil.

Oil is formed from the remains of plants and animals that lived on earth millions of years ago. The remains of ancient living things are called fossils. This is why oil is called a fossil fuel. Coal and natural gas are fossil fuels too.

Oil, coal, and natural gas all hold the chemical energy that was stored in those ancient plants and in the animals that ate the plants. When you drive in a car it is that stored energy that makes the car go.

Fossil fuels are easy to use. They are easy to store. They are easy to change into other forms of energy-heat, light, motion, and electricity. They are so handy that people in many places around the earth use fossil fuels to supply almost all the energy they need.

Now fossil fuels are beginning to be used up. That's why people worry about running out of energy.

But as long as the sun shines, the earth will not run out of energy. The sun pours more energy onto the earth than we can ever use. Most of that energy comes to us as heat and light. Energy from the sun is called solar energy.

Anything to do with the sun is called solar. The word comes from the Romans' word for sun and their god of the sun, who was called Sol.

Solar energy is a safe kind of energy. It doesn't make pollution or have dangerous leftovers. That is why scientists and inventors are experimenting with ways of harnessing the sun to do some of the jobs fossil fuels have been doing.

But to make the sun do work like that they have to solve some problems.

They have to collect the sun's energy. Collecting sunshine isn't easy, unless you are a plant.

Sunshine isn't easy to store, either. You can't fill a tank with it or put it in the woodbox. You can't move it through a pipe or a wire. You can't just turn it on.

Still, people have been using solar energy to help do their work for a long time. There are old ways and new ways of catching sunshine and putting it to work.

Suppose you were living in a cold place and going to spend the winter in a cave. Would you choose a cave that faced the winter sun or a cave that faced away from it?

You might make the same choice if you were building a house in a cold place. You would probably build the house so the winter sun would pour in the windows to warm it. People have been building houses that way for a long time.

Is it possible to catch still more of the sun's heat in a house? Yes. Some houses also collect heat on the roof, move it indoors, store some, use some to make hot water, and use the rest for heating. A house like that is called a solar house.

People who build solar houses have learned how to do those things by observing how the earth itself uses solar energy.

Remember the beach?

Remember the hot sand and the hot rocks?

Some materials take in heat energy from the sun and hold it. They absorb the heat. Sand and rocks do this. So do some other solid materials, such as metals. Water absorbs the sun's heat too.

Color can also be important. Dark, dull colors absorb heat. They bounce it back. That's why dark clothes are warmer in the winter and light-colored clothes are cooler in the summer.

The longer it takes something to heat up, the longer that thing holds the heat. Materials that heat up fast cool off fast.

If you go back to the beach in the evening after sunset, the sand and the rocks, which heat up fast, will be cool. But the water, which heats up slowly, will still be warm.

It takes a long time for the sun to heat the water in a big lake or an ocean. But by the end of summer, a large body of water will have caught and stored enough heat from the sun to last for a good part of the winter. Water stores heat very well.

Unit Eleven

That's why land near a large body of water never gets quite as cold in the winter as land far away from the water. The stored heat in the water keeps the land around it warm.

Slowly, all winter long, heat from the water moves out into the cold air. Heat always moves that way—from a warmer place or thing to a cooler one. Once you know which way heat moves, you understand how things get hot and how they lose heat.

Remember when the hot sand on the beach burned your feet? Heat from the sand was moving into your cooler feet!

(1,287 words)

Exercises

1. [True, False, Not Given]

Decide whether the following statements are True, False or Not Given.

T (for True) if the statement agrees with the information given in the passage;
F (for False) if the statement doesn't agree with the information given in the passage;
NG (for Not Given) if the information is not given in the passage.

1) The author tells us that all the work in the world is done by stored fuel.
2) Oil, coal, and natural gas are called fossil fuels.
3) Fossil fuels will last forever.
4) Sunshine is easy to collect but not to store.
5) If you build a house in a cold place, you will probably put in windows to catch the light from the winter sun.
6) Both light-and-dark-colored things reflect heat.
7) Heat doesn't move.

2. [Blank-Filling]

For questions 1)–3), complete the sentences with the information given in the passage.

1) According to this story, all the energy we use comes from _____.
2) Energy from the sun is called _____.
3) People who build solar houses learn to use solar energy by _____.

Unit Twelve

Text 1 (Intensive Reading)

Background Tips: Professionalism

Merriam-webster defines professionalism as the conduct, aims, or qualities that characterize or mark a person. Being professional is also the first lesson for those medicine and business students. It requires the understanding of the job nature itself. Professionalism embraces a set of attitudes, skills, and behaviors, attributes and values that are expected from those to whom society has extended the privilege of being considered a professional. The core values of professionalism include: Honesty and Integrity, Altruism, Respect, Responsibility and Accountability, Compassion and Empathy, Dedication and Self-improvement.

Work
工作

It is physically impossible for a well-educated, intellectual, or brave man to make money the chief object of his thoughts; as physically impossible as it is for him to make his dinner the principal object of them. All healthy people like their dinner, but their dinner is not the main object of their lives. So all healthy-minded people like making money—ought to like and to enjoy the sensation of winning it; but the main object of their lives is not money; it is something better than money.

A good soldier, for instance, mainly wishes to do his fighting well. He is glad of his pay—very properly so, and justly grumble when you keep him ten months without it; still, his main notion of life is to win battles, not to be paid for winning them.

So of doctors. They like fees no doubt—ought to like them; yet if they are brave and well educated, the entire object of their lives is not fees. They, on the whole, desire to cure the sick, and—if they are good doctors, and the choice is fairly put to them—would rather cure their patient and lose their fee than kill him and get it. And so with all other brave and rightly trained men; their work is first, their fee second, very important always, but still second.

But in every nation, there is a vast class of people who are cowardly, and more or less stupid. And with these people, just as certainly the fee is first and work second, as with

Unit Twelve

brave people the work is first and the fee is second.

And this is no small distinction. It is the whole distinction. It is the whole distinction in a man. You cannot serve two masters; you must serve one or the other. If your work is first with you, and your fee second, work is your master.

Observe, then, all wise work is mainly threefold in character. It is honest, useful, and cheerful. I hardly know anything stranger than that you recognize honesty in play, and do not in work. In your lightest games you have always someone to see what you call "fair play". In boxing you must hit; in racing, start fair. Your watchword is fair play; your hatred, foul play. Did it ever strike you that you wanted another watchword also, fair work, and another hatred also, foul work?

(399 words)

Word List

object	[ˈɒbdʒɪkt]	n.	目标,目的
principal	[ˈprɪnsɪp(ə)l]	adj.	主要的,最重要的
sensation	[senˈseɪʃən]	n.	感觉
grumble	[ˈgrʌmbl]	v.	抱怨
notion	[ˈnəʊʃən]	n.	观念,想法
cure	[kjʊə]	v.	治愈
cowardly	[ˈkaʊədlɪ]	adj.	胆小的,怯懦的
distinction	[dɪˈstɪŋkʃən]	n.	区别,差别
threefold	[ˈθriːfəʊld]	adv.	三倍
cheerful	[ˈtʃɪəful]	adj.	快乐的,高兴的
watchword	[ˈwɒtʃwɜːd]	n.	标语;口号
hatred	[ˈheɪtrɪd]	n.	憎恶,憎恨
foul	[faʊl]	adj.	犯规的;肮脏的
strike	[straɪk]	v.	给人……印象,让人觉得……

Idioms & Expressions

on the whole	总的来说;大体上;基本上

Exercises

1. [Definitions]

Match the words in the box with their meanings. Write the word that stands for the definition in the appropriate answer space.

object	principal	sensation	grumble	notion
cure	cowardly	distinction	threefold	cheerful
watchword	hatred	foul	strike	

1) _____ : an angry feeling of extreme dislike for someone or something.
2) _____ : to make someone well again after they have been ill.
3) _____ : a clear difference or separation between two similar things.
4) _____ : lacking courage.
5) _____ : the purpose of a plan, action, or activity.
6) _____ : to keep complaining in an unhappy way.
7) _____ : to give somebody a particular impression.
8) _____ : a word or phrase that expresses an attitude or belief.
9) _____ : a feeling that you get from one of your five senses.
10) _____ : most important.
11) _____ : to do something to another player that is against the rules of the game.
12) _____ : an idea, belief, or opinion.
13) _____ : three times as much or as many.
14) _____ : happy, or behaving in a way that shows you are happy.

2. [Sample Sentences]

Use the new words and phrases you have learned from the box in the following sentence. Change the form where necessary.

1) The basketball player _____ again.
2) As he was always _____ he had the nickname "Smiler".
3) The _____ of the game is to improve children's math skills.
4) Why _____ at me about your own stupid mistakes?
5) Their _____ stems from envy.
6) When I left the hospital I was completely _____.
7) He didn't have a slightest _____ of what I meant.
8) Today the _____ is "Learn through Playing".
9) He was _____ by her air of confidence.
10) A _____ should be made between the primary and secondary tasks.

11) Try it. Don't be such a _____.
12) The answer is _____: time, team, and himself.
13) I knew the train had stopped, but I had the _____ that it was moving backwards.
14) The Nile is one of the _____ rivers of Africa.

3. 【Translation】

A. Translate the following English sentences into Chinese.

1) He was clever and cheerful and brave in his actions, but mild and quiet in his ways.

2) If we want to keep fit, we must always remember that prevention is better than cure.

3) Love overlooks defects and hatred magnifies shortcomings.

4) He was fouled inside the penalty area.

5) She had remained cheerful and energetic throughout the trip.

B. Translate the following Chinese sentences into English by using the word in the bracket.

1) 他们是非不分。(distinction)

2) 我感觉到一种幸福感。(sensation)

3) 教育的目的在于培养品德。(object)

4) 勇敢的敌人胜过懦怯的朋友。(cowardly)

5) 他们声称已经发现了一种治疗此病的药物,但此事尚未得到证实。(cure)

4. 【Writing】

For this part, you can try to write a composition on the topic How to Succeed in a Job Interview? You should write at lest 120 words, and base your composition on the outline given in Chinese below:

Outline: 1) 面试在求职过程中的作用
2) 取得面试成功的因素:仪表、举止谈吐、能力、专业知识、自信、实事求是……

Reading Skills: 默读

专家认为，做阅读理解不应该是读，而应该是看。默读有利于发展阅读者的内部语言，有利于强化理解，有利于提高阅读速度。测试表明，我们朗读时，一分钟能念 125 个字就已很不错了，而默读时，每分钟可读 150 个字以上，有人阅读小说时甚至可达每分钟 600 字。

默读时一定要做到如下三点：①全神贯注。这是有效阅读最需要的心理素质。②积极思维。默读有利于思维活动的开展，有利于深层理解。③减少回视。回视率高不仅限制了速度，也会对内容的理解产生支离破碎的影响。

培养默读习惯最好的方法是扩大视幅快读，让你的嘴跟不上你的阅读速度；我们也可用手指压在嘴上或按住喉部，这样就会逐渐改掉嘴唇抖动的坏习惯。

Practice

As one comes to some crossroads, he or she sees a sign which says that drivers have to stop when they come to the main road ahead.① At other crossroads, drivers have to go slow, but they do not actually have to stop unless, of course, there is something coming along the main road; and at still others, they do not have either to stop or to go slow, because they are themselves on the main road.

Mr. Williams, who was always a very careful driver, was driving home from work one evening when he came to a crossroad. It had a "SLOW" sign. He slowed down when he came to the main road, looked both ways to see that nothing was coming, and then drove across without stopping completely.

At once he heard a police whistle (口哨声), so he pulled into the side of the road and stopped.② A policeman walked over to him with a notebook and a pen in his hand and said, "You didn't stop at that crossing."

"But the sign there doesn't say 'STOP'." answered Mr Williams, "It just says 'SLOW', and I did go slow."

The policeman looked around him, and a look of surprise came over his face.③ Then he put his notebook and pen away, scratched (抓) his head and said, "Well, I'm in the wrong street！"

难句注释

① a sign which says that drivers have to stop when they come to the main road ahead.
一个让驾驶员到了主干道就得停下来的标牌。

② pull into the side of the road and stop 转向路边并停了下来。

③ The policeman looked around him, and a look of surprise came over his face.
这个警察朝他的周围看了看，脸上露出惊讶的表情。

Total words: 231
Reading time: _____
Reading speed: _____

Text 2 (Extensive Reading)

Zoo
动物园

The children were always good during the month of August. This was especially so when it began to get near the twenty-third of August, Professor Hugo's Interplanetary Zoo came to the Chicago area. The great silver spaceship would settle down in a hug parking area. It would remain there during its annual six-hour visit.

Long before daybreak large crowds would gather. Lines of children and adults, each one clutching his or her dollar, would wait restlessly to see the Professor's Interplanetary Zoo. Everyone was eager to see what race of strange creatures the Professor had brought this year.

In the past they had been treated to three-legged creatures from Venus. Or tall, thin men from Mars. Or snake-like horrors from some even more distant planet.

This year, as the large silver spaceship settled down to earth in the huge parking area just outside of Chicago, the children watched with awe. They saw the sides of the spaceship slide up to reveal the usual cages made of thick bars. Inside the cages were some wild, small, horse-like animals that moved with quick, uneven motions and kept chattering in a high-pitched tone.

The citizens of Earth clustered around as Professor Hugo's crew quickly collected a dollar from everyone in the audience. Soon the good Professor, himself, made an appearance. He was wearing; his many-colored caped and top hat.

"Peoples of Earth," he called into his microphone.

The crowd's noise died down and he continued. "Peoples of Earth," he went on, "this year we have a real treat for your dollar. Here are the little-known horse-spider people of Kaan—brought to you across a million miles of space at great expense. Gather around the amazing horse-spider people of Kaan. See them, study them, listen to them. Tell your friends about them. But hurry! My spaceship can remain here for only six hours!"

And the crowds slowly filed by, horrified and fascinated by these strange creatures that looked like horses, but ran up the walls of their cages like spiders. "This is certainly worth a dollar," one man remarked. "I'm going home to tell my wife."

All day long it went like that. Finally, then thousands of people had filed by the barred cages which were built into the side of the spaceship. Then, as the six-hour time limit ran out, Professor Hugo once more took the microphone in his hand.

"We must go now," said the professor, "but we will return again next year on this date.

And if you enjoyed Professor Hugo's Interplanetary Zoo this year, phone your friends in other cities. Tell them about it. We will land in New York tomorrow. Next week we go on to London, Paris, Rome, Hong Kong, and Tokyo. Then we must leave for other worlds!"

He waved farewell to them. And as the ship rose from the ground, the earth peoples agreed that this had been the very best Zoo yet....

Two months and three planets later, the silver spaceship of Professor Hugo settled at last onto the familiar jagged rocks of Kaan. The horse-spider creatures scurried away in a hundred different directions as they began seeking their homes among the rocks.

In one, the she-creature was happy to see the return of her mate and little one, she babbled a greeting in the strange Kaan language. Then she hurried to embrace them. "You were gone a long time," she said. "Was it good?"

The he-creature nodded. "Our little one enjoyed it especially," he said. "We visited eight worlds and saw many things."

The little one ran up the wall of the cave. "The place called Earth was the best. The creatures there wear garments over their skins, and they walk on two legs."

"But isn't it dangerous?" asked the she-creature.

"No," the he-creature answered. "There are bars to protect us from them. We stay right in the ship. Next time you must come with us. It is well worth the nineteen 'commocs' it costs."

The little one nodded. "it was the very best Zoo ever."

(673 words)

Word List

- interplanetary [ˌɪntəˈplænɪtərɪ] adj. 星际的;行星间的;太阳系内的
- spaceship [ˈspeɪsʃɪp] n. 宇宙飞船
- annual [ˈænjuəl] adj. 一年一次的,年度的,每年的
- daybreak [ˈdeɪbreɪk] n. 黎明,拂晓
- restlessly [ˈrestləslɪ] adv. 不安静地
- creature [ˈkriːtʃə] n. 生物,动物,人
- Venus [ˈviːnəs] n. 金星
- Mars [mɑːz] n. 火星
- uneven [ʌnˈiːvən] adj. 不平坦的,不均匀的
- chatter [ˈtʃætə] v. 喋喋不休,唠叨
- high-pitched [haɪˈpɪtʃt] adj. 声调高的
- cluster [ˈklʌstə] v. 聚集
- amazing [əˈmeɪzɪŋ] adj. 令人惊奇的
- horrified [ˈhɒrɪfaɪd] adj. 感到恐惧的,受惊吓的
- fascinated [ˈfæsɪneɪtɪd] adj. 感到着迷的,被强烈吸引的
- jagged [ˈdʒægɪd] adj. 有缺口的,参差不齐的

Unit Twelve

○ babble	['bæbəl]	v.	模糊不清地说,咿呀学语
○ embrace	[ɪm'breɪs]	v.	拥抱
○ garment	['gɑːmənt]	n.	衣服

Idioms & Expressions

file by	成队走过	wave farewell to somebody	向某人告别
scurry away	快跑走		

Exercises

1. [Questions]

Based on the information provided in the text, answer the following questions briefly.

1) What was the cost to see Professor Hugo's Zoo?

2) What was the "treat" Professor Hugo had this year for the people of Chicago?

3) How long did the spaceship remain in Chicago?

4) How many people had visited Professor Hugo's Interplanetary Zoo before the spaceship left Chicago?

5) How long had it taken Professor Hugo to complete his tour?

2. [Multiple Choices]

Choose the right answer from the four choices marked A, B, C, and D.

1) Professor Hugo's Interplanetary Zoo came to the Chicago are _____.
   A. once every two years   B. twice a year
   C. once a year   D. once a month

2) As the crowds filed by and saw the creatures that Professor Hugo had brought, the people _____.
   A. were bored   B. felt cheated
   C. were horrified   D. felt curious

3) Professor Hugo's next stop with his Interplanetary Zoo was going to be _____.
   A. New York   B. London
   C. Paris   D. Tokyo.

4) When Professor Hugo had completed his interplanetary tour, he went back to _____.
   A. Mars   B. Venus   C. Earth   D. Kaan
5) A horse-spider man and his child enjoyed their long trip during which they visited _____
   A. eight worlds   B. six worlds   C. four worlds   D. one world

Text 3 (Fast Reading)

Sleeping and Dreaming
睡眠与做梦

In a way, you're already an expert on sleeping and dreaming. After all, you do it every night! Before you start interpreting your dreams and the dreams of your friends, take a few minutes to learn about what happens every time you close your eyes and sleep.

Non-REM and REM sleep

There are two different types of sleep: REM, or rapid-eye-movement sleep, known as "dreaming sleep"; and non-REM sleep, known as "quiet" sleep. During non-REM sleep, your body is at rest. It is capable of movement, but your brain stops sending messages to your body to move, so you usually lie still. Your heartbeat and breathing are normal. The mind is also at rest during non-REM sleep. There is very little dreaming, if any at all.

During REM sleep, your mind becomes very active. This is when you do almost all of your dreaming. Your body also becomes more active. Behind closed eyelids, your eyes dart back and forth rapidly as if you were watching a hyper-speed tennis match. Your heart rate and breathing speed up too.

Ironically, despite this increased activity, your body is basically paralyzed during REM sleep. The most you're able to do is twitch your hands, feet and face. The rest of your muscles are unable to move. The brain signals sent to tell your muscles to move are blocked in the spinal cord. (That's why any sleepwalking you do is done during non-REM sleep.)

This may, in part, explain that scary feeling you may have experienced in a dream when you try to escape from someone or something, only to find you're rooted to the spot. But maybe it's a good thing you can't move around freely while you dream. Otherwise, one might in the middle of a dram about your current crush, you might awaken to find yourself knocking at his or her front door in an effort to act out your dream!

The Sleep Cycle

Even though you don't always remember your dreams, you dream every night. Your brain is a dram machine, producing over two hours' worth of dreams during eight hours of sleep. Some research shows that most people experience anywhere from three to nine dreams a night.

When you first begin to fall asleep, you are in non-REM sleep. There are four stages to non-REM sleep: Stage 1 begins when you first feel drowsy and start to fall asleep. You then pass through stages 2, 3 and 4. Each stage puts you into a deeper and deeper sleep.

After reaching stage 4, the deepest stage of sleep, you return through stages 3 and 2 back to stage 1. you then enter REM sleep and begin dreaming.

REM sleep is a light state of sleep. But even if your sleep is disturbed—let's say the alarm clock goes off—you may not wake up easily if you're in the middle of a really interesting dream. Or, you may work the alarm clock into your dream before it finally rouses you out of your sleep.

This entire non-REM/REM cycle takes about 90 minutes and is repeated throughout the night.

Dreaming time

During the first few non-REM/REM cycles, you don't spend much time dreaming. The first REM period may last only five or ten minutes. As the night progresses, however, you spend more and more time in REM sleep and less in non-REM sleep. By the end of the night you may be spending as much as hour at a time in REM sleep.

Adults spend 25 percent of their nightly sleep in the REM state. Babies spend up to 50 percent in REM sleep. No one knows why babies need more REM sleep, but experts believe that it somehow helps with a baby's development. Kinds also spend slightly more time in REM sleep than adults. However, according to Richard Ferber, director of pediatric sleep disorders at the Children's Hospital in Boston, by the time you hit your teens, your dream time is 25 percent.

The Importance of Dreaming

Dreams can be important tools in examining how you feel about yourself and the world. Despite all the research done on sleep and dreaming, however, no one yet knows why people have REM sleep or why the dream. But because everyone dreams every night, researchers conclude that REM sleep and dreaming serve some sort of important function in the human mind. What research has shown is that if people go without REM sleep (alcohol and some medications deprive people of REM sleep), they become irritable, anxious and have trouble concentrating. So it appears that everyone needs REM sleep and dreams.

Making Sense of Your Dreams

Some dreams are very straightforward. For example, if you're anxious about an upcoming science test and you dream that your pen runs out of ink in the middle of an important exam and you can't finish it, the dream is most likely a reflection of the anxiety you're feeling. The exam in your dream probably stands for the science test you will soon be taking.

But often the messages of dreams are more mysterious. Your first thought is, what does that dream mean? Dreams have their own logic, but it's almost always not the logic you use when you're awake. This is why dreams can be so confusing.

Universal Sleep Symbols

You have a dream that you're walking down a long road. In your hand, you're clutching an old, battered suitcase, packed with all of your most cherished possessions.

Your best friend has a similar dream of walking down a road with a suitcase. Do these images in the dream—the road, the suitcase—mean the same thing in your dram as they mean in your pal's dream?

In part, maybe. Carl Gustav Jang was the first dream theorist to introduce the idea that dream images may stand for the same things in everybody's dreams. Today, many dream experts believe this to be true to a certain extent. For example, one dream expert, Tony Crisp, examined thousands of dreams over 22 years and, in the 1990, drew up his own book of meanings for popular dream images in *Dream Dictionary*. He found that images in one person's dreams often mean the same as in the next person's. These images and their meanings make up his dictionary. He also emphasized, however, the need for people to examine dreams for their own personal meanings as well.

If you were to go to your local bookstore and look in the "Dreams" section, you'd find many dream dictionaries. Most of the experts who write these books have come up with the same meanings for certain dream images. For example, in most dream dictionaries, you'll find that a road in your dream generally stands for your journey through life.

While you are interpreting the objects in your dreams, you should not place too much importance on any one object. Instead, try to look at your dream in general and how the objects relate to each other.

(1,161 words)

Exercises

1. [True, False, Not Given]

Decide whether the following statements are True, False or Not Given.

T (for True) if the statement agrees with the information given in the passage;

F (for False) if the statement doesn't agree with the information given in the passage;

NG (for Not Given) if the information is not given in the passage.

1) People do almost all of their dreaming during non-REM sleep.

2) The deepest stage of sleep in the sleep cycle is reached in Stage 4.

3) The entire non-REM/REM cycle of sleep takes 90 minutes.

4) Based on this selection, you can conclude that dreaming is somewhat important.

5) The meaning of some dreams may be realized after hours or even days or weeks of careful and deep consideration.

6) The first dream theorist to introduce the idea that dream images may stand for the same thing in everybody's dreams was Tony Crisp.

7) A road in someone's dream generally stands for the way to a new but uncertain life for that person.

Unit Twelve

2. 〖Blank-Filling〗

For questions 1)–3), complete the sentences with the information given in the passage.

1) During Non-REM sleep, you body is _____ while during REM sleep, your body becomes very _____.

2) When you first begin to fall asleep, you are in _____.

3) Some dreams are very _____, but often the messages of dreams are more _____.

Unit Thirteen

Text 1 (Intensive Reading)

Background Tips: Success

When the Success Journey becomes difficult, remember these words: "We make a living by what we get, but we make a life by what we give"
— Winston Churchill

"Effort only fully releases its reward after a person refuses to quit."
—Napoleon Hill

"One of the greatest discoveries a man makes, one of his great surprises, is to find he can do what he was afraid he couldn't do." —Henry Ford

"All great deeds and all great thoughts have a ridiculous beginning."
—Albert Camus

"You were born to win, but to be a winner you must plan to win, prepare to win, and expect to win."
—Zig Ziglar

It's Never Too Late for Success
成功之路，永不言迟

You and your parents can stop worrying—Pasteur, Edison, Darwin and lots more were far from being geniuses in their teens.

History books seldom mention it, but the truth is that many of our greatest figures were practically "beatniks" when they, were teenagers. They were given to daydreaming, in decision, hebetude (plain dullness), and they shoed no promise of being doctors, lawyers or India chiefs.

So, young men and women, if you suffer from the same symptoms, don't despair. The world was built by men and women whose parents worried that they would "never amount to a hill of beans." You don't hear too much about their early failure because parents prefer to cite more inspiring examples.

So it goes. You have the Wright brothers, who were brilliant at engineering in their early teens, and you have Thomas Alva Edison, whose teacher tried to get him out of the class because his brain was "addled". You have the Nobel Prize physicist Enrico Fermi, who at 17 read enough mathematics to qualify for a doctor's degree. And you have the great Albert

142

Unit Thirteen

Schweitzer, who wavered between music and the church until he was 30. Then he started his medical studies.

Charles Darwin's early life was a mess. He hated school and his father once shouted: "You care for nothing but shooting dogs and rat catching, and you will be a disgrace to yourself and all your family!" He was sent to Glasgow to study medicine, but he couldn't stand the sight of blood. He was sent to divinity school and barely managed to graduate. Whereupon he chucked the whole business and shipped to South Seas on the famous exploring ship-eagle. On that voyage, one of history's greatest scientists was born. It was here that he collected; the material for the book that would revolutionize biological science—*The Origin of the Species*.

And added to all the aforementioned paradoxes you have a small army of child prodigies who were graduated from college when they were 15, and are now obscure clerks in accounting departments. And you have a small army of men who were too stupid or indolent to get into or finish college and who are today presidents of the firms that hire the prodigies.

So who's to say what about youth? Any young boy or girl who knows what he wants to do in life is probably the better off for it. but no teenager needs despair of the future. He has that one special advantage over the greatest man alive-time.

(421 words)

Word List

daydream	[ˌdeɪdriːm]	v.	做白日梦
symptom	['sɪmptəm]	n.	症状
despair	[dɪ'speə]	v.	绝望
inspiring	[ɪn'spaɪərɪŋ]	adj.	鼓舞人心的，令人振奋的
addled	['ædl]	adj.	糊涂的，愚蠢的
mess	[mes]	n.	混乱，脏乱
disgrace	[dɪs'greɪs]	n.	丢脸，耻辱
divinity	[dɪ'vɪnɪtɪ]	n.	神学；神性；神
chuck	[tʃʌk]	v.	抛弃，放弃
revolutionize	[ˌrevə'luːʃənaɪz]	v.	彻底改革；产生革命性变化
aforementioned	[ə'fɔː'menʃənd]	adj.	上述的；前述的
paradox	['pærədɒks]	n.	自相矛盾的话，似是而非的隽语
prodigy	['prɒdɪdʒɪ]	n.	神童，奇才
obscure	[əb'skjʊə]	adj.	不著名的，无名的
indolent	['ɪndələnt]	adj.	懒惰的；好逸恶劳的

Idioms & Expressions

| amount to | 等于,相当于 | a hill of beans | 一点;丝毫;无价值的东西 |
| an army of | 一大群 | better off | 情况好起来,生活富裕起来 |

Exercises

1. [Definitions]

Match the words in the box with their meanings. Write the word that stands for the definition in the appropriate answer space.

daydream	symptom	despair	inspiring	addled	mess
disgrace	divinity	chuck	revolutionize	aforementioned	paradox
prodigy	obscure	indolent			

1) _____ : confused; unable to think clearly.

2) _____ : the loss of other people's respect because you have done something they strongly disapprove of.

3) _____ : to feel that there is no hope at all.

4) _____ : mentioned before in an earlier part of a document, article, book.

5) _____ : a situation that seems strange because it involves two ideas or qualities that are very different.

6) _____ : not well known and usually not very important.

7) _____ : to completely change the way people do something or think about something.

8) _____ : to think about something pleasant, especially when this makes you forget what you should be doing.

9) _____ : lazy.

10) _____ : a young person who has a great natural ability in a subject or skill.

11) _____ : to throw something away because you do not want it any more.

12) _____ : the study of God and religious beliefs; a god.

13) _____ : something wrong with your body or mind which shows that you have a particular illness.

14) _____ : a dirty or untidy state.

15) _____ : giving people a feeling of excitement and a desire to do something great.

Unit Thirteen

2. [Sample Sentences]

Use the new words and phrases you have learned from the box in the following sentence. Change the form where necessary.

1) He was born around 1650 but his origins remain _____.
2) New fuel-cell components will _____ the auto industry.
3) I must _____ out all those old magazines.
4) None of the _____ evidence shall serve as the basis of establishment of facts before it has been ascertained and verified.
5) My brain feels _____.
6) Fever is a _____ of illness.
7) The _____ is that fishermen would catch more fish if they fished less.
8) I _____ of ever passing my driving test.
9) He was an _____ man, who lived only to eat, drink, and play at cards.
10) They say a _____ should be around 10 years old and have mastered an adult skill.
11) He sat in the classroom, _____ about the holidays.
12) His _____ speech elevated the audience.
13) The workers cleaned up the _____ before they left.
14) All prophets are human and never part of _____: they are simply recipients of revelation from God.
15) The minister was _____ by the hint of scandal.

3. [Translation]

A. Translate the following English sentences into Chinese.

1) The man who can meet despair and defeat with a cheer, there's the man of God's choosing.

2) It is better to die than to live when life is a disgrace.

3) The beauty of nature has the features of divinity, human-analogy, and sociality.

4) Be fond of sleep, fond of company, indolent, lazy and irritable—this is a cause of one's downfall.

5) An additional condition or symptom in the course of a disease, not necessarily connected with the disease.

B. Translate the following Chinese sentences into English by using the word in the bracket.

1) 她凝视窗外,陷入白日梦中。(daydream)

2) 高价往往是短缺的信号。(symptom)

3) 如果你现在取消,就会破坏我所有的计划。(mess)

4) 如此富足的国家竟有如此多的穷人,这是个矛盾的现实。(paradox)

5) 原子能的使用将使人类未来的生活产生巨变。(revolutionize)

4.【Writing】

For this part, you are allowed thirty minutes to write a composition on the topic Reading Selectively or Extensively? You should Write at least 120 words, and base your composition on the outline (given in Chinese) below.
1) 有人认为读书要有选择
2) 有人认为应当博览群书
3) 我的看法

Reading Skills: 阅读速度

一个人的阅读能力的高低决定了他能否快速高效地吸收有用信息。合理的快速阅读可以使阅读者思想高度集中,在阅读中积极思维,不时作出归纳、演绎、对比、推测,正确理解篇章大意。没有一定的阅读速度,就不能顺利地输入信息,阅读理解的成效也会大大地降低。

英语要求每分钟读 60 个字,但我们在平常练习时应达到并超过这个基本标准,以便在英语中能给自己挤出更多时间去进行思考。我们要培养快速阅读的能力,就必须克服指读、回读、重读等不良习惯,不要把注意力过度集中在孤立的单词上,以致于对整句、整段的意思把握不清。与此同时,我们还应注意运用多种阅读技巧,如略读、扫读、跳读等来搜寻关键词、主题句,理清文章脉络,把握语篇实质。

Practice

When someone says, "Well, I guess I'll have to face the music①", it doesn't mean that he is planning to go to hear a singer or attend a concert. It is something far less unhappy than you are called in by your leader to explain why you did this and that or why you did not do this or that.②

At some time or another, every one of us has to "face the music", especially (尤其) as children. We can all remember father's angry words "I want to talk to you". And only because we did not listen to him. What a bad thing it was!

In the middle or at the end of every term, we students have to "face the music". The result of the exam will decide whether we will face the music or not. If...that means parents cold faces and contempt (轻视) of the teachers and classmates.

"To face the music" is well known to every American, young or old. It is at least 100 years old. It really means that you have to do something, no matter (无论) how terrible the whole thing might be, because you know you have no choice.

难句注释

① I guess I'll have to face the music.
   我想这下我得自食其果了。
   face the music 指由于自己的决定或行为而接受批评、承担后果等。

② It is something far less unhappy than you are called in by your leader to explain why you did this and that or why you did not do this or that.
   这要比你被老板喊进去解释为什么这样做,或者为什么不那样做难过得多。

Total words: 200
Reading time: _____
Reading speed: _____

Text 2 (Extensive Reading)

Meet the President
认识总统

What is a President?

Every four years, the American people elect a person to one of the most important jobs in the world, president of the United States. But just what is a president?

In 1776, when American's 13 colonies declared themselves a new nation, they needed a leader to help strengthen the cause of freedom and independence. Up until that time, many leaders of other countries were kings and queens who had inherited their power or had taken control of their countries by force. America, which had been ruled by the King of England, King George III, was a new nation with different ideas. Americans needed their own system of government... and a different kind of leader. The 13 colonies even anted a new title for that leader and chose the Latin word praesidens, which means "to preside" or "to rule."

In 1787, the people chose representatives to act as "delegates" at a Constitutional Convention. At this meeting, it was decided that America's new leader would be chosen according to the will of the people, and would govern by a written code called The Constitution, which we still live by today.

How is our president different from other leaders?

These are many ways in which America's president is different from other world leaders:

- He is elected to office every four years, with a maximum of two terms (eight years) in office. Some countries allow presidents to be elected over and over again, or limit them to a single term.
- The title and duties of president cannot be inherited, even though America's presidents have sometimes been related. In cases where the president is no longer able to carry out his (or, hopefully, someday her) elective duties, the role of president passes to the vice president.
- A president is bound by the same laws as every other American. If he breaks the law, he can be fined, arrested, or removed from office.

What are the three branches of American government?

America's system of government has three branches: executive, legislative, and judicial.

The president leads the executive branch, which includes many agencies and the president's Cabinet departments.

The legislative branch contains the two houses of Congress—the House of Representatives and the Senate. The House of Representatives has 435 elected members representing each state in the nation according to its population, with at least one representative from each state. They are elected every two years. The senate has 100 members, consisting of two representatives from each state, who are elected to serve a six-year term.

The judicial branch is headed by the Supreme Court, which oversees the federal judicial system and decides issues of Constitutional law.

Because these three branches of government are separate, they help keep too much power from being given to any one person, including the president himself.

Who can be president?

Americans have always been proud to say that "anyone can grow up to become president." Our presidents have come in all shapes and sizes. They have all had different lives and experiences. Many were lawyers or military leaders before being elected to the White House. Others have been teachers, shopkeepers, farmers... even movie stars. After leaving office, some of America's presidents have been forgotten, while others are remembered all over the world.

The rules for being able to run for president are very simple. A president must be born a U.S. citizen, be at least 35 years old, and have lived in the United States for at least 14 years. That's it!

What are the duties of the president?

The duties and powers of a president, according to the United States Constitution, are as follows:

1. The president is Commander-in-Chief of the armed forces.
2. He meets with the leaders of foreign countries.
3. He has the power to make treaties with other countries.
4. He has the power to appoint ambassadors and judges.

Unit Thirteen

5. He must make certain America's laws are upheld.
6. He has the power to grant pardons and reprieves to criminals.
7. He is required to report to Congress on "the State of Union," although he is not required to report on any particular subject or at any particular time during the year.

(706 words)

Word List

colony	[ˈkɒlənɪ]	n.	殖民地
inherit	[ɪnˈherɪt]	v.	继承
representative	[ˌreprɪˈzentətɪv]	n.	代表
delegate	[ˈdelɪɡət]	n.	代表
convention	[kənˈvenʃən]	n.	大会
govern	[ˈɡʌvən]	v.	统治
code	[kəud]	n.	法规,法典
bind	[baɪnd]	v.	约束,捆绑
arrest	[əˈrest]	v.	逮捕,拘捕
executive	[ɪɡˈzekjutɪv]	adj.	行政的
legislative	[ˈledʒɪslətɪv]	adj.	立法的
judicial	[dʒu(ː)ˈdɪʃəl]	adj.	司法的
agency	[ˈeɪdʒənsɪ]	n.	行政机构(或部门)
Cabinet	[ˈkæbɪnɪt]	n.	内阁
Senate	[ˈsenɪt]	n.	参议院(美)
oversee	[ˌəuvəˈsiː]	v.	监督,管理
commander-in-chief		n.	总司令
ambassador	[æmˈbæsədə]	n.	大使
uphold	[ʌpˈhəuld]	v.	支持,维护
grant	[ɡrɑːnt]	v.	授予,承认
pardon	[ˈpɑːdn]	n.	原谅,赦免
reprieve	[rɪˈpriːv]	n.	缓刑

Exercises

1. [Questions]

Based on the information provided in the text, answer the following questions briefly.

1) How does America's new leader chosen originally?

2) If the president is no longer able to carry out his elective duties, what should others do?

3) Which branch of government contains the two houses of Congress? What are the two houses of Congress?

4) What is one benefit of keeping the three branches separate?

5) What're the rules for being able to run for president?

2. 【Multiple Choices】

Choose the right answer from the four choices marked A, B, C, and D.

1) In what year was the Constitutional Convention held?
   A. 1760　　　B. 1776　　　C. 1787　　　D. 1781

2) America's president is different from other world leaders in that he _____
   A. may be elected over and over again.
   B. is limited to a single term in office.
   C. the duties of president can be inherited by the vice president.
   D. is limited to a maximum of two terms (eight years) in office D.

3) Which of the following is not one of the duties or powers of the president?
   A. To make certain U.S. laws are upheld.
   B. To oversee the judicial system B.
   C. To make treaties with other countries.
   D. To grant pardons and reprieves to criminals.

4) Members of the United States Senate are elected to serve for a term of_____.
   A. two years　　B. four years　　C. six years　　D. eight years

5) Which branch is the government decides issues of Constitutional law?
   A. judicial　　B. executive　　C. legislative　　D. none of these

Text 3 (Fast Reading)

The Lion, the Witch, and the Wardrobe
狮子,女巫和衣橱

Once there were four children whose names were Peter, Susan, Edmund and Lucy. This story is about something that happened to them when they were sent away from London during the war because of the air-raids. They were sent to the house of an old Professor who lived in the heart of the country, ten miles from the nearest railway station and two miles from the nearest post office. He had no wife and he lived in a very large house with a housekeeper called Mrs. Macready and three servants. (Their names were Ivy, Margaret, and Betty, but they did not come into the story much.) He himself was a very old man with shaggy white hair, which grew over most of his face as well as on his head, and they liked him almost at once; but on the first evening when he came out to meet them at the front door he was so odd-looking that Lucy (who was the youngest) was a little afraid of him, and Edmund (who was the next youngest) wanted to laugh and had to keep on pretending he was blowing his nose to hide it.

As soon as they had said good night to the Professor and gone upstairs on the first night, the boys came into the girls' room and they all talked it over.

"We've fallen on our feet and no mistake," said Peter. "This is going to be perfectly splendid. That old chap will let us do anything we like."

"I think he's an old dear," said Susan.

"Oh, come off it!" said Edmund, who was tired and pretending not to be tired, which always made him bad-tempered. "Don't go on talking like that."

"Like what?" said Susan, "And anyway, it's time you were in bed."

"Trying to talk like Mother," said Edmund. "And who are you to say when I'm going to bed? Go to bed yourself."

"Hadn't we all better go to bed?" said Lucy. "There's sure to be a row if we're heard talking here."

"No, there won't," said Peter. "I tell you this is the sort of house where no one's going to mind what we do. Anyway, they won't hear us. It's about ten minutes' walk from here down to that dining room, and any amount of stairs and passages in between."

"What's that noise?" said Lucy suddenly. It was a far larger house than she had ever been in before and the thought of all those long passages and rows of doors leading into empty rooms was beginning to make her feel a little creepy.

"It's only a bird, silly," said Edmund.

"It's an owl," said Peter. "This is going to be a wonderful place for birds. I shall go to bed now. I say, let's go and explore tomorrow. You might find anything in a place like this. Did you see those mountains as we came along? And the woods? There might be eagles. There might be stags. There'll be hawks."

"Badgers!" said Lucy.

"Snakes!" said Edmund.

"Foxes!" said Susan.

But when morning came, there was a steady rain falling, so thick that when you looked out of the window you could see neither the mountains nor the woods nor even the stream in the garden.

"Of course it would be raining!" said Edmund. They had just finished breakfast with the professor and were upstairs in the room he had set apart for them—a long, low room with two windows looking out in one direction and two in another.

"Do stop grumbling, Ed," said Susan. "Ten to one it'll clear up in an hour or so. And in the meantime we're pretty well off. There's a wireless and lots of books."

"Not for me," said Peter. "I'm going to explore in the house."

Everyone agreed to this and that was how the adventures began. It was the sort of house that you never seem to come to the end of, and it was full of unexpected places. The first few doors they tried led only into spare bedrooms, as everyone had expected that they would; but soon they came to a very long room full of picture and there they found a suit of armor, and after that was a room all hung with green, with a harp in the corner; and then came three steps down and five steps up, and then a kind of little upstairs hall and a door that led out onto the balcony, and then a whole series of rooms that led into each other and were lined with books—most of them very old books and some bigger than a Bible in a church. And shortly after that they looked into a room that was quite empty except for one big wardrobe; the sort that has a looking glass in the door. There was nothing else in the room at all except a dead blue bottle on the windowsill.

"Nothing there!" said peter, and they all trooped out again—all except Lucy. She stayed behind because she thought it would be worthwhile trying the door of the wardrobe, even though she felt almost sure that it would be locked. To her surprise it opened quite easily, and two mothballs dropped out.

Looking into the inside, she saw several coats hanging up—mostly long fur coats. There was nothing Lucy liked so much as the smell and feel of fur. She immediately stepped into the wardrobe and got in among the coats and rubbed her face against them, leaving the door open, of course, because she knew that it is very foolish to shut oneself into any wardrobe. Soon she went further in and found that there was a second row of coats hanging up behind the first one. It was almost quite dark in there and she kept her armed stretched out in front of her so as not to bump her face into the back of the wardrobe. She took a step further in—then two or three steps—always expecting to feel woodwork against the tips of her fingers. But she could not feel it.

"This must be a simply enormous wardrobe!" thought Lucy, going still further in and pushing the soft folds of the coats aside to make room for her. Then she notices that there was something crunching under her feet. "I wonder is that more mothballs?" she thought, stooping down to feel it with her hands. But instead of feeling the hard, smooth wood of the floor of the wardrobe, she felt something soft and powdery and extremely cold. "This is very queer," she said, and went on a step or two further.

Next moment she found that what was rubbing against her face and hands was no longer soft fur but something hard and rough and even prickly. "Why, it is just like branches of trees!" exclaimed Lucy. And then she saw that there was a light ahead of her, not a few inches away where the back of the wardrobe ought to have been, but a long way off.

Unit Thirteen

Something cold and soft was falling on her. A moment later she found that she was standing in the middle of a wood at nighttime with snow under her feet and snowflakes falling through the air.

Lucy felt a little frightened, but she felt very inquisitive and excited as well. She looked back over her shoulder and there between the dark three trunks, she could still see the open doorway of the wardrobe and even catch a glimpse of the empty room from which she had set out. (She had, of course, left the door open, for she knew that it is a very silly thing to shut oneself into a wardrobe.) It seemed to be still daylight there. "I can always get back if anything goes wrong," thought Lucy. She began to walk forward, crunch-crunch, over the snow and through the wood and toward the other light.

In about ten minutes she reached it and found that it was a lamppost. As she stood looking at it, wondering why there was a lamppost in the middle of a wood and wondering what to do next, she heard a pitter-patter of feet coming toward her. And soon after that a very strange person stepped out from among the trees into the light of the lamppost.

(1,398 words)

Exercises

1. [True, False, Not Given]

Decide whether the following statements are True, False or Not Given.

T (for True) if the statement agrees with the information given in the passage;

F (for False) if the statement doesn't agree with the information given in the passage;

NG (for Not Given) if the information is not given in the passage.

1) From the way it is written, the story is a funny story.
2) The story takes place in the countryside far from London.
3) The house where the children are staying is large, dark, and damp.
4) Peter decided to try the door of the wardrobe before leaving the room.
5) Lucy feels a little sad about finding herself in such a strange place.
6) The children are very happy about the place they are staying.
7) It was raining in the place beyond the wardrobe.

2. [Blank-Filling]

For questions 1)–3), complete the sentences with the information given in the passage.

1) From what the children do in this story who do you think is the most curious about things?
   _____

2) Through the wardrobe Lucy came to a _____

3) What did Lucy see near the lamppost? _____.

153

Unit Fourteen

Text 1 (Intensive Reading)

Background Tips: British and American Difference

Grassroots tell some cultural differences between British and American people in a funny way:

— If British people and Americans look alike, you can tell who is the American and who is the British by looking at their cars. The American car is always huge.
— You can tell too, if you look at how much they owe to the bank and credit cards. Americans do not own, they just pay for a living.
— If you ask an American what is America, the answer is the USA. The British will think you are talking about North, Central and South America altogether.
— In America you use disposable stuff even at home. In the UK you will wash your plate and fork.
— In America you will drink coffee (never instant coffee), in the UK you will drink tea (never iced tea).

The English and the Americans
英国人和美国人

The contrasting English and American patterns have some remarkable implications, particularly if we assume that man, like other animals, has a built-in need to shut himself off from others from time to time. An English student in one of my seminars typified what happens when hidden patterns clash. He was quite obviously experiencing strain in his relationships with Americans. Nothing seems to go right and it was quite clear from his remarks that we did not know how to behave. An analysis of his complaints showed that a major source of irritation was that no American seemed to be able to pick up the subtle clues that there were times when he didn't want his thoughts intruded on. As he stated it, "I'm walking around the apartment and it seems that whenever I want to be alone my roommate starts talking to me. Pretty soon he's asking 'What's the matter?' and wants to know if I'm angry. By then I am angry and say something."

It took some time but finally we were able to identify most of the contrasting features of the American and British problems that were in conflict in this case. When the American

Unit Fourteen

wants to be alone he goes into a room and shuts the door—he depends on architectural features for screening. For an American to refuse to talk to someone else present in the same room, to give them the "silent treatment", is the ultimate form of rejection and a sure sign of great displeasure. The English, on the other hand, lacking rooms of their own since childhood, never developed the practice of using space as a refuge from others. They have in effect internalized a set of barriers, which they erect and which others are supposed to recognize. Therefore, the more the Englishman shuts himself off when he is with an American the more likely the American is to break in to assure himself that all is well. Tension lasts until the two get to know each other. The important point is the spatial and architectural needs of each are not the same at all.

(353 words)

Word List

contrast	[ˈkɒntræst]	n.	对比,对照
pattern	[ˈpætən]	n.	方式,形式;图案,样式;
remarkable	[rɪˈmɑːkəbl]	adj.	显著的,非凡的;引人注目的
implication	[ˌɪmplɪˈkeɪʃən]	n.	可能的影响;暗示,含意
seminar	[ˈsemɪnɑː]	n.	研讨会
typify	[ˈtɪpɪfaɪ]	v.	作为……的典型
clash	[klæʃ]	n.	碰撞;冲突,抵触
strain	[streɪn]	n.	紧张,张力;过度劳累
irritation	[ˌɪrɪˈteɪʃən]	n.	激怒,烦恼
intrude	[ɪnˈtruːd]	v.	侵入,闯入
architectural	[ˌɑːkɪˈtektʃəl]	adj.	建筑的,建筑学的
screen	[skriːn]	v.	掩蔽,庇护
ultimate	[ˈʌltɪmət]	adj.	极端的;最终的
refuge	[ˈrefjuːdʒ]	n.	避难(处),庇护(所)
internalize	[ɪnˈtɜːnəlaɪz]	v.	使内化
barrier	[ˈbærɪə]	n.	障碍物,栅栏

Idioms & Expressions

shut off	关掉,切断;使隔离	from time to time	偶尔,有时
break in	强行进入;非法闯入		

Exercises

1. [Definitions]

Match the words in the box with their meanings. Write the word that stands for the definition in the appropriate answer space.

contrast	pattern	remarkable	implication	seminar
typify	clash	strain	irritation	intrude
architectural	screen	ultimate	refuge internalize	barrier

1) _____: to hide or protect something/ somebody by placing something in front of or around them.

2) _____: to interrupt someone or become involved in their private affairs in an annoying and unwanted way.

3) _____: a class at a university or college for a small group of students and a teacher to study or discuss a particular subject.

4) _____: a situation in which two events happen at the same time in a way that is inconvenient.

5) _____: the feeling of being annoyed about something, especially something that happens repeatedly or for a long time.

6) _____: most extreme; best, worst, greatest, most important.

7) _____: connected with architecture.

8) _____: unusual or surprising and therefore deserving attention or praise.

9) _____: shelter or protection from someone or something.

10) _____: to make a feeling, an attitude, or a belief part of the way you think and behave.

11) _____: a possible effect or result of an action or decision.

12) _____: a type of fence or gate that prevents people from moving in a particular direction.

13) _____: to be a typical example of something.

14) _____: the regular way in which something happens, develops, or is done.

15) _____: worry that is caused by having to deal with a problem or work too hard over a long period of time.

16) _____: to compare two things, ideas, people etc to show how different they are from each other.

2. [Sample Sentences]

Use the new words and phrases you have learned from the box in the following sentence. Change the form where necessary.

1) Mum's illness has put a _____ on the whole family.
2) Don't _____ your own views upon others.
3) Dark glasses _____ his eyes from the sun.
4) She _____ the bored housewife.
5) He broke the vase on purpose to express his _____.
6) They failed to consider the wider _____ of their actions.
7) The black furnishings provide an interesting _____ to the white walls.
8) He have get over the language _____.
9) He has a fixed _____ of behavior.
10) The old professor had presided over a _____ for theoretical physicists.
11) A thunderstorm forced him to take _____ at a hut.
12) This kind of _____ style depresses me.
13) His achievements in art are _____.
14) An armed _____ is unavoidable.
15) The innovation process is to accept, activate, _____ and construct knowledge.
16) This race will be the _____ test of your skill.

3. [Translation]

A. Translate the following English sentences into Chinese.

1) The development of the site will have implications for the surrounding countryside.

2) The color of the curtains clashed with the color of the carpet.

3) You can't screen your children from the real life forever.

4) Violence is the last refuge of the incompetent.

5) Taxes are the biggest barrier to free trade.

B. Translate the following Chinese sentences into English by using the word in the bracket.

1) 他的白头发与黑皮肤形成了鲜明的对比。(contrast)

2) 这个地方以其美丽如画的景色著称。(remarkable)

3) 车辆的噪声对城市居民是无休无止的骚扰。(irritation)

4) 我们的最终目标是消除所有核武器。(ultimate)

5) 如果你很忙的话,我就不打扰了。(intrude)

4.【Writing】

For this part, you are allowed 30 minutes to write a poster recruiting volunteers. You should write at least 120 words following the outline given below:
1) 校学生会将组织一次英美文化周,现招募志愿者
2) 本次志愿者活动的目的、内容、安排等
3) 报名条件及联系方式

Reading Skills：扩大视幅

扩大视幅是高效阅读的一种技巧,它是指在阅读过程中,我们要扩大眼睛在阅读材料上每停留一次所能感知的文字的广度。阅读的过程,实际上是一个积极思维、迅速将文字符号转换为词义的过程。一般说来,我们的视幅总长度可达到4-5厘米。所以我们在阅读过程中,要尽可能扩大视线在文章每一行的覆盖范围,将尽可能多的单词收入视线范围之内。眼睛所注视的范围越大,输入大脑的文字内容也就越多,我们的阅读速度自然也就越快。

我们平时在阅读时,不能逐词阅读,要不断训练自己从"点读"过渡到"句读"、"段读",让我们的识别幅度覆盖一个完整的思维单位,学会整体认读、整体理解句子意思,并要熟悉句子的结构和词语的搭配习惯,切忌读破句。

Practice

Different countries and different people have different manners. We must find out their customs, so that they will not think us ill mannered. Here are some examples of the things that a well mannered person does or does not do.

If you visit a Chinese family you should knock at the door first. When the door opens, you'll not move before the host says "Come in, please!". After you enter the room, you wouldn't sit down until the host asks you to take a seat. When a cup of tea is put on a tea table before you or sent to your hand, you'll say "Thank you"① and receive it with your two hands, not one hand, or they'll think you are ill mannered.

Before entering a house in Japan, it is good manners to take off your shoes. In European countries, even though shoes sometimes become very dirty, this is not done.② In a Malay (马来西亚的) house, a guest never finishes the food on the table. He leaves a little to show that he has had enough. In England, a guest always finishes a drink or the food to show that he has enjoyed it. This will make the host, especially (尤其) the hostess pleased.

Text 2 (Extensive Reading)

Stargazing Basics
观星常识

If you do not know any constellations, the sky can be a confusing place. So, before you head outside to study the stars, read about what a constellation is and how knowing the constellations can help you find your way easily around the sky.

What is a constellation?

A constellation is not only a pattern of stars, but it is also a specific area of the sky and includes everything that lies within its boundaries. Think of a state (or province, if you are in Canada). Each state has its boundaries, and everything within those boundaries is part of that state. The boundaries of the constellations were decided by a committee of astronomers in 1928. These boundaries are shown on some star charts. Everything in the sky—whether a star, nebula, or galaxy—is in one constellation or another.

What is a star?

The constellations are marked by stars. We think of the stars as both tiny and faint because that is how they look to us, but they are neither. They are enormous and brilliant—and they are very far away.

Stars are like our sun. Our sun is a globe of hot gas almost a million miles across—so big that if the earth were the size of a Ping-Pong ball, the sun would be the size of your bedroom. If the sun were hollow, you would need more than 1,000,000 Earths to fill it. The sun is certainly big compared to anything else we know, but it is just an average-sized star. The stars look tiny only because they are so very distant.

Like people, each star is different. Some stars are many times the size and brightness of our sun, but others are much smaller. Astronomers express distances to stars with light-years. A light-year is a unit of distance, not a unit of time. It is the distance that a beam of light travels in one year. Light travels at the enormous speed of 186,200 miles per second—fast enough to travel seven times around the earth or almost from the earth to the moon in only one second! A beam of light travels to the earth from the sun or a nearby planet in a few minutes. In one year light travels almost 6 trillion miles—about 65,000 times the distance from the earth to the sun.

The closest star we see from northern North America is Sirus, which is a little over eight light-years (50 trillion miles) distant. The stars of the Big Dipper are all about 100 light-years away. The most distant object you can see without a telescope is the Andromeda Galaxy, which is over 2 million light-years away.

If our sun were light-years away instead of light-minutes, it, too, would appear as faint as the stars in the night sky. Because it takes time for light to travel, we see a star as it was long ago, when its light began its journey to earth. We see old starlight.

How often do the constellations move?

The constellations are always in motion!

As you sit and read, the earth is carrying you and this book in two directions at once. The earth is constantly spinning and makes one complete rotation every 24 hours. It makes a complete trip around the sun once a year. Although we do not feel these motions, we see the result of them in the sky. The spin of the earth gives us night and day, while the rotation around the sun gives us our different seasons. Both of these movements cause you to see different constellations throughout the night and at different times of the year.

As the earth spins toward the east, carrying you along with it, the sky seems to turn toward the west. We say that the stars rise in the east and set in the west, although we know that it is the earth that is turning. This causes us to face different parts of the sky at different times of the night. If you watch the sky for several hours, you will see that stars (as well as the planets, the sun, and the moon) rise in the east, travel westward across the sky, and eventually set in the west. Stars that are in the east early in the evening are in the west late at night.

At the same time, the earth is orbiting around the sun. the stars we see at night lie in the opposite direction from the sun. (When stars lie in the same direction as the sun, they are in the daytime sky and we cannot see them.) As the earth moves around the sun, the part of the sky that lies opposite the sun changes month by month. The constellations we see at night change with the seasons.

As the earth orbits the sun, it looks like the sun moves around the sky. The part of the sky that is hidden by the sun changes month by month. As the earth moves around the sun, the part of the sky is blocked by the sun changes. Constellations become invisible behind the sun, only to reappear again a few months later. Remember: the earth's orbital motion causes us to see different constellations throughout the year.

(876 words)

Word List

• constellation	[ˌkɒnstəˈleɪʃn]	n.	星座
• boundary	[ˈbaʊndərɪ]	n.	分界线,边界
• astronomer	[əˈstrɒnəmə]	n.	天文学家
• nebula	[ˈnebjʊlə]	n.	星云
• galaxy	[ˈgæləksɪ]	n.	星系,银河
• hollow	[ˈhɒləʊ]	adj.	空心的,中空的
• trillion	[ˈtrɪljən]	num.	万亿
• Sirus			天狼星

Unit Fourteen

- Big Dipper   北斗七星
- Andromeda   [æn'drɔmidə]   仙女座
- spin   [spɪn]   v.   使旋转
- rotation   [rəu'teɪʃən]   n.   自转,旋转
- orbit   ['ɔːbɪt]   v.   环绕……轨道运行
- block   [blɒk]   v.   阻碍,阻止

Exercises

1. 【Questions】

Based on the information provided in the text, answer the following questions briefly.

1) If the sun were the size of your bedroom, the earth would be the size of a _____.

2) What is a light-year?

3) What is the most distant object you can see from Earth without a telescope?

4) What does the author mean when he say that we see old starlight when we look at the stars?

5) What causes us to see different constellations throughout the year?

2. 【Multiple Choices】

Choose the right answer from the four choices marked A, B, C, and D.

1) The author compares the boundaries of a constellation to the boundaries of a _____.
   A. galaxy   B. state   C. country   D. frontier
2) Which is the following is an accurate statement about stars?
   A. All stars are larger than the sun.
   B. All stars are smaller than the sun.
   C. All stars are equal to the sun.
   D. Some stars are larger than the sun while others are much smaller.
3) How far can light travel in one year?
   A. approximately 65,000 miles.
   B. about 186,300 miles
   C. almost 6 trillion miles.
   D. about 65,000 times the distance from the earth to the moon.

4) What gives us night and day?

   A. The rotation of the moon around the earth

   B. The rotation of the earth around the sun

   C. The spinning motion of the earth

   D. The spinning motion of the moon.

5) The stars we see at night lie _____.

   A. in the same direction as the sun

   B. in the opposite direction from the sun.

   C. between the earth and the sun.

   D. in the solar system.

Text 3 (Fast Reading)

The Strange Voyage of the Mary Celeste
"玛丽·莎莉丝特"号奇怪的航行

Sailors believe that it is bad luck to change a ship's name. "Let her stay as she was born," they say. Certainly the troubles aboard the good ship Amazon began when her name was changed to the Mary Celeste. Twice she ran aground. She sprang leaks. And her owners were always losing money on her.

But none of these incidents can compare with what happened to the Celeste in 1872. In November of that year, she set sail from New York on a routine trip to England. Beneath her decks she carried a cargo of wood alcohol. The alcohol was highly explosive. But because it was safely stored in wooden barrels, no one gave it a second thought. Besides, the seas were calm, and the weather was good. Everyone expected to be in England within the month.

Two weeks later, in the middle of the Atlantic, the Mary Celeste was spotted by a ship called the Dei Gratia. Though the Celeste was under full sail, no one could be seen on deck.

"Something is wrong with that ship," said Captain David Morehouse. "Lower a bloat, and we'll board her."

As soon as the boarding party reached the Celeste, the sailors shouted for the crew.

There was no answer.

They searched her from stern to bow.

But no one was there.

What had happened to the crew? Where had everyone gone? The weather was good. There were no leaks in the ship. And the cargo of alcohol was intact. Yet, for some reason, the men were gone. They had left in a hurry, too. A half-eaten breakfast was still on the table. The ship's compass and other valuables had been left behind. And in one of the cabins was the beginning of a letter: Fanny, my dear wife is all it said.

The ship's log was located, but it gave no clues to the crew's fate. The last entry had been recorded a week earlier, and it made no mention of possible troubles.

Almost everything was in order, but here were a few exceptions. There were strange, bloodstained gashes on the rail. A hatch was open. The lifeboat was missing. And the sounding rod was down. That meant someone had been checking the depth of the sea.

The Dei Gratia towed the Celeste to England. Within a week, a hearing was held.

The boat was checked again—for signs of a leak, a fire, or an explosion. None were found. The crew of the Dei Gratia was questioned by the court. Finally, the judge ruled.

"It's a clear case of murder," he said. "The way I see it, the crew got drunk. They killed the captain and threw his body overboard. Then they climbed into the lifeboat, hoping the Celeste would sink. She didn't sink, but perhaps the lifeboat did."

Few people believed the judge's explanation. For one thing, the "blood" on the rail turned out to be rust. Furthermore, the Celeste's captain had been well liked. Men who had sailed with him reported that he was hard-driving but fair. And it simply didn't make sense for the crew to abandon ship.

Over the years, many people have tried to solve the mystery. Here are a few of their explanations:

The captain and the first mate were swimming a race around the ship. The crew got out on a platform to cheer them on. Sharks ate the swimmers. At the same moment, the platform fell into the sea, and everyone drowned. (Very farfetched!)

The ship came upon the lost continent of Atlantis. The crew sailed into a little harbor and dropped the sounding rod to test the depth of the water. Everyone got off the ship to look around. Suddenly, Atlantis sank back into the sea, and everyone drowned. (This, too, seems farfetched. No one has ever proved that Atlantis exists.)

A giant squid attacked the ship. Everyone was eaten. (A few giant squids have been sighted, and this might explain the gashes on the rail. However, such an attack would have caused more damage. And there certainly would have been some signs of a struggle.)

Everyone died of a mysterious disease. (Where were the bodies?)

The sailors were all killed by pirates. (As far as anyone knew, there were no pirates in the area at the time. Besides, nothing of value was missing.)

The Dei Gratia crew killed the sailors to collect the salvage money for recovering the Celeste. (The men didn't seem like killers. And the amount of money they got was pitifully small.)

The men found a leak and thought the ship was about to sink. They took to the lifeboat. Then, either the lifeboat sank or the ship sailed away without them. (It is hard to believe the captain would have made such a grave error. He knew the ship and the sea well. He would have known that the danger was not great. Besides, there was no sign of a leak.)

The captain thought the alcohol below-decks was about to explode. He opened a hatch to air out the hold. Then everyone took to the life boat to wait for the danger to pass but suddenly a wind sprang up. The Celeste sailed away by herself. The lifeboat sank, and everyone drowned. (This doesn't explain why the sounding rod was down. But otherwise it makes the most sense.)

No trace of the crew was ever found. We may never know their fate. We do know, however, what happened to the Mary Celeste. Her final days were spent under a cloud of suspicion and mistrust. No on wanted to sail on her. Few people wanted to own her.

Finally, in 1884, the Mary Celeste set sail for her last time. On a cloudless day, off Haiti, she smashed into the rocks. The wreck had been staged. The captain had set up the whole thing so that he could collect the insurance money. In due time the truth came out, and the captain was thrown in jail. He was the last person trapped in the web of bad luck spun by the ill-fated Mary Celeste.

(1,023 words)

Exercises

1. [True, False, Not Given]

Decide whether the following statements are True, False or Not Given.

T (for True) if the statement agrees with the information given in the passage;

F (for False) if the statement doesn't agree with the information given in the passage;

NG (for Not Given) if the information is not given in the passage.

1) The selection you just read was about a ship that disappeared while sailing from New York to England.

2) The selection is about something that happened in the 1700s.

3) Things were broken as though there had been a fight when the ship was found.

4) The judge at the hearing thought that the captain's death was a "clear case" of murder.

5) Over the years, a few people have solved the mystery.

6) The ship finally smashed into the rocks.

7) None of the explanations given in the story for the crew's disappearance makes sense.

2. [Blank-Filling]

For questions 1)–3), complete the sentences with the information given in the passage.

1) _____ was on the ship when it was found.

2) The cargo that the ship was carrying was _____.

3) Why do sailors believe that a ship's name should not be changed? _____.

Unit Fifteen

Text 1 (Intensive Reading)

Background Tips: Work & Happiness

The single most efficient way to increase your productivity is to be happy at work. No system, tool or methodology in the world can beat the productivity boost that you get from really, really enjoying your work.

Here are the 10 most important reasons why happiness at work is the number one productivity booster.

1. Happy people work better with others.
2. Happy people are more creative.
3. Happy people fix problems instead of complaining about them.
4. Happy people have more energy.
5. Happy people are more optimistic.
6. Happy people are more motivated.
7. Happy people get sick less often.
8. Happy people learn faster.
9. Happy people worry less about making mistakes—and consequently make fewer mistakes.
10. Happy people make better decisions.

Work and Happiness
工作和快乐

  Whether work should be placed among the causes of happiness may perhaps be regarded as a doubtful question. There is certainly much work which is exceedingly irksome, and an excess of work is always very painful I think, however, that, provided work is not excessive in amount, even the dullest work is to most people less painful than idleness. There are in work all grades, from mere relief of tedium up to the profoundest delights, according to the nature of the work and the abilities of the worker. Most of the work that most people have to do is not in itself interesting, but even such work has certain great advantages. To begin with, it fills a good many hours of the day without the need of deciding what one shall do. Most people, when they are left free to fill their own time according to their own choice, are at a loss to think of anything sufficiently pleasant to be worth doing. And whatever they decide on, they are troubled by the feeling that something else would have been pleasanter. To be able to fill leisure intelligently is the last product of civilization, and at present very few people have reached this level. Moreover the exercise of choice is in itself tiresome. Except to people with unusual initiative it is positively agreeable to be told what to do at each hour of the day, provided the orders are not too unpleasant. Most of the idle rich suffer unspeakable boredom as the price of their freedom from drudgery. At times they may find relief by hunting big game in Africa, or by flying round the world, but the number of such sensations is limited, especially after youth is past. Accordingly the more intelligent rich men work nearly as hard as if they were poor, while rich women for the most part keep themselves busy with innumerable trifles of whose earthshaking importance they are firmly persuaded.

Work therefore is desirable, first and foremost, as a preventive of boredom, for the boredom that a man feels when he is doing necessary though uninteresting work is nothing in comparison with the boredom that he feels when he has nothing to do with his days. With this advantage of work another is associated, namely that makes holidays much more delicious when they come. Provided a man does not have to work so hard as to impair his vigor, he is likely to find far more zest in his free time than an idle man could possibly find.

(424 words)

Word List

exceedingly	[ɪkˈsiːdɪŋlɪ]	*adv.*	非常地,极度地
provided	[prəˈvaɪdɪd]	*conj.*	如果,假如
idle	[ˈaɪdl]	*adj.*	无所事事的,闲散的
tedium	[ˈtiːdɪəm]	*n.*	单调乏味,冗长
profound	[prəˈfaʊnd]	*adj.*	深切的,深远的,深刻的
sufficient	[səˈfɪʃənt]	*adj.*	充足的,足够的
tiresome	[ˈtaɪəsəm]	*adj.*	令人厌烦的;讨厌的
initiative	[ɪˈnɪʃətɪv]	*n.*	主动(性)
agreeable	[əˈgriːəbl]	*adj.*	令人愉快的,惬意的
drudgery	[ˈdrʌdʒərɪ]	*n.*	辛苦乏味的工作;苦工
innumerable	[ɪˈnjuːmərəbl]	*adj.*	无数的,数不清的
trifle	[ˈtraɪfəl]	*n.*	小事,琐事;微不足道的东西
earthshaking	[ˈɜːθʃeɪkɪŋ]	*adj.*	震撼世界的,惊天动地的
preventive	[prɪˈventɪv]	*n.*	预防,预防措施
impair	[ɪmˈpeə]	*v.*	损害,损伤
vigor	[ˈvɪgə]	*n.*	活力,精力
zest	[zest]	*n.*	热情,乐趣

Unit Fifteen

Idioms & Expressions

be regarded as   被认为是……   at a loss   不知所措
in comparison with   和……相比

Exercises

1. [Definitions]

Match the words in the box with their meanings. Write the word that stands for the definition in the appropriate answer space.

exceedingly	provided	idle	tedium	profound	sufficient
tiresome	initiative	agreeable	drudgery	innumerable	trifle
earthshaking	preventive	impair	vigor	zest	

1) _____ : something of little value, substance, or importance.
2) _____ : very great; felt or experienced very strongly.
3) _____ : the act of stopping something bad from happening.
4) _____ : extremely.
5) _____ : the ability to make decisions and take action without waiting for someone to tell you what to do.
6) _____ : hard boring work.
7) _____ : the feeling of being bored because the things you are doing are not interesting and continue for a long time without changing.
8) _____ : very many, or too many to be counted.
9) _____ : to damage something or make it not as good as it should be.
10) _____ : used to say that something will only be possible if something else happens or is done.
11) _____ : eager interest and enjoyment.
12) _____ : as much as is needed for a particular purpose.
13) _____ : not working or producing anything.
14) _____ : physical or mental energy and determination.
15) _____ : having a very great effect and of great importance.
16) _____ : pleasing to the mind or senses especially as according well with one's tastes or needs.
17) _____ : making you feel annoyed or impatient.

2. [Sample Sentences]

Use the new words and phrases you have learned from the box in the following sentence. Change the form where necessary.

1) We must transform passivity into _____.
2) Labor-saving devices have emancipated women from kitchen _____.
3) He entered into the work with _____.
4) The two families established a _____ friendship.
5) Great and _____ historical changes have taken place in China in the 20th century.
6) Don't _____ away your precious time
7) The illness had _____ his ability to think and concentrate.
8) He is _____ suspicious of all his neighbors.
9) She longed for something to relieve the _____ of everyday life.
10) The recipe is _____ for six people.
11) The police were able to take _____ action and avoid a possible riot.
12) We'll buy everything you produce, _____ of course the price is right.
13) Buying a house can be a very _____ business.
14) He is a young lad with plenty of _____.
15) We spent a most _____ day together.
16) The stars in the night sky are _____.
17) Don't waste your time at these _____.

3. [Translation]

A. Translate the following English sentences into Chinese.

1) Let's awaken tomorrow with all our zest and zeal by embracing and creating life.

2) The lesson is profound; we'll never recommit the same error.

3) The tiresome lecture seemed endless; nearly half of the audience dozed off.

4) Technology was supposed to take away a lot of the drudgery from our lives, and free us up to relax.

5) Not all of us have to possess earthshaking talent. Just common sense and love will do.

B. Translate the following Chinese sentences into English by using the word in the bracket.

1) 时间就是生命,懒人消耗时间就是消耗自己的生命。(idle)

2) 他们有足够的食品和衣服以满足所需。(sufficient)

3) 人类曾经创造了无数的奇迹。(innumerable)

4) 这点小事不足挂齿。(trifle)

5) 垃圾污染环境,损害健康。(impair)

4.【Writing】

For this part, you are allowed 30 minutes to write a composition on the topic My View on Job-hopping. You should write at least 120 words according to the outline given below in Chinese:

1) 有些人喜欢始终从事一种工作,因为……
2) 有些人喜欢经常更换工作,因为……
3) 我的看法

Reading Skills: 抓主干,理枝叶

长难句增加,是近年英语阅读理解试题不可忽视的现象之一。英语的长句可分为两类:含有数量较多的定语或状语的简单句和含有数量较多的各种从句的并列句或复合句。阅读长句的基本方法是抓主干,理枝叶。抓主干就是抓句子的主体部分,也就是主语和谓语,它们是传达信息的主要载体;理枝叶就是分析句子的附加部分,不论它们有多长,有多复杂,它们都是辅助成分,我们只要明确它们与主体的关系就可以了。如:

The moon is so far from the earth that even if huge trees were growing on the mountains, and elephants were walking about, we could not see them through the most powerful telescopes which have ever been invented.

这个长句的主干就是 **The moon is far from the earth**,其他部分,如状语从句、定语从句等,都是为突出主题服务的。

Practice

The Winter Olympics, which is also called the White Olympics, were first held as a separate competition in 1924 at Chamonix Mont Blanc, France. At this time, many colorful stamps are published to mark the great games. The first stamp marking the opening of the White Olympics was issued (发行) on January 25, 1932 in the United States to celebrate the third White Olympics [①] From then on, issuing stamps during the White Olympics became a tradition.

To observe the fourth Winter Olympic Games,[②] a group of stamps were published in Germany in November, 1935. The five rings of the Olympics were printed on the front of the sportswear. It was the first time that the symbol (象征) appeared on stamps of the Winter Olympics.

In the 1950s, the stamps of this kind became more colorful. When the Winter Olympics came, the host countries as well as the non host countries published stamps to mark those games.

China also published four stamps in February, 1980, when the Chinese sportsmen began to march into the area of the White Olympics.

Japan is the only country in Asia that has ever held the White Olympics. Altogether 14,500 million stamps were sold to raise funds (经费) for this sports meet.

Different kinds of sports were printed on these small stamps. People can enjoy the beauty of the wonderful movements of some athletics.

难句注释

① The first stamp marking the opening of the White Olympics was issued on January 25, 1932 in the United States to celebrate the third White Olympics.
为了庆祝第3届冬季奥运会，纪念其开幕的第一枚邮票于1932年1月25日在美国发行。

② to observe the fourth Winter Olympic Games 为了庆祝第四届冬季奥运会。
observe 意为"举行；庆祝"。

Total words: 226
Reading time: _____
Reading speed: _____

Text 2 (Extensive Reading)

The Scientific Method
科学研究的方法

Science is based on wondering. You begin to be a scientist when you ask questions.
- Why did that happen?
- What would be different if I change this one thing?
- How did that happen?
- When did that occur?
- How is this different from that?

You become a scientist when you try to find answers to your questions by using the scientific method.

When you follow the scientific method, your science project begins with a hypothesis—a question and your own informed guess at an answer, which you test by following your procedure. A procedure is the steps you take to do an experiment or field work, which leads you to confirm—or not confirm—your hypothesis. You look at the actual results, compare them with your expectations, and write your conclusion based on what you have found out.

In your report, you describe how you followed the scientific method, step by step. At the end of your report, you will mention new questions you would like to look into and things you would like to try based on what you have learned from your results.

Let's take some time to understand the scientific method, the backbone of a science project. The scientific method has four parts:

Observation

You notice something in the world that you want to know more about. You then ask a question about it. This question is what you try to uncover an answer to in your science project.

Hypothesis

You predict why, when, where, or how whatever you observed happened, based on information you already have. Sometimes this takes the form of an "if... then" statement. A hypothesis is often called an "educated guess" because you base your prediction on facts you already know.

Testing

You test your hypothesis with a procedure. You can do either an experiment, where everything except the particular thing being tested is carefully controlled, or field work, where you study your subject in the natural world. Careful observations and measurements are recorded in both testing procedures.

Conclusion

You state whether or not your hypothesis was correct, based on the results of your testing. If your hypothesis is proven wrong, try to explain why. Also, make any further predictions your results could point to, and describe any changes to your procedure you think would give more accurate results or be helpful to further research.

Procedure

The procedure is the practical part of the scientific method—it's the steps you take to test your hypothesis.

The purpose of science is to discover things about the world with accuracy, truth, and objectivity. Scientists

- test ideas;
- weigh evidence carefully;
- come to conclusions cautiously;
- make conclusions based on facts.

An important part of the scientist's process of discovery is the procedure followed. A procedure is like a recipe—it's a list of steps. The steps you plan to take to test your hypothesis must be clearly written out so that anyone could repeat what you have done. Your procedure

- gives step-by-step directions on what to do;
- lists all the materials and equipment you use;
- provides any instructions you need to build or use equipment.

Experiment and Field Work

Scientist tests their hypotheses either through experiment or field work.

Experiment

Experimental observations are made in a controlled environment that you create. How? You make a simpler, smaller-scale version of the part of the real world you want to study. You focus your attention on just a few things, instead of on everything that can happen.

In an experiment, a scientist tries to look at how just one thing affects a subject. The tricky part is creating an environment in which only that one thing changes. That is why you often see scientists using test tubes, petri dishes, and other small, enclosed settings for their experiment. It is much easier to control things in such environments.

Field Work

In field work, a scientist goes into an uncontrolled environment, a specific place in the world, and records exactly what is observed there at the time. Because you are studying a unique situation every time, field work is almost always new and original.

The tricky part with field work is that while you are recording your observations, you must make sure that you yourself are not interfering with your subject simply by being there. For instance, you cannot count birds in a tree if you scare any (or all) away while you try to count them.

(745 words)

Word List

hypothesis	[haɪˈpɒθɪsɪs]	n.	假设
backbone	[ˈbækbəʊn]	n.	支柱,基础
predict	[prɪˈdɪkt]	v.	预言
objectivity	[əbˈdʒektɪv]	n.	客观性
recipe	[ˈresɪpi]	n.	食谱,处方
field work			现场工作,野外工作
scale	[skeɪl]	n.	等级,级别;规模,范围
tricky	[ˈtrɪki]	adj.	复杂的;棘手的;难处理的
interfere	[ˌɪntəˈfɪə]	v.	干涉,妨碍
scare	[skeə]	v.	使害怕,惊吓

Exercises

1. 【Questions】

Based on the information provided in the text, answer the following questions briefly.

1. What is a hypothesis?

2. How many parts are there to the scientific method? What are they?

3. What would you do in the part of "Observation"?

4. What is the purpose of science?

5. What is most important part in field work?

2. 〖Multiple Choices〗

Choose the right answer from the four choices marked A, B, C, and D.

1) You begin to be a scientist when you _____.
   A. ask questions about things you wonder about
   B. find answers to questions you wonder about
   C. do experiments to prove why something happens
   D. test your hypothesis by following your procedure

2) When doing a science project following the scientific method, you should first _____.
   A. write a report describing how you will follow the scientific method
   B. do an experiment or field work
   C. state your hypothesis
   D. ask questions to the one who have already known the answer

3) The author compares the procedure used in the scientific method to a _____.
   A. report   B. recipe   C. guidebook   D. directory

4) When should you use a controlled environment?
   A. When doing an experimental observation.
   B. When doing field work.
   C. Before stating your hypothesis.
   D. Before making conclusions based on facts.

5) Which of the following statements is true of both an experimental observation and field work?
   A. It is almost always new and original because you are studying a unique situation every time.
   B. You focus your attention on just a few things, instead of on everything that can happen.
   C. Careful observations and measurements are recorded.
   D. You tries to look at how just one thing affects a subject.

Text 3 (Fast Reading)

Fishing
垂钓

Have you ever seen a fish jump in the middle of a pond? Do you know what it's doing? It's catching bugs and flies that float on the surface of the water. A sparkle in the water means a fish is feeding, too, turning sideways to dislodge bits of food from the bottom with its mouth. The sun reflecting off the fish's silvery sides makes the sparkle.

If you see a fish tail splash in a shallow stream, you'll know that a trout is feeding on underwater insects that cling to the rocky bottom. A v-shaped wave through the water could be a large fish chasing a smaller one. And a loud glunk in a splashy circle may be a big hungry fish gobbling up a frog or a swimming mouse.

It's always a good idea to watch the water for a while before you begin fishing. If you can figure out what the fish are feeding on, offer it to them on your hook, and you'll catch more fish.

Bait fishing

All you need for bait fishing is a line on a pole, a couple of hooks, and some split-shot sinkers. Most of you who fish use earthworms as bait, but in their natural diet, fish eat very few worms. There are more abundant foods, like the underwater insects, living with them in the pond or stream.

The next time you are fishing in a clear stream, turn over some rocks and you will find insects clinging to the undersides. These insects, called nymphs, are good fish bait. But a nymph on a very small hook and squeeze a split-shot sinker on your line a foot above it. The weight will drift the bait along the bottom of the stream, where the fish normally look for nymphs.

Whatever bait you choose, remember to make it appear natural to the fish. If your sandwich leaped off the plate and danced across the table, you would hesitate to eat it. The same is true of fish. They are wary of any food that doesn't look and act natural.

Always use a hook smaller than your bait, so the fish won't see it. If you want the bait to sink, squeeze a split-shot onto the line. If you want it to float, take off the sinker. Watch the water and see how different insects behave; then imitate them with your bait.

When you are fishing, be as quiet as possible. Fish can't hear you talking, but they can feel the slightest movement in the water and the vibrations from any thumping sounds you make on the bank or in a boat. Stay low so the fish won't see you, and try not to make any sudden movements. All of these things will alarm the fish and stop them from feeding.

Unit Fifteen

Lure Fishing

Artificial lures are designed to attract fish to your line by imitating the motions or sounds of foods they usually eat. There are metal lures that will wiggle, wobble, and flash like shiny minnows when pulled through the water. And there are wooden or plastic lure, called plugs, that will float on the water and dive momentarily when you reel them in. a plug acts like an injured fish—an easy, tempting meal that a hungry fish will rarely pass up.

Some plugs are weighted inside, so they'll sink to the bottom and then swim back to the surface as you reel in your line. In this way they imitate the movements of crayfish, salamanders and other bottom-dwelling creatures.

Lures that make sounds are good for fishing at dusk or at night, when the water is still and visibility is low. One of the simplest of these is the popping plug. A popper floats quietly until you give it a jerk. Then its hollowed front cups the surface water, making a loud pop that sounds like a frog jumping. Nearby fish will inspect the noise every time. And getting a fish's attention is the most important step in catching it.

There are other plugs that are designed to crawl through the water as you pull them in. A crawling plug looks and sounds like a swimming mouse.

Whatever kind of lure you choose, just a fishing pole and string won't do. You'll need a rod and reel. Cast your line and wait ten seconds to let the water clam down. Then reel it in slowly, without stopping. Keep reeling even if you feel a tug on the line. Fish expect their food to try and escape!

Fishing with a lure is like working the strings of a marionette. It's tricky at first. But the more you practice, the better you'll become at making the lure—or the marionette—look like the real thing.

Fly fishing

Another way to catch insect-eating fish is to use a lure called a fly. Flies are made of feathers and fur tied on tiny hooks. Tied light and bushy, they will float on the water like winged insects, and fish will jump right out of the water to get them. This is called dry fly fishing. Tied wooly and heavy, they will sink below the surface and swim along like underwater insects. These "wet" flies catch the most fish.

You don't need special equipment just to try fly fishing. You can buy some inexpensive flies at a tackle shop and use them on your own pole or rod. Simply tie one to your line and crouch by the edge of the water. Lower the fly until it gently touches the surface and let it float along. You'll get a close-up view of the fish, when it sips in the fly and tries to swim away with it. Or you can let the fly get waterlogged and sink. Fish will try and swallow it as it drifts to the bottoms.

Fishing time is anytime—rain or shine, day or night. You can fish in the spring, when the waters are cold and the fish are scrappy. You can fish in the lazy days of summer under the shade of a willow or in autumn when the big fish are feeding before the freeze-up. You can even fish in the winter through a hole in the ice.

Whatever the season, fishing can lead to a deeper understanding of stream or pond life—not to mention providing you and your family with many delicious dinners!

(1,064 words)

Exercises

1. [True, False, Not Given]

Decide whether the following statements are True, False or Not Given.

T (for True) if the statement agrees with the information given in the passage;

F (for False) if the statement doesn't agree with the information given in the passage;

NG (for Not Given) if the information is not given in the passage.

1) The best way to learn what fish are eating is to watch the water for a while.

2) In this story you learn that there are three ways to fish, with hook, line, and sinker.

3) Whatever you use on your fishing hook, you should remember to make it look artificial.

4) While fishing you should always leave your fishing pole and go hide behind a rock or bush.

5) The author tells us that the lures are live insects.

6) Fishing time is only in good weather.

7) Fishing lures are made to imitate the motions or sounds of foods that fish usually eat.

2. [Blank-Filling]

For questions 1)–3), complete the sentences with the information given in the passage.

1) The author tells us that one of the best baits to use for fishing is _____.

2) The most important step in catching a fish is _____.

3) What are the two types of fly fishing the author talks about?

Unit Sixteen

Text 1 (Intensive Reading)

Background Tips: McDonald's & Starbucks

McDonald's
Type: Public (NYSE:MCD)
Founded: May 15, 1940 in San Bernardino, California
McDonald's Corporation, 1955 in Desplaines, Illinois
Founders: Dick and Mac McDonald, (McDonald's restaurant concept)
Ray Kroc, (McDonald's Corporation founder)
Headquarters: Oak Brook, Illinois, USA
Number of locations: 31,000+ worldwide
Area served: Worldwide
Key people: James A. Skinner (Chairman) & (CEO)
Industry: Restaurants
Products: Fast Food
(hamburgers ● chicken ● french fries ● soft drinks ● coffee ● milkshakes ● salads ● desserts ● breakfast)
Last updated: Dec 31, 2008
Period Length: 12 Months
Market cap: US$ 60.07 billion
Revenue: ▲ US$ 23.5 billion
Operating income: ▼ US$ 6.4 billion
Net income: ▼ US$ 4.3 billion
Total assets: ▲ US$ 28.461 billion
Total equity: ▼ US$ 13.382 billion
Employees: 390,000

Starbucks:
Type: Public (NASDAQ: SBUX)
Founded: In 1971 across from Pike Place Market in Seattle, Washington
Founders: Zev Siegel, Jerry Baldwin and Gordon Bowker
Headquarters: Seattle, Washington, USA
Key people: Howard Schultz, Chairman, President and CEO
Martin Coles, President, Starbucks International

Troy Alstead, Chief Financial Officer
Stephen Gillett, Chief Information Officer

Industry: Restaurants
Retail Coffee and Tea
Retail Beverages
Entertainment

Products: Whole Bean Coffee
Boxed Tea
Made-to-order beverages
Bottled beverages
Baked Goods
Merchandise
Frappuccino beverages
Smoothies

Services: Coffee

Last updated: Dec 31, 2008
Period Length: 12 Months
Revenue: ▲ US$ 10.4 billion
Operating income: ▲ US$ 504 million
Net income: ▲ US$ 315.5 million
Total assets: US$ 5.53 billion

McDonald's Targets Starbucks
麦当劳叫板星巴克

McDonald's, the fast-food company, is heating up competition with the Starbucks Coffee Company. McDonald's plants to put coffee bars in its fourteen thousand restaurants in the United States. Fewer than a thousand now offer specialty coffee drinks like lattes and cappuccinos.

Just like Starbucks, each coffee bar would have its own barista, the person who makes and serves the drinks. Company documents reported by the *Wall Street Journal* said the plan would add one billion dollars a year in sales.

McDonald's has enjoyed several years of strong growth. The company had almost twenty-two billion dollars in sales in 2006. Still, the move to compete against Starbucks carries some risk. Some experts say it could slow down service at McDonald's restaurants. And some people who are happy with McDonald's the way it is now may not like the changes.

Unit Sixteen

As early as 2001, the company tested McDonald's in the United States to sell specially coffee at McDonald's restaurants. But the drinks were not available at the drive-through windows that provide two-thirds of its business. McDonald's thinks its new plan has a greater chance of success.

Starbucks, on the other hand, has faced slower growth and increasing competition. Its stock has lost about half its value since last January.

Starbucks has about 10,000 stores in the United States. Its high-priced coffee drinks have names like Iced Peppermint, White Chocolate Mocha, and Double Chocolate Chip Frappuccino. Lately Starbucks has added more foods, including breakfast foods, and put drive-through windows in some stores.

Several days ago, the company replaced its chief executive officer, bring back former C.E.O. Howard Schultz. He remains chairman of the board. He joined Starbucks in 1982, when it had just four stores. He is credited with building the Seattle Company into an international success store.

But a year ago he warned that its fast growth had led to what he called the watering down of the Starbucks experience. Some neighborhoods have a Starbucks on every block or two. Now, Starbucks will speed up it international growth while slowing its expansion in the United States.

Millions of People have a taste for Starbucks. But last year, McDonald's Premium coffee got some good press. Testers from Consumer Reports thought it tasted better than Starbucks, and it cost less.

(378 words)

Word List

target	[ˈtɑːgɪt]	v.	把……作为目标,靶子
competition	[ˌkɒmpɪˈtɪʃən]	n.	竞争,竞赛
specialty	[ˈspeʃəltɪ]	n.	专业,特制
lattes	[ˈlɑːteɪ]	n.	拿铁咖啡
cappuccino	[kæpʊˈtʃiːnəu]	n.	卡布奇诺咖啡
compete	[kəmˈpiːt]	v.	比赛,竞争
risk	[rɪsk]	n.	冒险,风险
available	[əˈveɪləbl]	adj.	可用到的,可利用的
stock	[stɒk]	n.	股票,股份
replace	[rɪˈpleɪs]	v.	取代,替换,代替
remain	[rɪˈmeɪn]	v.	保持,逗留,残存
credit	[ˈkredɪt]	v.	相信,信任
peppermint	[ˈpepəmɪnt]	n.	胡椒薄荷,薄荷油
premium	[ˈpriːmɪəm]	adj.	特级的,特佳的
expansion	[ɪkˈspænʃən]	n.	扩充,膨胀,扩张

Idioms & Expressions

heat up	加热，升温	slow down	（使）慢下来，减速
credit with	认为某人有（某种优点或能力等）		
lead to	导致，通向		
water down	加水冲淡，稀释，减弱某事物的作用		
speed up	（使某事物）加速		

Exercises

1. 【Definitions】

Match the words in the box with their meanings. Write the word that stands for the definition in the appropriate answer space.

target	compete	specialty	risk	available	replace
remain	credit	premium	expansion	stock	

1) _____ : of superior quality or value.
2) _____ : the possibility of suffering harm or loss; danger.
3) _____ : to strive with another or others to attain a goal, such as gaining an advantage or winning a victory.
4) _____ : the number of shares that each stockholder possesses.
5) _____ : a reputation for sound character or quality; standing.
6) _____ : to take or fill the place of.
7) _____ : to continue in the same state or condition.
8) _____ : the act or process of expanding.
9) _____ : present and ready for use; at hand; accessible.
10) _____ : an item or a product of a distinctive kind or of particular superiority.
11) _____ : to cause to have an effect on a particular, intentionally limited group.

2. 【Sample Sentences】

Use the new words and phrases you have learned from the box in the following sentences. Change the form where necessary.

1) The young tennis player has often _____ against famous players, but so far he has always been beaten.
2) The new city, Brasilia, _____ Rio de Janeiro as the capital of Brazil in 1960.
3) Steel production was _____ for 60,000 tons last year.

4) This type of new car needs _____ gas as its power.
5) Attention, please. These tickets are _____ on (the) day of issue only.
6) He _____ his life when he saved the child from the fire.
7) She invested all her money into _____ and shares.
8) The company planed to _____ their business into the foreign market.
9) The death of the innkeeper still _____ a mystery.
10) His success brings _____ to his family.
11) French pastry is the chef's _____ .

3. 【Translation】

A. Translate the following English sentences into Chinese.

1) McDonald's the fast-food company, is heating up competition with the Starbucks Coffee Company.

2) McDonald's thinks its new plan has a greater chance of success.

3) He is credited with building the Seattle Company into an international success store.

4) But a year ago he warned that its fast growth had led to what he called the watering down of the Starbucks experience.

5) Now, Starbucks will speed up its international growth while slowing its expansion in the United States.

B. Translate the following Chinese sentences into English by using the words in the bracket.

1) 福利开支正在削减,所以它只应该用于最需要的那部分人。(target)

2) 有什么东西能取代母亲的爱和关怀吗? (replace)

3) 他决心不管发生什么事都忠于球队。(remain)

4) 政府正要把物价下跌说成是自己的功劳。(credit)

5) 这些批评已经被修改得很温和,以免冒犯人。(water down)

4. 【Writing】

Write a composition of about 150-200 about your opinions on fastfood.
Your composition should be put into three paragraphs and the outline should be like this:

Title: Fastfood is My Favorite or Fastfood is junk food.
Introduction: Express your ideas on fastfood: Do you love it or dislike it? Do you think fastfood is a kind of good food or bad food for people nowadays? Do you think that its advantages are more than its disadvantages or just on the contrary.
Development: Give enough examples to support and prove your ideas.
Conclusion: Restate your ideas on fastfood but use different sentences from the introduction.

Reading Skills: 英语阅读中的重点句式（1, 2）

在英语文章的写作当中，作者经常要用各种手段来突出自己的主题和观点。我们把与文章主题、观点及关键信息相关的语句称为重点句式。而作者用来突出解释和分析主题观点的一些手法如举例、引用、列数字、下定义等均为补充说明性的次要句子。在阅读理解过程中，为了能提高阅读的速度和抓住文章的要点与主旨，我们可以利用各种阅读方法，分清文章中的主次信息，将次要的、解释分析性、意义补充说明性的词句先略过去不读，重点阅读和掌握那些有关中心思想和主题观点性的句子。我们将阅读中的重点句式归结为以下几类：

1. 带转折词的句子

在英语文章中，带转折词的句子通常用来表达与上下文内容不同或相反的含义，作者往往喜欢用这种句子来突出自己的观点或主题。因此，在阅读文章时，我们应该重点掌握这种句子。表达转折关系的词汇和短语常见有：

but, yet, however, nonetheless, nevertheless, rather, in any case, though, although, while, in fact, as a matter of fact 等。

2. 带总结归纳词的句子

英语文章中的总结归纳句子常用在段落和文章的结尾部分。用以下结论、做总结、对全文的中心思想和基本大意进行总结概括。因此，这种带总结归纳词的句子通常与文章的主题要点有直接的联系。在阅读文章时，要关注这种词句，这样做，对正确把握文章的观点和主旨有很大的帮助。表达总结归纳的单词和短语有：**thus, so, therefore, accordingly, consequently, as a result, in a word, in summary, in brief** 等。

Text 2 (Extensive Reading)

Is EU Lost in Translation?
欧盟在翻译中迷失了吗？

The European Union operates in 20 official languages now. With annual translation costs set to rise to US $1.3 billion, some people question whether EU institutions are becoming overburdened by multilingualism.

Parliamentary sessions are conducted with 20 languages simultaneously. With further countries to join the EU, the body is due to accommodate several more languages by 2010. Some analysts fear the effectiveness of its institutions could be getting lost in translation.

Even before expansion in 2004, the EU ran the world's largest translation operation—twice as big as that of the United Nations, which has six official languages.

EU institutions currently require around 2,000 written-text translators. They also need 80 interpreters per language per day, half of which operate at the European Parliament. The total annual cost of EU multilingualism will soon rise from US$ 875 million dollars to US$ 1.3 billion dollars.

The European Parliament (EP) requires some 60 interpreters to help elected politicians from the 25 member states understand each other. These interpreters work in soundproofed booths, translating the words of Members of European Parliament (MEP). Even so, unfamiliar words or phrases can leave interpreters lost for words.

Comic misunderstandings can arise that become part of Brussels lore. For instance, during an agricultural working group session, "frozen semen" was translated into French as "frozen seamen".

Another MEP recalls how the expression "out of sight, out of mind" became "invisible lunatic" after a computer-aided translation.

On a more serious note, Stevenson said, "Because it is deemed a fundamental right to be able to communicate with your electors in your own tongue, the parliament now has to work in 20 different languages." This exercise currently consumes tens of thousands of tons of paper a year, as every word spoken has to by typed up and filed in mountainous archives.

The EC says it's essential that legislation is published in the official languages of all member states, because EU citizens can't be expected to comply with laws they don't understand.

However, the resulting translation workload has meant problems for both the EC and individual member states. For example, Estonia's government reported major difficulties in ratifying some European legislation because of poor translation of EU laws.

Richard Rowe, spokesperson for the EC's Directorate-General for Translation, says that the legal requirement that all EU legislation is simultaneously published in all official languages has been suspended until enough Maltese-speaking translators can be trained.

"Apart from the problem of the lack of qualified candidates for some languages, we are under budgetary constraints, which means we cannot recruit all the translators we need in an ideal world until 2006," Rowe added.

Yet the spokesman said the EC is taking measures to speed up and simplify its written translation work, which last year amounted to more than 1.5 million pages.

"One simplification measure the commission has already adopted is to impose a reduction in the length of tests sent to us for translation," he noted. Now these tests should not exceed 15 pages in length.

Most EC translators also have access to a powerful computer application called Translator's Workbench, which stores all previous work.

"The translator faced with a new assignment feeds it into the system and gets back a text in which the memory suggests translations of phrases, sentences, or even whole paragraphs that have been translated in the past," Rowe said. "We always recycle previous work wherever possible."

He adds that internal EC work is conducted largely in just three languages—English, French, and German—for reasons of efficiency and economy. In the longer term, such an approach may be the way forward throughout the EU, according to Giles Chichester, a British MEP.

"In practice, the institutions are trying to move towards one dominant language, with one or two other working languages," he said. "Let nature take its course."

Unofficially English is the language of choice within the EU. It is now used for drafting around 60 percent of all paperwork. English is also widely spoken as a second language in Europe, especially in Scandinavian and Eastern European countries. In Malta, the vast majority of residents understand English.

Officially, however, and EU dominated by English would be unacceptable politically. The French are particularly sensitive to its increased use, while multilingualism is considered a vital cornerstone of the European Parliament.

"Members are elected and represent the public because of their political stances, not their languages skills," said Rowe, "So in the interests of democracy and transparency, the service provided to them has to be much more multilingual."

In fact, the amount of translation and interpretation work could multiply further if various political groups get their way. Catalan is spoken by some even million Europeans, mostly in Spain. Yet it doesn't have official status within the EU. Similarly the Irish and Welsh are lobbying for official recognition of their native Celtic tongues.

(810 words)

Word List

legislative	['ledʒɪslətɪv]	adj.	立法的,立法机关的
headquarter	['hed,kwɔːtə]	n.	总部
parliament	['pɑːləmənt]	n.	国会,议会
simultaneously	[,sɪməl'teɪnɪəslɪ]	adv.	同时地
soundproofed	['saʊndpruːft]	adj.	隔音的
booth	[buːð]	n.	货摊,售货亭,棚
lunatic	['luːnətɪk]	adj.	精神错乱的,疯狂的
deem	[diːm]	v.	认为,相信
comply	[kəm'plaɪ]	v.	顺从,答应,遵守
ratify	['rætɪfaɪ]	v.	批准,认可

Unit Sixteen

• suspend	[səˈspend]	v.	延缓
• budgetary	[ˈbʌdʒɪtəri]	adj.	预算的
• constraint	[kənˈstreɪnt]	n.	约束,强制
• amount	[əˈmaʊnt]	v.	总计,等于
• assignment	[əˈsaɪnmənt]	n.	分配,任务,(课外)作业
• dominate	[ˈdɒmɪneɪt]	v.	支配,占优势
• democracy	[dɪˈmɒkrəsi]	n.	民主主义,民主政治
• transparency	[trænˈspærənsi]	n.	透明度,透明,幻灯片
• multiply	[ˈmʌltɪplaɪ]	v.	繁殖,乘,增加
• lobby	[ˈlɔbi]	v.	游说,对(议员)进行疏通
• archive	[ˈɑːkaɪv]	v.	存档
• impose	[ɪmˈpəʊz]	v.	征税,强加

Idioms and & Expressions

according to	依照	out of sight, out of mind	眼不见,心不烦
apart from	远离,除……之外	take measures	设法,着手
in the long term	从长远来看	in practice	在实践中,实际上
let nature take its course	顺其自然	comply with	遵守,服从
lobby for	向(政府,议员等)游说		

Exercises

1. [Questions]

Based on the information provided in the text, answer the following questions briefly.

1) How much will the total annual cost of EU multilingualism soon rise?

2) According to the EC, why the legislation is published in the official languages of all member states?

3) What measures has the EU taken to speed up and simplify its written translation work?

4) Why can't English become the only official language?

5) What is the future of the translation and interpretation work in EU?

2. [Multiple Choices]

Choose the right answer from the four choices marked A, B, C and D.

1) Before expansion in 2004, how many languages did the EU operate?
   A. 20　　　　B. 6　　　　C. 12　　　　D. 18

2) How many interpreters do EU institutions need per language per day to serve at the European Parliament.
   A. 2,000　　　B. 40　　　　C. 80　　　　D. 1000

3) Which one of the following statements is not the problem that the EU is facing with in the language translation?
   A. EU institutions are becoming overburdened by multilingualism.
   B. The translation costs are also a big burden to the EU.
   C. Unfamiliar words or phrases can leave interpreters lost for words.
   D. EU can not accept any more new member states.

4) Which one of the following statements is not the reason that English can not become the only official language of EU?
   A. Because it is a fundamental right to be able to communicate with the electors in their mother languages.
   B. Because multilingualism is considered a vital cornerstone of the EP.
   C. Because in the interests of the democracy and transparency, the service provided to them has to be much more multilingual.
   D. Because all the member states strongly object to regarding English as the only official language.

5) What measurements has EU taken to speed up and simplify its translation work?
   A. Imposing a reduction in the length of the texts sent for translation.
   B. The translators have access to powerful computer application.
   C. All the internal EC work now is conducted in just three languages-English, French and German.
   D. Both A and B.

Text 3 (Fast Reading)

Secrets of Self-Made Millionaires
成为百万富翁的秘密

Passion pays off

　　In 1996, Linda Victoria and her husband were barely making ends meet. Like so many of us, Linda was eager to discover her purpose, so she splurged on a session with a life coach. "When I told her my goal was to make $30,000 a year, she said I was setting the bar too low. I need to focus on my passion, not on the paycheck."

Linda, who lives with her son in Alexandria, Minnesota, owned a gift basket company and earned just $16,000 a year. She noticed when she let potential buyers taste the food items, the baskets sold like crazy. Linda thought: Why not sell the food directly to customers in a fun setting?

With $7,000 in savings, a bank loan and a friend's investment, Linda started packaging gourmet foods in a backyard shed and selling them at taste-testing parties. It wasn't easy. "I remember sitting outside one day, thinking we were three months behind on our house payment, I had two employees I couldn't pay, and I ought to get a real job. But then I thought: No, this is your dream. Recommit and get to work."

She stuck with it, even after her husband died 4 years later. "I live by the law of abundance, meaning that even when there are challenges in life, I look for the win-win," she says.

The positive attitude worked: Linda's backyard company, Tastefully Simple, is now a direct-sale business, with $125 million in sales last year. And Linda was named one of the top 25 female business owners in North America by Fast Company magazine.

According to the research by Thomas J. Stanley, author of The Millionaire Mind, over 80% of millionaires say they never would have been successful if their vocation wasn't something they cared about.

Grow your money

Most of us know the never-ending cycle of living paycheck to paycheck. "The fastest way to get out of that pattern is to make extra money for the specific purpose of reinvesting in yourself," says Loral Langemeier, author of *The Millionaire Maker*. In other words, earmark some money for the sole purpose of investing it in a place where it will grow dramatically—like a business or real estate.

There are endless ways to make extra money for investing—you just have to be willing to do the work. "Everyone has a marketable skill," says Langemeier. "When I started out, I had a tutoring business, seeing clients in the morning before work and in my lunch break."

A little moonlighting cash really can grow into a million. 25 years ago, Rich Sikorski dreamed of owning a personal training business. "I rented a tiny studio where I charged $15 an hour," he says. When money started trickling in, he squirreled it away instead of spending it, putting it all back into the business. Rick's 400-quare-foot studio is now Fitness Together, a franchise based in Highlands Ranch, Colorado, with more than 360 locations worldwide. And he's worth over $40 million.

When extra money rolls in, it's easy to think: Now I can buy that new TV. But if you want to get rich, you need to pay yourself first, by putting money where it will work hard for you—whether that's in your retirement fund, a side business or investment like real estate.

No guts, no glory.

Last summer, David Lindahl footed the bill for 18 relatives at a fancy mansion in the Adirondacks. One night, his dad looked out at the scenery and joked, "I can't believe we used to call you the black sheep."

At 28, David was broke, living in a small apartment near Boston and wondering what to do after 10 years in a local rock band. "I looked around and thought: If I don't do something, I'll be stuck here forever."

He started a landscape company, buying his equipment on credit. When business literally froze over that winter, a banker friend asked if he'd like to renovate a foreclosed home. "I'm a terrible carpenter, but I needed the money, so I want to some free seminars at Home Depot and figured it out as I went," he says.

After a few more renovations, it occurred to him: Why not buy the homes and sell them for profit? He took a risk and bought his first property. Using the proceeds, he bought another, and another. 12 years later, he owns apartment buildings, worth $143 million, in 8 states.

The biggest secret? Stop spending

Every millionaire we spoke to has one thing in common: not a single one spends needlessly. Real estate investor David Lindahl drives a Ford Explorer and says his middle-class neighbors would be shocked to learn how much he's worth. Fitness mogul Rick Sikorski can't fathom why anyone would buy bottled water. Steve Maxwell, the finance teacher, looked at a $1.5 million home but decided to buy one for half the price because "a house with double the cost wouldn't give me double the enjoyment."

It's not a fluke: According to the 2007 Annual Survey of Affluence & Wealth in America, some of the richest people "spend their money with a middle-class mind-set." They clip coupons, wait for sales and buy luxury items at a discount.

No kidding! Talk show host Tyra Banks herself the Queen of Cheap and keeps perfume samples from magazine ads in her purse for quick touch-ups.

Sara Blakely, founder of the $100 million shapewear company Spanx, gets her hair trimmed at Supercuts.

And Warren Buffett, the third richest person in the world, according to Forbes, lives in the same Omaha, Nebraska, home he bought 4 decades ago for $31,500.

(973 words)

Exercises

1. [True, False, Not Given]

Decide whether the following statements are True, False or Not Given.

T (for True) if the statement agrees with the information given in the passage;

F (for False) if the statement doesn't agree with the information given in the passage.

NG (for Not Given) if the information is not given in the passage.

1) Linda's backyard company, Tastefully Simple, is now a direct-sales business, with $125 million in sales last year.
2) The fastest way to get out of the never-ending circle of living paycheck to paycheck is to make more money for the special purpose of reinvesting in yourself.
3) Rick's 400-square-foot studio is now Fitness Together with more than 360 locations all over the world.
4) If you want to get rich, you need to pay yourself first, by putting money where it will work hard for you.
5) David Linda started his business with guts and he now owns apartment building, worth $143 million, in 8 states.
6) The biggest secret of getting rich is not to spend money freely and excessively.
7) According to the Annual Survey, some of the richest people spend their money with a top-class mind-set.

2. [Blank-Filling]

For questions 1)–3), complete the sentences with the information given in the passage.

1) According to the research by Thomas J. Stanley, over 80% of millionaires say they never would have been successful if their profession _____.
2) There are many ways to make extra money for investing—you need to _____.
3) Every millionaire has one thing in common: _____.

Unit Seventeen

Text 1 (Intensive Reading)

Background Tips: Hypothermia

Hypothermia (from Greek) is a condition in which an organism's temperature drops below that required for normal metabolism and bodily functions. In warm-blooded animals, core body temperature is maintained near a constant level through biologic homeostasis. But, when the body is exposed to cold, its internal mechanisms may be unable to replenish the heat that is being lost to the organism's surroundings.

Hypothermia is the opposite of hyperthermia, the condition that causes heat exhaustion and heat stroke.

Want to Stay Warm in Winters? Think COLD
在冬天想要保暖，想想"COLD"吧

Winter in many places means ice skating, sledding and snowball fights. But unless someone is prepared, outdoor fun can also mean frostbite and hypothermia. So it seems necessary for us to talk about how to stay warm, dry and safe.

Frostbite is damage that happens when skin is exposed to extreme cold for too long. It mainly happens on the hands, feet, nose and ears.

People with minor cases of frostbite that affect only the skin may not suffer any permanent damage. But if deeper tissue is affected, a person is likely to feel pain every time the area gets cold.

If blood vessels are damaged, people can suffer an infection, gangrene. Sometimes, doctors have to remove frostbitten areas like fingers and toes.

Hypothermia happens when the body cannot produce as much heat as it loses. The condition comes on slowly. Signs include uncontrollable shaking, unusually slow breathing and difficulty thinking clearly. If not treated, hypothermia can be deadly.

The best way to avoid cold-related injuries is to be prepared for the outdoors. Here is a simple way to remember four basic steps to staying warm. Think of COLD-C.O.L.D.

The C stands for cover. Wear a hat and scarf to keep hear from escaping through the head, neck and ears. And wear mittens instead of gloves. Gloves may not keep hands as warm because they separate the fingers.

Unit Seventeen

The O stands for overexertion. Avoid activities that will make you sweaty. Wet clothes and cold weather are a bad mix.

L is for layers. Wearing loose, lightweight clothes, one layer on top of another, is better than a single heavy layer of clothing. Also, make sure outerwear is made of water resistant and tightly knit material.

Can you guess what the D in COLD stands for? D is for dry. In other words, stay as dry as possible. Pay attention to the places where snow can enter, like the tops of boots, the necks of coats and the wrist areas of mittens.

And a couple of other things to keep in mind, one for children and the other for adults. Eating snow might be fun but it lowers the body's temperature. And drinking alcohol might make a person feel warm, but what it really does is weaken the body's ability to hold heat.

(383 words)

Word List

frostbite	['frɒstbaɪt]	n.	冻伤,霜寒
hypothermia	[ˌhaɪpəʊ'θɜːmɪə]	n.	降低体温
expose	[ɪk'spəʊz]	v.	使暴露,使曝光
extreme	[ɪk'striːm]	adj.	极端的,尽头的,最后的
minor	['maɪnə]	adj.	较小的,次要的,二流的
affect	[ə'fekt]	v.	影响,感动,侵袭
permanent	['pɜːmənənt]	adj.	永久的,持久的
tissue	['tɪsjuː]	n.	组织,薄的纱织品
vessel	['vesəl]	n.	导管,容器,船
infection	[ɪn'fekʃən]	n.	传染,影响,感染
gangrene	[ˌgæŋgriːn]	n.	坏疽,腐败
remove	[rɪ'muːv]	v.	移动,开除,移交
treat	[triːt]	v.	治疗,对待,款待
injury	['ɪndʒərɪ]	n.	伤害,侮辱
mitten	['mɪtn]	n.	棒球手套,拳击手套
overexertion	['əʊvərɪg'zəʃən]	n.	努力过度,用力过度
layer	['leɪə]	n.	层,阶层
sweaty	['swetɪ]	adj.	出汗的,吃力的
resistant	[rɪ'zɪstənt]	adj.	抵抗的,有抵抗力的
weaken	['wiːkən]	v.	削弱,变弱
alcohol	['ælkəhɒl]	n.	酒,酒精

Idioms & Expressions

be likely to	可能	be prepared for	准备做……
stand for	代表,代替,象征,支持	in other words	换句话说
make sure	确定,确信,证实	keep ... in mind	牢记……
pay attention to	注意	be made of	由……制成,做成
come on	发展,生长,赶快		

Exercises

1. [Definitions]

Match the words in the box with their meanings. Write the world that stands for the definition in the appropriate answer space.

| expose | extreme | minor | affect | permanent | infection |
| remove | treat | injury | resistant | weaken | |

1) _____ : damage or harm done to or suffered by a person or thing.
2) _____ : having or showing resistance.
3) _____ : to make visible.
4) _____ : to have an influence on or effect a change in.
5) _____ : the act or result of being infecting, or a disease spread by infecting.
6) _____ : to give medical aid to (someone).
7) _____ : to do away with; eliminate.
8) _____ : lasting or remaining without essential change.
9) _____ : to make or become weak or weaker.
10) _____ : being in or attaining the greatest or highest degree; very intense.
11) _____ : lesser or smaller in amount, extent, size, importance, rank, or seriousness.

2. [Sample Sentences]

Use the new words and phrases you have learned from the box in the following sentences. Change the form where necessary.

1) I have a _____ job here.
2) The crime of the corrupt officials must _____ without any reserve.
3) He lives at the _____ edge of the forest.
4) One of the boys in the class had a fever and he soon _____ other children.
5) The young actress was given a _____ part in the new play.

6) The engineer felt that he hadn't _____ fairly
7) He _____ the mud form his shoes.
8) The driver of the car received serious _____ to the legs and arms.
9) She _____ as the illness grew worse.
10) This article will _____ my thinking.
11) The new type of disease is _____ to antibiotics.

3. 【Translation】

A. Translate the following English sentences into Chinese.

1) If deeper tissue is affected, a person is likely to feel pain every time the area gets cold.

2) Hypothermia happens when the body cannot produces as much heat as it loses.

3) The best way to avoid cold-related injuries is to be prepared for the outdoors.

4) Wearing loose, lightweight clothes, one layer on top of another, is better than a single heavy layer of clothing.

5) Drinking alcohol might make a person feel warm, but what it really does is weaken the body's ability to hold heat.

B. Translate the following Chinese sentences into English by using the words in the brackets.

1) 他的名字詹姆斯·B·克拉克中的 B 代表什么？(stand for)

2) 如果没有煤，可以用石油来代替。(instead)

3) 她是最有希望得奖的女孩。(likely)

4) 留在屋里，不要让皮肤在太阳下暴晒。(expose)

5) 由于那次重大的失误，他被免职了。(remove)

4. 【Writing】

Write a summary of about 150-200 words on how to keep warm and prevent your body from hypothermia.

The summary should include the following points:
1) A brief definition of hypothermia and its symptoms.

2) Some improper methods to keep warm.
3) The right methods to keep warm.

Reading Skills: 英语阅读中的重点句式 (3, 4)

3. 带有表达观点、做总结概括的动词的句子

带有表达观点、做总结概括的动词的句子往往与文章的主题、作者支持或反对的观点等重要内容有关。因此,在阅读英语文章时应留心这些句子的理解和把握,表示提观点、下结论、做总结的动词有：

believe, think, deem, argue, assume, in one's opinion, as far as sb be concerned, suggest, imply, indicate, show, conclude, draw the conclusion that, find that, discover that 等。

4. 问句

英语文章中的问句与汉语文章中的问句比较类似。从其作用上来分,共有三种:一种是真实的疑问句,即作者不清楚问题的答案,提出问题,询问读者以求得到答案。这种真实问句在阅读理解文章中出现的情况比较少。第二种是设问句,即作者自问自答式的问句,作者之所以要先提出问题,然后由自己给出问题的答案,其目的是为了引起读者的注意,给读者一个关注作者阐述的重点主题的提示。第三种问句是反意疑问句也叫做反问句,即作者明知某件事,却要反问一下这个问题,从而达到强调和突出重点的效果。我们阅读到的大部分英语文章中出现的问句通常不是设问句,就是反问句。问句中的内容和问题的答案其实往往就是文章作者要介绍的主题或观点。因此,在阅读理解所读文章时,要对这些具有特殊含义和作用的问句有所关注和领悟。

Text 2 (Extensive Reading)

Pockety Women Unite
穿口袋服装的女士们团结起来

Pockets are what women need more of. The women's movement in the past decade has made giant strides in achieving greater social justice for females, but there's a great deal of work yet to be done. And it can't be done without pockets.

It has been commonly thought that men get the best jobs and make the most money and don't have to wash the dinner dishes simply because they're men, that cultural traditions and social conditioning have worked together to give them a special place in the world

Unit Seventeen

order.

While there is undoubtedly some truth to this, the fact remains that no one has investigated the role that pockets have played in preventing women for attaining the social status and rights that could and should be theirs.

Consider your average successful executives. How many pockets does he wear to work? Two in the sides of his trousers, two in the back, one on the front of his shirt, three on his suit coat, and one on the inside of the suit coat. Total: nine.

Consider your average woman dressed for office work: If she is wearing a dress or skirt and blouse, she is probably wearing zero pockets, or one or two at the most. The pantsuit, that supposedly liberating outfit, is usually equally pocketless.

Now, while it is always dangerous to generalize, it seems quite safe to say that, on the whole, the man of the world, at any-given time, are carrying about a much greater number of pockets than are the women of the world. And it is also quite clear that, on the whole, the men enjoy more power, prestige, and wealth than women do.

Everything seems to point to a positive correlation between pockets, power, prestige, and wealth. Can this be?

An examination of the function of the pocket seems necessary. Pockets are for carrying money, credit cards, identification (including access to those prestigious clubs where people presumably sit around sharing powerful secrets about how to run the world), important messages, pens, keys, combs, and impressive-looking handkerchiefs.

All the equipment essential to running the world. And held close to the body. Easily available. Neatly classified. Pen in the inside coat pocket. Keys in the back left trouser pocket. Efficiency. Order. Confidence.

What does a woman have to match this organization? A purse.

The most hurried examination will show that a purse, however large or important-looking, is no match for a suitful of pockets. If the woman carrying a purse is so lucky as to get an important phone number or market tip from the executive with whom she is lunching, can she write it down? Can she find her pen? Perhaps she can, but it will probably be buried under three old grocery lists, two combs, a checkbook, and a ward of Kleenex. All of which she will have to pile on top of the lunch table before she can find the pen.

Will she ever get another tip from this person of power? Not likely. Now she has lost any psychological advantage she may have had. He may have been impressed with her intelligent discussion of the current economic scene before she opened her handbag, but four minutes later, when she is still digging, like a busy little prairie dog, for that pen, he is no longer impressed.

He knows he could have whipped his pen in and out of his pocket and written fourteen important messages on the table napkin in the time as she is still searching?

What can a pocketless woman do?

Two solutions seem apparent. The women can form a pocket lobby (Pocket Power?) and march on the New York garment district. Or in the event that effort fails (and well it might, since it would, by necessity, have to be run by a bunch of pocketless women) and alternate approach remains.

Every man in the country for his next birthday finds himself the lucky recipient of one of those very stylish men's handbags, and to go with it, one of those no-pocket body shirts.

(675 words)

Word List

decade	['dekeɪd]	n.	十年,十
stride	[straɪd]	n.	步幅
achieve	[ə'tʃiːv]	v.	完成,达到
justice	['dʒʌstɪs]	n.	正义,公平,司法
investigate	[ɪn'vestɪgeɪt]	v.	调查,研究
attain	[ə'teɪn]	v.	达到,获得
executive	[ɪg'zekjʊtɪv]	n.	执行者,主管人员
liberate	['lɪbəreɪt]	v.	解放,释放
outfit	['aʊtfɪt]	n.	全套装配,用具,配备
generalize	['dʒenərəlaɪz]	v.	归纳,概括,推广
prestige	[pre'stiːʒ]	n.	声望,威望,威信
correlation	[ˌkɒrɪ'leɪʃən]	n.	相互关系,相关性
identification	[aɪˌdentɪfɪkeɪʃən]	n.	辨认,鉴定,证明
presumably	[prɪ'zjuːməblɪ]	adv.	推测起来,大概
essential	[ɪ'senʃəl]	adj.	本质的,基本的,精华的
classify	['klæsɪfaɪ]	v.	分类,分等
pile	[paɪl]	v.	堆积,累积
grocery	['grəʊsərɪ]	n.	食品杂货店
whip	[wɪp]	v.	鞭打,突然移动
napkin	['næpkɪn]	n.	餐巾纸,餐巾
garment	['gɑːmənt]	n.	衣服,外衣,服装
recipient	[rɪ'sɪpɪənt]	n.	容纳者,容器
alternate	['ɔːltɜːneɪt]	adj.	轮流的,预备的

Idioms & Expressions

prevent ... from	预防,防止	on the whole	大体上,基本上
access to	有权使用,可进入		
a wad of	一块(布),一沓(纸);一捆(钞票)等		
be impressed with	被打动(感动)	a bunch of	一群,一帮,一束,一串

Unit Seventeen

Exercises

1. 【Questions】

Based on the information provided in the text, answer the following questions briefly.

1) What are reasons commonly given to explain why men hold better positions in society than women?

2) How many pockets does the average successful male executive wear to work?

3) How many pockets does the average women wear for office work?

4) According to the author, why do people need pockets?

5) According to the author, what is the correlation between power and pockets?

2. 【Multiple Choices】

Choose the right answer from the four choices marked A, B, C and D.

1) Which of the following statements are not right according to the passage?
   A. Women's movement has made great success in the past decade.
   B. Pockets are very important for women's achieving social justice.
   C. Men earn more money and have better jobs than women.
   D. No one has proved that pockets prevented women from getting some rights.

2) Among the function of the pocket, which one is not included in the passage?
   A. Carrying money.
   B. Carrying pens and keys.
   C. Carrying messages.
   D. Carrying identification card.

3) What does the author think is the disadvantage of the women's purse?
   A. It is too small and can't be put into everything that women need.
   B. It is a little large and can't be put into the pocket.
   C. It is so beautiful that women don't want to put it into pockets.
   D. It is no match for the clothes sometimes.

4) What could the man do when the woman needs a pen to write something but can't find it according to the passage?
   A. Lending the woman his pen.
   B. Using his pen to write the message himself.
   C. Waiting until the woman finds her pen.
   D. Giving the woman his name card.

5) What does the author propose for women's pocket problems?

   A. Giving men special birthday gift-very stylish handbags with pocketless shirts.

   B. Buying clothes with many pockets.

   C. Carrying smaller purse.

   D. Wearing trousers instead of skirts.

Text 3 (Fast Reading)

The Role of Supplements in Health and Nutrition
添加剂在健康和营养中的角色

Supplements may not be the darling of the media they once were, but the importance of vitamins and minerals and herbal and specialty supplements (VMHS) to consumer's health and wellness lifestyles should not be overlooked nor their role diminished. Because of increasing consumer health consciousness (due in no small part to an aging population), the rise of "self-care" and "self-treatment", media attention and product proliferation, the supplement category continues to change and evolve—and remains complex.

Even the most advanced wellness consumers, who one might expect to shun any and all elements of the modern medical establishment, are still buying the one thing that symbolizes allopathic medicine to most of us: pills.

Past Hartman Group research has shown that consumers' movement from periphery to core along the wellness continuum increases their likelihood of using dietary supplements. Some of the triggers that get people started may include nutritional needs, health conditions (such as high cholesterol or arthritis) and aging. The lack of knowledge about supplements initially inhibits some consumers from buying supplements. Additional inhibitors include price and the perceived lack of scientific proof of the efficacy of these products.

Consumers continue to purchase and use nutritional supplements, but with less intensity and exploratory nature than what we saw in 2000. Today, mid-level and core consumers appear to have identified key supplements that they use with some regulatory (ranging from three times per week to daily) and have decreased their exploratory shopping for new supplements. We also find new interest in key supplements such as green tea, probiotics and Omegas.

Consumers have dramatically increased the number of phrases and behaviors that define "wellness" to them from 2000 to 2005. Particularly notable is "taking supplements", which is now seen as the path of wellness by 43% of consumers, nearly double the number in 2000 (23%).

Unit Seventeen

The language map illustrate the most predominate ways in which consumers think and talk about health and wellness. The map progresses from bottom to top, with the bottom representing consumers who are less involved in health and wellness (periphery wellness consumers) and the top representing those who are most involved in health and wellness (core wellness consumers). This map depicts several interesting shifts and changes from 2000. We find that wellness consumers still begin the journey with the desire to eat well, but with more intention towards living a healthier lifestyle.

The predominant themes of the language being used for periphery to core are represented by the black areas. The grayed "bubbles" represent secondary themes that run throughout the language analysis and support the primary themes. The white areas are supporting quotes, thoughts, tactics, activities, examples, etc. to what the primary themes mean to consumers.

At the bottom, periphery wellness consumers have little or no brand recognition of supplements and knowledge is very limited. Moving up the ladder, brand awareness and knowledge increases among mid-level wellness consumers, but only moderately. At the top, brand awareness and supplement knowledge is at its zenith among core wellness consumers.

In general, except for the use of vitamins and minerals on an occasional basis, periphery wellness consumers have a much lower involvement with products outside of the traditional food groups.

As one moves towards the core, or top on the language map, the importance of specialty supplements to consumers increases more, relative to the other supplement categories, than the frequency in which consumers use the products. In practical terms this means that consumers' use of the specialty supplements lags behind vitamins, minerals, and herbal and supplements.

Cultural preferences to health products

Most American consumers address general health concerns (e.g., stay in shape, eating well, eating balanced meals, etc.) with daily, lifestyle routines and practices rather than targeted, acute responses (e.g., taking medication). At this level, most Americans use a vague watching behavior (e.g., "I watch my sugar intake") or, if they are more evolved wellness consumers, they incorporate lots of fresh foods into their diet to address current and long-term health. What they tend not to use is a specific plan of action requiring health products that target a specific health condition.

When consumers are experiencing chronic or acute health problems (allergies, diabetes, high blood pressure, stroke, osteoporosis, etc.), we find that they definitely shift from more general watching behaviors and high level dietary overhauls (with the requisite focus on avoiding "bad things") to more proactive and targeted health behaviors. In the case of this proactive test, those with diagnosed chronic conditions generally take medications and, if pushed, also alter their overall diet to avoid ingredients that might exacerbate their condition.

However, most consumers with chronic health conditions, we find, will end up turning to alternative medicine—to different pills. Overwhelmingly, respondents chose pills (72%)

compared to the next most popular format beverages (26%). Consumers view dietary supplements as a key symbolic component that they use in their lives to challenge the hold that they view pharmaceutical companies have over them. The most successful dietary supplement products are those that focus on offering up modes of control, including prevention, for which modern medicine offers either poor solutions, last-minute solutions, or no solutions at all. This fits well with what consumers report as the most commonly used supplements including vitamin C, calcium, fiber and vitamins B, E and D. These supplements use levels reflects consumer concerns about and increasing roles for products that offer antioxidants, bone and digestive health, as well as overall perceived "increase in wellness". (922 words)

Exercises

1. [True, False, Not Given]

Decide whether the following statements are True, False or Not Given.

T (for True) if the statement agrees with the information given in the passage;

F (for False) if the statement doesn't agree with the information given in the passage.

NG (for Not Given) if the information is not given in the passage.

1) The most advanced wellness consumers avoid many elements of the modern medical establishment.
2) Today the intensity of using nutritional supplements has increased.
3) The mid-level wellness consumers believe taking supplements is the path to longevity.
4) The periphery wellness people never use products outside of the traditional food groups.
5) Specialty supplement is used much less than the other supplements.
6) Most Americans now use a specific plan of action requiring health products that target a specific health condition.
7) Most consumers with chronic health conditions will end up taking medications.

2. [Blank-Filling]

For questions 1)–3), complete the sentences with the information given in the passage.

1) The triggers that get people using dietary supplements may include nutrition needs, aging and _____.
2) Wellness consumers still begin the journey with the desire to eat well, but with more intention towards _____.
3) The key symbolic component that the consumers use in their lives is _____.

Unit Eighteen

Text 1 (Intensive Reading)

Background Tips: Numerology

Numerology is any of many systems, traditions or beliefs in a mystical or esoteric relationship between numbers and physical objects or living things.

Numerology and numerological divination were popular among early mathematicians, such as Pythagoras, but are no longer considered part of mathematics and are regarded as pseudomathematics by most modern scientists. This is similar to the historical development of astronomy out of astrology, and chemistry from alchemy.

Today, numerology is often not associated with numbers, but with the occult, alongside astrology and similar divinatory arts.

Number definitions

There are no set definitions for the meaning of specific digits. Common examples include:

0. Everything or absoluteness. All
1. Individual. Aggressor. Yang.
2. Balance. Union. Receptive. Yin.
3. Communication/interaction. Neutrality.
4. Creation.
5. Action. Restlessness.
6. Reaction/flux. Responsibility.
7. Thought/consciousness.
8. Power/sacrifice.
9. Highest level of change.
10. Rebirth.

Numerology—Using Numbers to Predict the Future
数字命理学——使用数字预测未来

Just as some people think that certain numbers are lucky or unlucky, others believe that we can use numbers to understand our personalities, or predict what will happen to us in the future. Numerology is a way of using numbers to describe a person's character, and to make predictions about future life events. Numerologists use the numbers 1 to 9, 11 and 22—also known as the "master" numbers—to help a person understand his or her personality, life goals, and destiny.

Numerologists consider your Life Path number to be the most significant because this number describes your character. To find this number, add together all the numbers in your date of birth. For example, a person born on April 25, 1985 would add the month (4), to the numbers of the date (2+5), plus the numbers of the birth year (1+9+8+5). If the final number is a double figure, it is added again until a number between 1 and 9, 11 or 22 is reached. In this case the total is 34, so this person's Life Path number is 7 (3+4). Numerologists believe that people with this number are peaceful, affectionate people who can also be very reserved.

Your Expression number describes your talents and predicts how you should use these to fulfill your destiny in life. Numerologists assign a number between 1 and 9 to each of the letters in your name. These numbers are then added together in the same way as before to find your Expression number. Numerologists can also do calculations to predict when the most challenging periods of your life will be.

Numerologists also believe that the day a person is born is important. Each day of the month has a character description. People born on the fourth are said to be responsible, honest, and stubborn. People born on the fifteenth have very strong attachments to family and home. Those who celebrate their birthday on the thirtieth are artistic, creative, and imaginative, and often make good writers.

If we calculate the numerical value of our name and birth date, numerologists believe that we can learn more about our personalities. They also believe that we can predict our destinies, how our lives will progress, and what challenges we may face along the way. To the numerologists, numbers can be used in many more ways than we think.

(393 words)

Word List

prediction	[prɪˈdɪkʃən]	n.	预言,预报
destiny	[ˈdestɪnɪ]	n.	命运,定数
significant	[sɪɡˈnɪfɪkənt]	adj.	有意义的,重大的,重要的
peaceful	[ˈpiːsfʊl]	adj.	和平的,安宁的
affectionate	[əˈfekʃənɪt]	adj.	亲爱的,挚爱的
reserved	[rɪˈzɜːvd]	adj.	保留的,包租的
fulfill	[fʊlˈfɪl]	v.	履行,实现,完成(计划)等
assign	[əˈsaɪn]	v.	分配,指派
calculate	[ˈkælkjʊleɪt]	v.	计算,考虑,计划,打算
responsible	[rɪˈspɒnsɪbl]	adj.	有责任的,负责的
stubborn	[ˈstʌbən]	adj.	顽固的,难应付的

Unit Eighteen

○ attachment	[əˈtætʃmənt]	n.	附件,附加装置
○ celebrate	[ˈselɪbreɪt]	n.	庆祝,表扬,赞美
○ artistic	[ɑːˈtɪstɪk]	adj.	艺术的,有美感的,风雅的
○ creative	[krɪˈeɪtɪv]	adj.	创造性的
○ imaginative	[ɪˈmædʒɪnətɪv]	adj.	想象的,虚构的
○ personality	[ˌpɜːsəˈnælɪtɪ]	n.	个性,人格,人物
○ progress	[ˈprəʊgres]	v.	前进,进步,进行
○ challenge	[ˈtʃælɪndʒ]	n.	挑战

Idioms & Expressions

in the way of	以……的方式(方法);关于……的方面
make prediction about	对……做出预测
be known as	被认为是
have attachment to	对……喜爱,爱慕,依恋

Exercises

1. [Definitions]

Match the words in the box with their meanings. Write the world that stands for the definition in the appropriate answer space.

prediction	personality	destiny	significant	affectionate	fulfill	assign
calculate	stubborn	attachment	creative	imaginative	progress	

1) _____ : to give out as a task; allot.

2) _____ : the pattern of collective character, behavioral, temperamental, emotional, and mental traits of a person.

3) _____ : to advance; proceed.

4) _____ : something foretold or predicted; a prophecy.

5) _____ : having the ability or power to create.

6) _____ : a bond, as of affection or loyalty; fond regard.

7) _____ : having a lively imagination, especially a creative imagination.

8) _____ : to bring into actuality; effect.

9) _____ : the inevitable or necessary fate to which a particular person or thing is destined; one's lot.

10) _____ : to ascertain by computation; reckon.
11) _____ : a bond, as of affection or loyalty; fond regard.
12) _____ : unreasonably, often perversely unyielding; bullheaded.
13) _____ : having or likely to have a major effect; important.

2. [Sample Sentences]

Use the new words and phrases you have learned from the box in the following sentences. Change the form where necessary.

1) There has been a _____ improvement in the company's safety record.
2) The economists _____ an increase in the rate of inflation.
3) If he's lazy, he'll never _____ his ambition to achieve anything.
4) She has already formed a strong _____ to her baby brother.
5) Though their _____ differed, they got along as friends.
6) The building of the largest bridge across the river in Adia is in _____.
7) The monitor was _____ to take notes for the meeting.
8) Human beings are _____ animals.
9) It was the great man's _____ to lead his country to freedom.
10) When the princess saw the little poor child, she gave him a _____ hug.
11) You can _____ my surprise when they told me the news.
12) Our price has already been closely _____. There is no room for reduction.
13) She won't do what I ask—she's very _____.

3. [Translation]

A. Translate the following English sentences into Chinese.

1) Numerology is a way of using numbers to describe a person's characters, and to make predictions about future life events.

2) Your Expression number describes your talents and predicts how you should use these to fulfill your destiny in life.

3) People born on the fifteenth have very strong attachments to family and home.

4) If we calculate the numerical value of our name and birth date, numerologists believe that we can learn more about our personalities.

5) Numerologists believe that people with this number are peaceful, affectionate people who can also be very reserved.

B. Translate the following Chinese into English by using the words in the bracket.

1) 同我们一样,他们也提前完成了任务。(fulfill)

2) 他向我挑战要我跟他再打一场网球。(challenge)

3) 科学家能准确地计算出太空船什么时候抵达月球。(calculate)

4) 公共汽车司机应对乘客的安全负责。(responsible)

5) 两国政府确定了下一轮谈判的日期。(assign)

4.【Writing】

Write a composition of about 200 words on the meaning of numbers. The composition should include the following points:

1) Numbers have different meanings in different cultures...
2) Different nations have their own lucky and unlucky numbers. These numbers show the particular cultural and social forms. Give some examples to explain the differences especially between China and the Western countries.
3) Express your opinions on numbers: Do you believe in that special numbers can bring you good or bad luck?

Reading Skills: 英语阅读中的重点句式 (5, 6)

5. 文章中段落的首尾句

英语文章中除了前面提到的四种句子外,文章中的每个段落的第一句和最后一句这种在特殊位置的句子通常也很重要,他们所表达的内容不是与文章全文的主题中心有关,就是与文章每个段落的段落大意有关。因此,重点阅读这些语句也会帮助大家迅速了解要点信息,抓住文章的主要内容。

6. 其他阅读中的重点句式

在进行英语文章阅读时,除了要多关注前面两课讲过的五种重点句式,还有一些特殊的句子对于把握文章大意和回答相关的问题也非常重要。如强调句,这种句子常用来突出主题和要点;如用词较少、结构明了的简单句和简短句,作者常用这种简洁明了的句子来明确表达出自己的观点和态度。因此,我们在进行英语文章的阅读和理解时,应该分清主次内容,把握要点句式和关键信息。

Text 2 (Extensive Reading)

Internet Addiction
网 络 成 瘾

The Internet is fast becoming just another part of everyday life, much like the TV and the computer itself. What started as something amazing, exciting, and often out of reach, has become commonplace and freely available. Technology is advancing at an amazing rate. I can remember when 56k connection were the new exciting fad that everyone just got to have, and now you're almost abnormal if you still chug along with your trusty dialup. The Net has become integrated into our lives, as people are becoming dependent on its services. The advent of the Internet has its threatening side thought. It has been found that some people are becoming addicted to the online world.

A recent news story reported that the Finnish army has sent some of its conscripts home due to the fact that they are unable to handle the compulsory six months in the army without access to their computers. When computers and the Internet are becoming an integral component or even the main focus of leisure, education, and work time, it's not hard to see how losing access can really affect someone. I can see this new technology getting blamed for all sorts of woes in the future much in the same way television has in the present.

Internet addiction comes in many forms. The common areas of Internet addiction that are often listed are cyber-sex, cyber-relations, gaming, information addiction, and the simple addiction to computers and Internet in general. Information addiction is an interesting concept to me. Basically the sheer volume of information freely available online has led to some people desperately "needing" to find out more and more. To me, getting people obsessed with learning seems kind of a good thing, but it can form a similar sort of mentality to drug addiction where the user is always searching for their next "hit" which becomes harder and harder to find. Often the depth of information available is actually lacking. We tend to skim information online by just picking out a few points and then moving on. I've found in my own case that it's something quite hard to concentrate on a page long enough to read it in its entirety. I tend to read a little until I get the basic idea and then move on. This process has carried over into the "real world" in some way with newspapers rarely keeping may interest long enough to actually get through a whole article of any real length. I've witnessed similar experiences with friends and families and I think that attention spans are gradually getting shorter.

This means that probably more than half of the people who come across this article have stopped reading by now. Their interest has waned and they've moved on to the next tidbit. I could probably get away with padding the end of this article with the word "chicken" and it would go relatively unnoticed due to the skimming nature of article reading.

　　A quick Internet search will reveal that Internet addiction is actually more of a problem than many would choose to believe. There are several websites and foundation on the Web dedicated to helping people get over their Internet addiction. I found that humorously ironic... websites dedicated to helping people get over Internet addiction ... it's kind of like printing anti-drinking messages on the inside bottom of a beer can. The cynic in me can't help but wonder about the validity of these online services. A common question in the "Could You Be Addicted to the Internet?" questionnaires is "Do you have trouble controlling the urge to make purchases online?", and then they encourage you to send them $90 to book an online chat room counseling session!

　　It shouldn't be too hard to work out if you're addicted to the Internet. Do you find that when you get offline you're frequently surprised by the amount of time that has passed? Do you find yourself staying home because you'd rather use the Internet than do something else? Do people comment on the amount of time you spend online? If this is ringing a bell then you may have to look at what you're doing.

　　I don't know how severe Internet addiction can get. Presumably it's as problematic as any other addiction. I shouldn't downplay it or the therapy institutions out there offering help. I will take a guess and say that, at least to some degree, people simply being aware of what can happen can probably prevent it. Don't be afraid to do something if you notice problems in yourself or a friend. Just try cutting back on your usage for a while until it's under your control. Like any other problem, don't be afraid to get friends involved. If it's particularly serious you could try installing a parental control program that limits your access to the Internet, and get a friend to choose and keep the disabling password secret from you. Stay aware, alert, and in control and your Internet use can and will be a beneficial part of life.

(839 words)

Word List

commonplace	['kɒmənpleɪs]	adj.	平常的,普通的,平庸的
fad	[fæd]	n.	时尚,一时的爱好
abnormal	[æb'nɔːməl]	adj.	反常的,变态的
chug	[tʃʌg]	v.	发出轧轧声
integrate	['ɪntɪgreɪt]	v.	结合,使成整体,使一体化
threaten	['θretn]	v.	恐吓,威胁
handle	['hændl]	v.	处理,操作,运用
access	['ækses]	n.	通路,访问,入门
integral	['ɪntɪgrəl]	adj.	完整的,整体的
component	[kəm'pəʊnənt]	n.	成分

leisure	[ˈleʒə]	n.	空闲,闲暇,悠闲,安逸
cyber	[saɪbə]	adj.	(前缀)计算机的,网络的
sheer	[ʃɪə]	adj.	纯粹的,绝对的,彻底的
desperately	[ˈdespərɪtlɪ]	adv.	拼命地,绝望地
obsess	[əbˈses]	v.	迷住,使困扰
witness	[ˈwɪtnɪs]	v.	目击,作证,证明
concentrate	[ˈkɒnsəntreɪt]	v.	集中,浓缩
span	[spæn]	n.	跨度,跨距,范围
tidbit	[ˈtɪd,bɪt]	n.	珍闻,小栏报道
reveal	[rɪˈviːl]	v.	显示,揭示,暴露
dedicate	[ˈdedɪkeɪt]	v.	献身,致力
ironic	[aɪˈrɒnɪk]	adj.	说反话的,讽刺的
cynic	[ˈsɪnɪk]	n.	愤世嫉俗者
questionnaire	[ˌkwestʃəˈneə]	n.	调查表,问卷
comment	[ˈkɒment]	n.	评论,意见
therapy	[ˈθerəpɪ]	n.	治疗

Idioms & Expressions

be addicted to...	沉溺于,对……上瘾	all sorts of	各种各样的
be obsessed with	被……缠住/迷住	pick out	挑选
concentrate on	集中于,全神贯注于……	come across	来到,偶遇
get over	克服,熬过,恢复		
ring a bell	唤醒,回忆起,引起反应		

Exercises

1. 〖Questions〗

Based on the information provided in the text, answer the following questions briefly.

1) What do people think of the Internet nowadays?

2) What are the common areas of Internet addiction?

3) How does the Internet change people's habits?

4) Is it easy to get over Internet addiction? Why and why not?

5) What do you think you should get along with the Internet?

2. [Multiple Choices]

Choose the right answer from the four choices marked A, B, C and D.

1) Why the Finnish Army had to send some of the conscripts home?
    A. Because they are unable to do the compulsory service.
    B. Because they are unable to handle the computer.
    C. Because they are unable to handle the life without computer.
    D. Because they have no leisure time to play the computer.

2) The sheer volume of information freely available online has led to _____.
    A. read the entity of a long passage
    B. skim the information online by just picking out a few points
    C. rarely read newspaper
    D. people's longer attention span

3) Quick Internet search will reveal that Internet addiction is _____.
    A. to get people obsessed with online learning
    B. troublesome cyber-relations
    C. humorous and ironic
    D. a bigger problem than many people believe

4) Printing anti-drinking messages on the inside bottom of a beer can is _____.
    A. ironic   B. valid   C. amusing   D. effective

5) Which one is not to help you prevent the addiction of Internet?
    A. Installing a personal control system.
    B. Ask your friend to change your password.
    C. Notice the problem of your friends.
    D. Find the beneficial part of the Internet.

6) According to the passage, which statement is not right?
    A. The Internet is becoming part of everyday life like TV and computer.
    B. Computer and TV are main focus of leisure, education and work time.
    C. Internet makes us more focused.
    D. Internet addiction is similar to the sort of mentality of drug addiction.

Text 3 (Fast Reading)

Can Animals Sense Earthquakes?
动物能感知地震吗？

The belief that animals can predict earthquakes has been around for centuries.

In 373 B.C., historians recorded that animals, including rats, snakes and weasels, deserted the Greek city of Helice in droves just days before a quake devastated the place.

Accounts of similar animal anticipation of earthquakes have surfaced across the centuries since. Catfish moving violently, chickens that stop laying eggs and bees leaving their hive in a panic have been reported. Countless pet owners claimed to have witnessed their cats and dogs acting strangely before the ground shook-barking or whining for no apparent reason, or showing sighs of nervousness and restlessness.

But precisely what animals sense, if they feel anything at all, is a mystery. One theory is that wild and domestic creatures fell the Earth vibrate before humans. Other ideas suggest they detect electrical changes in the air or gas released from the Earth.

Earthquakes are a sudden phenomenon. Seismologists have no way of knowing exactly when or where the next one will hit. An estimated 500,000 detectable quakes occur in the world each year. Of those, 100,000 can be felt by humans, and 100 cause damage.

One of the world's most earthquake-prone countries is Japan, where devastation has taken countless lives and caused enormous damage to property. Researchers there have long studied animals in hopes of discovering what they hear or feel before the Earth shakes in order to use that sense as a prediction tool.

American seismologists, on the other hand, are skeptical. Even though there have been documented cases of strange animal behavior prior to earthquakes, the United States Geological Survey, a government agency that provides scientific information about the Earth, says a reproducible connection between a specific behavior and the occurrence of a quake has never been made.

"What we're faced with is a lot of anecdotes," said Andy Michael, a geophysicist at USGS. "Animals react to so many things—being hungry, defending their territories, mating, predators—so it's hard to have a controlled study to get that advanced warning signal."

In the 1970s, a few studies on animal prediction were done by the USGS, "but nothing concrete came out of it," said Michael. Since that time the agency has made no further investigations into the theory.

Researchers around the world continue to purse the idea, however. In September 2003 a medical doctor in Japan made headlines with a study that indicated erratic behavior in dogs, such as excessive barking or biting, could be used to forecast quakes.

There have also been examples where authorities have forecast successfully a major earthquake, based in part on the observation of the strange antics of animals. For example, in 1975 Chinese officials ordered the evacuation of Haicheng, a city with one million people, just days before a 7.3-magnitude quake. Only a small portion of the population was hurt or killed. If the city had not been evacuated, it is estimated that the number of fatalities and injuries could have exceeded 150,000.

The Haicheng incident is what gave people hope that earthquakes might be predictable, says Michael, and what promoted the animal behavior studies by the USGS.

It was later discovered, though, that a rare serried of small tremors, called foreshocks, occurred before the large quake hit the city.

"It was the foreshock sequence that gave the sold prediction." Michael said.

Still, the Chinese have continued to look at animal behavior as an aid to earthquake prediction. They have had several notable successes and also a few false alarms, said Rupert Sheldrake, a biologist and author of the books, *Dogs that Know When Their Owners Are Coming Home* and *The Sense of Being Stared At*.

A reproducible connection between animal and earthquakes could be made, he said, but "as the Chinese have discovered, not all earthquakes cause unusual animal behavior while others do. Only through research could we find out why there might be such differences."

Sheldrake did his own study looking at animal reactions before major tremors, including the Northridge, California quake in 1994, and the Greek and Turkish quakes in 1999.

In all cases, he said, there were reports of peculiar behavior beforehand, including dogs howling in the night mysteriously, caged birds becoming restless, and nervous cats hiding.

Geologists, however, dismiss these kinds of reports, saying it's "the psychological focusing effect", where people remember strange behavior only after an earthquake or other catastrophe has taken place. If nothing had happened, they contend, people would not have remembered the strange behavior.

Sheldrake disagrees, "Comparable patterns of animal behavior prior to earthquakes have been reported independently by people all over the world," he said. "I cannot believe that they could all have made up such similar stories or that they all suffered from tricks of memory."

More research is needed and is long overdue, said Sheldrake, who proposes a special hotline or website where people could call or write in if they saw strange behavior in their animals. A computer would then analyze the incoming messages to determine where they originated. A sudden surge of calls or E-mails from a particular region might indicate that a quake was imminent.

The information would be checked to make sure the observations were not caused by other circumstances known to affect the behavior of animals, such as fireworks, or changes in weather. And to avoid issuing false warnings, Sheldrake said, the data would be used in conjunction with other monitoring devices such as seismological measurements.

"Such a project would capture the imagination of millions of people, encourage large-scale participation and research—and would be fun." He said. "What is holding this research back is not money but dogmatism and narrow-mindedness."

(940 words)

Exercises

1. [True, False, Not Given]

Decide whether the following statements are True, False or Not Given.

T (for True) if the statement agrees with the information given in the passage;

F (for False) if the statement doesn't agree with the information given in the passage.

NG (for Not Given) if the information is not given in the passage.

1) An estimated 500,000 detectable quakes occur in the world each year. Of those, 100,000 can be felt by humans, and 1,000 cause damage.

2) One of the world's most earthquake-prone countries is Japan, where devastation has taken countless lives and caused enormous damage to property.

3) The United States Geological Survey says a reproducible connection between a specific behavior and the occurrence of a quake has never been made.

4) In September 2003 a medical doctor in Japan made headlines with a study that indicated erratic behavior in dogs, such as excessive barking or biting, could be used to forecast quakes.

5) The Chinese have continued to look at animal behavior as an aid to earthquake prediction. They have had several successes and also a few false alarms.

6) Geologists say that people remember strange behavior only after an earthquake or other catastrophe has taken place. If nothing had happened, they contend, people would not have remembered the strange behavior.

7) Fireworks or changes in weather may also affect the behavior of animals.

2. [Blank-Filling]

For questions 1)–3), complete the sentences with the information given in the passage.

1) Before the earthquake, countless pet owners claimed to have witnessed their cats and dogs _____.

2) Before the large quake hit the city, it was later discovered that a rare series of small tremors, called _____, occurred.

3) Sheldrake did his own study looking at _____ before major tremors.

附录(Appendix)

2007年6月高等学校英语应用能力A级试题(阅读部分)

Part III Reading Comprehension (40 minutes)

Task 1

Directions: After reading the following passage, you will find 5 questions or unfinished statements, marked 36 to 40. For each question or statement there are 4 choices marked A, B, C and D. You should make the correct choice and mark the corresponding letter on the Answer Sheet with a single line through the center.

Everybody had an opinion about telecommuting (远程办公). "It won't work in most jobs", "It costs too much", "It reduces air pollution", "It helps people balance family and work responsibilities", and "Most people are doing it".

In reality, researchers continue to find strong growth and acceptance of telecommuting. Nearly two-thirds of the top 1000 companies in the world have a telecommuting program, and 92 percent say it reduces cost and improves worker productivity(生产力). The days of everyone commuting to the office five days a week are quickly disappearing.

Telecommuting involves a non-traditional work arrangement enabling workers to work at home or elsewhere, some or all of the time. This is not a new, novel, or untested way of working.

But is it for you? Telecommuting is not a panacea (万能药). Whether you are a manager, or an HR (Human Resources) specialist, there are decisions to make and actions to take before you begin a telecommuting arrangement.

Join us for any or all of the following meetings to get answers, information, and resources to develop and carry out a successful telecommuting arrangement. Each meeting offers you an informative presentation followed by the opportunity for a discussion with a panel of "experts" who have made telecommuting work for them.

36. How do people look at telecommuting according to the first paragraph?
    A. They are against it.   B. They don't care about it.
    C. They share the same view.   D. They differ in their opinions.
37. According to the response of most of the top 1000 companies, telecommuting _____.
    A. increases worker productivity   B. will disappear in the near future
    C. can not be accepted by the public D. is practiced in all the top companies

38. Which is the following statements is TRUE of telecommuting?

   A. It is up to the employees to accept it or not.

   B. It is getting popular in different companies.

   C. It is a new untested way of working.

   D. It is a traditional work arrangement.

39. Before beginning a telecommuting arrangement, the management should _____.

   A. appoint a new HR specialist to

   B. provide the facilities and conditions

   C. improve the company's productivity first

   D. decide whether it is suitable for the company

40. According to the last paragraph, meetings are held to _____.

   A. appreciate the efforts of the telecommuting companies

   B. discuss the employment of telecommuting experts

   C. help introduce the practice of telecommuting

   D. train people before they start telecommuting

Task 2

Directions: This task is the same as Task 1. The 5 questions or unfinished statements are numbered 41 to 45.

Rockwatch—The Best Club on Earth

　　If you are a young person and interested in geology (地质学), then Rockwatch is the club for you!

　　When you join New memberships receive a Rockwatch Rox file each. This has the information and top tips you will need to start enjoying geology.　It's designed to serve as your own field notebook as well.

　　In it you will find your membership card full color mini-map thumbs up guide fact cards.

Rockwatch Magazine

　　Our lively magazine is mailed to members three times a year. They can read reports and news from around the world, and articles on everything from diamonds to dinosaurs (恐龙), earthquakes to erosion (水土流失).

Rockwatch Events

　　With each magazine you will receive a Rockwatch events calendar. Rocky activities suitable for families are listed and include road shows and guided walks.

The Rockwatch Rock Artist

　　Are you an artist, or a photographer? This is your chance to become Rockwatch Rock Artist of the Year and win amazing prizes in our annual competition.

Special Offer

　　Rockwatch members can have specially discounted Wildlife Watch memberships. Watch is the biggest environmental action club for young people, with 100 groups across the country. You can join both clubs together by filling in the boxes in the membership form.

41. New Rockwatch Rox Club members will obtain a special file when they _____.
    A. do field work			B. join the club
    C. buy a field notebook		D. start studying geology
42. Rockwatch is a magazine telling about things related to _____.
    A. geology			B. agriculture
    C. politics			D. economics
43. What activities are specially arranged for Rockwatch members interested in photograph?
    A. Guided walks.		B. Rocky activities.
    C. Yearly competitions.		D. Academic workshops.
44. When applying for Wildlife Watch membership, a Rockwatch member can enjoy _____.
    A. free membership		B. a special discount
    C. a Rock Artist prize		D. guided road shows
45. You may join both Rockwatch and Wildlife Watch clubs by _____.
    A. calling the two clubs	B. providing references
    C. applying separately		D. filling in one form

Task 3

Directions: The following is an advertisement. After reading it, you should complete the information by filling in the blanks marker 46 to 50 in not more than 3 words in the table below.

NUROFEN RECOVERY (纽洛芬去痛片)

Please read these instructions carefully before you take this medicine.

Nurofen Recovery dissolves(溶解) quickly on the tongue without the need to use water. It delivers effective relief from headaches.

You should not take Nurofen Recovery if:

— you have had an allergic (过敏的) reaction to aspirin (阿司匹林)
— you have had a worsening of asthma (哮喘) when taking aspirin or similar medicines
— you are under 12 years of age

Administration

Place a tablet on the tongue, allow it to dissolve and then swallow—no water is required.

Adults, the elderly and children of 12 years and older:

Take 2 tablets, then if necessary, take 1 or 2 tablets every 4 hours. Do not exceed 6 tablets in 24 hours. Not suitable for children under 12 years.

Warnings:

If you take too many tablets by mistake, contact your doctor as soon as possible.

If symptoms persist or if new symptoms occur, consult your doctor.

Possible side effects:

Stomach discomfort or pain, worsening of asthma or shortness of breath. If you experience any of these, stop taking the tablets and see your doctor.

NUROFEN RECOVERY

Function: delivering (46) _____ to live a healthier life

Doctors' advice and other (47) _____.

People not intended for:

1) patients with an allergic reaction to aspirin

2) patients having asthma when taking aspirin

3) children under the age of (48) _____

Dosage:

1) Staring Dose: 2 tablets

2) If necessary: take 1 or 2 tablets (49) _____

3) Maximum daily intake: 6 tablets

Possible side effects:

1) stomach discomfort

2) worsening of asthma

3) (50) _____

Task 4

Directions: The following is a list of terms frequently used in medical services. After reading it, you are required to find the items equivalent to (与……等同) those given in Chinese in the list below. Then you should put the corresponding letters in brackets on the Answer Sheet, numbered 51 through 55.

A ---------- Waiting and Boarding

B ---------- Luggage Delivery

C ---------- Inspection and Quarantine

D ---------- Getting a Boarding Pass

E ---------- Security Check

F ---------- Domestic Departure

G ---------- Over-sized Luggage Checked-in

H ---------- Goods Prohibited to be Hand-carried

I ---------- Duty-free Articles

J ---------- Customs Declaration Form

K ---------- Quantity Allowed to Take

L ---------- Regulations on Restriction of Liquids

M ---------- Temporary Boarding ID Card

N ---------- Guide to Outgoing Passengers

O ---------- Goods Prohibited to Exit the Country

P ---------- Restriction of Hand Carry-on Articles

Q ---------- Detection Passage

Example: (L) 限定液体物品的规定 _____ (C) 检查与检疫

51. 离港旅客指南 _____ 领取登机牌
52. 禁止携带出境的物品 _____ 大件行李托运
53. 候机／登机 _____ 禁止随身携带的物品
54. 限带物品数量 _____ 检查通道
55. 海关申报表 _____ 免税物品

Task 5

Directions: There is an advertisement blow. After reading it, you are required to complete the statements that follow the questions (No. 56 to No. 60). You should write your answers in no more than 3 words on the Answer Sheet correspondingly.

When you buy life insurance, you want a policy that fits your needs at a reasonable cost. Your first step is to determine how much life insurance you need. Next, you need to decide how much money you can afford to pay. Finally, you must choose the type of policy that meets your coverage (保险类别) goals and fits into your financial plan. Once you have completed these steps, you will be able to move ahead and contact several life insurance companies through an agent who will shop for the right type of policy for you.

There are many reasons for purchasing life insurance, among which are the following:
1. Insurance to provide family protection and financial security to surviving family members upon the death of the insured person.
2. Insurance to cover a particular need upon the insured's death such as paying off a mortgage or other debts.

56. What should you take into consideration when choosing a life insurance policy?
    Both your needs and the _____.
57. What's the relationship between the type of policy and your financial plan?
    The type of policy should meet your _____.
58. Who can help you buy the right type of policy from an insurance company?
    _____.
59. Who will benefit from the life insurance upon the death of the insured person?
    Surviving _____.
60. What is the second goal for buying life insurance?
    To pay off a mortgage or _____ after death.

2007年6月高等学校英语应用能力B级试题(阅读部分)

Part III Reading Comprehension (40 minutes)

Task 1

Directions: After reading the following passage, you will find 5 questions or unfinished statements, marked 36 to 40. For each question or statement there are 4 choices marked A, B, C and D. You should make the correct choice and mark the corresponding letter on the Answer Sheet with a single line through the center.

We've found that eating habits vary (变化) so much that it does not make sense to include meals in the price of our tours. We want to give you the freedom of choosing restaurants and ordering food that suits your taste and budget (预算).

As your hotels offer anything from coffee and toast to a full American breakfast at very reasonable prices, it will never be a problem for you to start the day in the way you like best. At lunch stops, your tour guide will show you where you can find salads, soups, and sandwiches.

Dinner time is your chance to try some local food. Sometimes the tour guide will let you have dinner at a restaurant of your own choice. At other times he or she will recommend a restaurant at your hotel. Years of research have taught us which restaurants reliably serve a good choice of delightful dishes at down-to-earth prices.

In Mexico, Alaska, and the Yukon, where your restaurant choice may be limited, we include some meals. The meals provided are clearly stated on the tour pages.

36. According to the passage, most meals are not included in the price of tours mainly because _____.

   A. meals make up a large part of the tour budget
   B. meal prices vary a lot from place to place
   C. people dislike menus offered by tour guides
   D. people have different eating habits

37. We can learn from the passage that _____.

   A. the hotels where you stay will offer you free breakfast
   B. dining information can be obtained from your tour guides
   C. you can have a complete choice of local dishes at the hotel
   D. a full list of local restaurants can be found on the tour pages

38. Which of the following statements is TRUE?

   A. Tour guides are supposed to arrange dinner outside the hotel.
   B. Tour guides' recommendations on food are unreliable.
   C. Tourists must have lunch in the hotels they stay in.
   D. Tourists may taste local dishes during dinner time.

39. The word "down-to-earth" (Line 4, Para.3) most probably means _____.

   A. changeable   B. expensive
   C. reasonable   D. fixed

40. Meals are included in the tour price in some places where _____.

   A. restaurant choice may be limited
   B. there are many nearby restaurants
   C. delightful dishes are not served
   D. food may be too expensive

Task 2

Directions: This task is the same as Task 1. The 5 questions or unfinished statements are numbered 41 to 45.

Some cities have planned their transportation systems for car owners. That is what Los Angeles did. Los Angeles decided to build highways for cars rather than spending money on public transportation.

This decision was suitable for Los Angeles. The city grew outward instead of upward. Los Angeles never built many tall apartment buildings. Instead, people live in houses with gardens.

In Los Angeles, most people drive cars to work. And every car has to have a parking space. So many buildings where people work also have parking lots.

Los Angeles also became a city without a Central Business District(CBD). If a city has a CBD, crowds of people rush into it every day to work. If people drive to work, they need lots of road space.

So Los Angeles developed several business districts and built homes and other buildings in between the districts. This required more roads and parking spaces.

Some people defend this growth pattern. They say Los Angeles is the city of the future.

41. According to the passage, Los Angeles is a city where _____.

   A. there is no public transportation system
   B. more money is spent on highways for cars
   C. more money is spent on public transportation systems
   D. public transportation is more developed than in other cities

42. "The city grew outward instead of upward" (Line1, Para.2) means _____.

   A. the city became more spread out instead of growing taller
   B. there were fewer small houses than tall buildings
   C. rapid development took place in the city center
   D. many tall buildings could be found in the city.

43. According to the passage, if a city has several business districts, _____.

   A. people won't have to drive to work every day
   B. there have to more roads and parking spaces

C. companies would be located in between the districts

D. there would be no need to build parking spaces within the districts

44. According to the growth pattern of Los Angeles, homes were mainly built _____.

   A. in the city center
   B. along the main roads
   C. around business districts
   D. within the business districts

45. The passage is mainly about _____.

   A. the construction of parking spaces in Los Angeles
   B. the new growth pattern of the city of Los Angeles
   C. the public transportation system in Los Angeles
   D. the problem of traffic jams in Los Angeles

Task 3

Directions: The following is an advertisement. After reading it, you should complete the information by filling in the blanks marker 46 to 50 in not more than 3 words in the table below.

Trip Reports

Many companies require their employees to hand in reports of their business trips. A trip report not only provides a written record of a business trip and its activities, but also enables many employees to benefit from the information one employee has gained.

Generally, a trip report should be in the form of a memorandum(内部通知), addressed to your immediate boss. The places and dates of the trip are given on the subject line. The body of the report will explain why you made the trip, whom you visited, and what you did. The report should give a brief account of each major event. You needn't give equal space to each event. Instead, you should focus on the more important events. Follow the body of the report with a conclusion.

A Trip Report

Reported by: an employee back from a business trip

Addressed to: his or her immediate (46) _____

Used for:

1. serving as a written record

2. giving helpful (47) _____ that can be shared by others

Written in the form of: a (48) _____

Information to be included in the report: _____

1. the places and dates of the trip on (49) _____

2. major event(s) during the trip in the (50) _____ of the report

3. conclusion

Task 4

Directions: The following is a list of terms frequently used in medical services. After reading it, you are required to find the items equivalent to (与……等同) those given in Chinese in the list below. Then you should put the corresponding letters in brackets on the Answer Sheet, numbered 51 through 55.

A ---- information desk
B ---- ticket office
C ---- half fare ticket
D ---- waiting room
E ---- excess baggage charge
F ---- baggage check-in counter
G ---- security check
H ---- platform underpass
I ---- ticket agent
J ---- departure board
K ---- railroad track
L ---- traffic light
M ---- railroad crossing
N ---- soft sleeping car
O ---- hard sleeping car
P ---- hard seat
Q ---- baggage-claim area

Example: (O) 行李认领处   (E) 超重行李费

51. 硬座   软座
52. 开车时间显示器   信号灯
53. 站台地下通道   候车室
54. 问询处   安全检查
55. 半价票   售票处

Task 5

Directions: There is an advertisement blow. After reading it, you are required to complete the statements that follow the questions (No. 56 to No. 60). You should write your answers in no more than 3 words on the Answer Sheet correspondingly.

Problems
    Probable causes
    Suggested solutions
    The display is showing the sign ":".
    There has been a power interruption.
    Reset (重新设置) the clock.
    The fan seems to be running slower than usual.

The oven has been stored in a cold area.

The fan will run slower until the oven warms up to normal room temperature.

The display shows a time counting down but the oven is not cooking.

The oven door is not closed completely.

Close the door completely.

You have set the controls as a kitchen timer (定时器).

Touch OFF/CANCEL to cancel the Minute Timer.

The turntable (转盘) will not turn.

The support is not operating correctly.

Check the turntable support is properly in place, and restart the oven.

The microwave oven will not run.

The door is not firmly closed.

Close the door firmly.

You did not touch the button "START".

Touch the button "START".

You did not follow directions exactly.

Follow the directions exactly.

56. What should you do if the display is showing the sign ":"?
    Reset _____.

57. What is the probable cause if the fan seems to be running slower than usual?
    The oven has been put in a _____.

58. What are you advised to do if you have set the controls as a kitchen timer?
    Touch OFF/CANCEL to cancel the _____.

59. What is the cause for the turntable to fail to run?
    _____ is not operating correctly.

60. What will happen if you do not touch the button "START"?
    The microwave oven _____.

2006年12月高等学校英语应用能力A级试题(阅读部分)

Part III Reading Comprehension (40 minutes)

Task 1

Directions: After reading the following passage, you will find 5 questions or unfinished statements, marked 36 to 40. For each question or statement there are 4 choices marked A, B, C and D. You should make the correct choice and mark the corresponding letter on the Answer Sheet with a single line through the center.

We don't have beds in the spacecraft, but we do have sleeping bags. During the day, when we are working, we leave the bags tied to the wall, out of the way. At bedtime we untie them and take them wherever we've chosen to sleep.

On most spacecraft flights everyone sleeps at the same time. No one has to stay awake to watch over the spacecraft; the craft's computers call us on the radio.

On the spacecraft, sleep-time doesn't mean nighttime. During each ninety-minute orbit (轨道) the sun "rises" and shines through our windows for about fifty minutes, then it "sets" as the spacecraft takes us around the dark side of the Earth. To keep the sun out of our eyes, we wear black sleep masks.

It is surprisingly easy to get comfortable and fall asleep in space. Every astronaut (宇航员) sleeps differently: some sleep upside down, some sideways, and some right side up. When it's time to sleep, I take my bag, my sleep mask and my tape player with earphones and float (漂浮) up to the flight deck (驾驶舱). Then I get into the bag, and float in a sitting position just above a seat, right next to a window. Before I pull the mask down over my eyes, I relax for a while, listening to music and watching the Earth go by under me.

36. When the astronauts are working, sleeping bags are fastened _____.
    A. on the wall   B. to their seats
    C. onto the flight deck D. anywhere they like
37. Why can all the astronauts sleep at the same time?
    A. They have to follow the same timetable.
    B. The radio will take care of the aircraft for them.
    C. There are enough sleeping bags in the spacecraft.
    D. There is no need for them to watch over the spacecraft.
38. To relax himself before sleep, the writer often _____.
    A. makes a bed   B. gets into his bag
    C. listens to music   D. wears a sleep mask
39. How long does it take the spacecraft to go round the Earth?
    A. Forty minutes.   B. Fifty minutes.
    C. Ninety minutes.   D. Twenty-four hours.
40. The best title for this passage is _____.
    A. Traveling in Space   B. Sleeping in the Spacecraft
    C. Equipment Used by Astronauts   D. The Earth Seen from Outer Space

Task 2

Directions: This task is the same as Task 1. The 5 questions or unfinished statements are numbered 41 to 45.

Whenever traveling on Shanghai Airlines (SAL) flights with paid tickets, you will earn air miles according to the class shown on your tickets. When you have accumulated enough air miles, you can apply for a premium (奖励) ticket or other premium items.

Passengers (12 years old and over) are eligible (合格的) to join SAL FFP(Frequent Flying Passenger) Club unless it is banned (禁止) by the law of the country where they live.

Please fill out the application form on the back and mail it to the Customer Service Center of SAL. SAL Customer Center will mail the membership card and manual to you within 30 working days after receiving your Application Form.

Please show your membership card when you check in at an airport.

Please retain a photocopy of the ticket, the original boarding pass as well as a photocopy of your receipts after traveling or making purchases at ASL partner businesses until you confirm the record has been charged to your account.

If you flew SAL 3 months before your registration of SAL FFP Club, please mail to SAL Customer Service Center a copy of your ticket and the original boarding pass with your card number on it for recording air miles.

The Application Form can be used by one person only, and copies are void (无效).

For more information, please refer to the SAL FFP Program Guide.

41. What does SAL stand for in this passage?
    A. Shanghai Airport.   B. Shanghai Airlines.
    C. Shenzhen Airport.   D. South Airlines.
42. Who can apply for a premium ticket form SAL according to the passage?
    A. A passage who has traveled several times by plane.
    B. A passenger who wants to travel on any airlines flight.
    C. A passenger who has traveled on Shanghai Airlines flights.
    D. A passenger who has accumulated enough air miles on SAL flights.
43. What's the legal age to join SAL FFP Club according to the passage?
    A. 11 and under   B. 12 and under
    C. 12 and over   D. 18 and over
44. Whom should the application form be sent to if you want to apply for SAL FFP Membership?
    A. SAL FFP Club   B. The SAL ticket office
    C. The SAL headquarters.   D. SAL Customer Service Center
45. When they check in at an airport, Club members should show _____.
    A. their boarding pass   B. their membership card..
    C. a photocopy of the ticket.   D. an application form.

Task 3

Directions: The following is an advertisement. After reading it, you should complete the information by filling in the blanks marker 46 to 50 in not more than 3 words in the table below.

DISCLAIMER: This e-mail is confidential and should not be used by anyone who is not the original intended recipient (收件人). If you have received this e-mail in error, please inform the sender and delete it form your mailbox or any other storage mechanism (存储器). Neither Macmillan Publishers Limited nor any of its agents accept any responsibility for any statements which are clearly the sender's own and not expressly (明确无误地) made on behalf of Macmillan Publishers Limited or one of its agents. Please note that neither Macmillan Publishers Limited nor any of its agents accept any responsibility for viruses that may be contained in the e-mail or its attachments and it is your responsibility to scan the e-mail and attachments (if any). No contracts may be concluded on behalf of Macmillan Publishers Limited or its agent by means of e-mail communication.

Macmillan Publishers Limited

Registered Office

Brunel Road, Houndmills

Basingstoke RG21 6XS

E-mail Disclaimer

From: (46) _____

User of the e-mail: the (47) _____.

No responsibility accepted by Macmillan for:

a) any (48) _____ which are the sender's own

b) (49) _____ possibly contained in this e-mail

c) contracts concluded by means of (50) _____

Task 4

Directions: The following is a list of terms frequently used in medical services. After reading it, you are required to find the items equivalent to (与……等同) those given in Chinese in the list below. Then you should put the corresponding letters in brackets on the Answer Sheet, numbered 51 through 55.

A--- Advanced Mathematics

B--- Experiment in College Physics

C--- Fundamentals of Laws

D--- Theory of Circuitry

E--- Circuit Measurement Technology

F--- Optimum Control

G--- Signal & Linear Systems

H--- Electrical Engineering Practice

I--- Experiment in Electronic Circuitry

J--- Principles of Microcomputers

K--- Motor Elements and Power Supply

L--- Auto-measurement Techniques

M--- Automatic Control Systems

N--- Microcomputer control Technology

O--- Basis of Software Techniques

P--- Principles of Mechanics

Q--- Digital Image Processing

Example: (A) 高等数学   (J) 微机原理

51. 自动控制系统   法律基础
52. 数字图像处理   电路测量技术
53. 软件技术基础   信号与线性系统
54. 自动检测技术   大学物理实验
55. 电工实习   微机控制技术

Task 5

Directions: There is an advertisement blow. After reading it, you are required to complete the statements that follow the questions (No. 56 to No. 60). You should write your answers in no more than 3 words on the Answer Sheet correspondingly.

Sunburst Hotel

Location: On Waikiki Beach facing the ocean on one of the main beaches on the island of Oahu.

Accommodation: A large complex including 32 houses, two 12-storey towers with 245 rooms and a 16-storey tower with 300 rooms. Room choices include one or two king or queen size beds or 2 double beds. Each room has a shower, hair-dryer, coffee maker, mini-fridge, in-room sage, phone, TV with pay movies and radio.

Facilities: Two restaurants, three bars and four loungers (休息厅) provide excellent food, relaxation and entertainment 24 hours a day. There are also a tour desk, gift shops, laundry facilities and pay parking. Our room service is prompt and reasonable.

Amusement: Two large swimming pools and a very large fitness (健身) center with three full-time staff.

Special feature: Children under 16 stay free when sharing with an adult (one adult per child). More than one child per adult is half price. Coupon (优惠券): All guests receive a coupon book upon check-in. It offers discounts on dining, shopping, entertainment and other activities.

56. Where is the hotel located on the island of Oahu?
   On _____.
57. How many rooms are there altogether in the tower buildings?
   There are altogether _____ rooms.
58. How is the room service in the hotel?
   _____.
59. How much will you pay for your second child if you take two children along?
   _____.
60. What's the use of the coupon book?
   With the coupon book, guests can get _____ on dining, shopping, etc. in the hotel.

2006年12月高等学校英语应用能力B级试题（阅读部分）

Part III Reading Comprehension (40 minutes)

Task 1

Directions: After reading the following passage, you will find 5 questions or unfinished statements, marked 36 to 40. For each question or statement there are 4 choices marked A, B, C and D. You should make the correct choice and mark the corresponding letter on the Answer Sheet with a single line through the center.

People who work night shifts are constantly fighting against an "internal clock" in their bodies. Quite often the clock tells them to sleep when their job requires them to remain fully awake. It's no wonder that more accidents happen during night shifts than at any other time. Light therapy (照光疗法) with a bright light box can help night-shift workers adjust their internal clock. However, many doctors recommend careful planning to help improve sleep patterns. For example, night-shift workers often find it difficult to sleep in the morning when they get off work because the body's natural rhythm (节律) fights back, no matter how tired they are. Some experts recommend that night-shift workers schedule two smaller sleep periods—one in the morning after work, and another longer one in the afternoon, closer to when the body would naturally need to sleep. It's also helpful to ask friends and family to cooperate by avoiding visits and phone calls during the times when you are sleeping.

36. Night-shift workers are those who _____.
　　A. have to rely on their internal clock　　B. need to re-adjust their clock
　　C. fall asleep late at night　　D. have to work at night

37. In order to remain fully awake at work, people working night shifts should _____.
　　A. have longer sleep periods after work　　B. make the light darker than usual
　　C. try to re-set their "internal clock"　　D. pay more attention to their work

38. Many doctors think it is helpful for night-shift workers _____.
　　A. to sleep with a bright light on　　B. to plan sleep patterns
　　C. to avoid being disturbed at work　　D. to sleep for a long time after work

39. Night-shift workers often find it difficult to sleep in the morning because _____.
　　A. their internal clock will not allow them to
　　B. they are often disturbed by morning visits
　　C. they are not trying hard enough to do so
　　D. they are too tired to go to sleep well

40. According to the passage, some doctors recommend that night-shift workers should _____.
　　A. have frequent visits and phone calls　　B. improve their family relationship
　　C. have two smaller sleep periods　　D. rely mainly on light therapy

Task 2

Directions: This task is the same as Task 1. The 5 questions or unfinished statements are numbered 41 to 45.

A few ways Greyhound can make your next trip even easier.

Tickets By Mail. Avoid lining up together, by purchasing your tickets in advance, and having them delivered right to your mailbox. Just call Greyhound at least ten days before your departure (1-800-231-2222)

Prepaid tickets. It's easy to purchase a ticket for a friend or family member no matter how far away they may be. Just call or go to your nearest Greyhound terminal (车站) and ask for details on how to buy a prepaid ticket.

Ticketing Requirement. Greyhound now requires that all tickets have travel dates fixed at the time of purchase. Children under two years of age travel free with an adult who has a ticket.

If your destination (目的地) is to Canada or Mexico.

Passengers traveling to Canada or Mexico must have the proper travel documents. U.S., Canadian or Mexican citizens should have a birth certificate, passport or naturalization (入籍) paper. If you are not a citizen of the U.S., Canada or Mexico, a passport is required. In certain cases a visa may be required as well. These documents will be necessary and may be checked at, or before, boarding a bus departing for Canada or Mexico.

41. From the passage, we can learn that "Greyhound" is probably the name of _____.
    A. an airline   B. a hotel
    C. a website   D. a bus company

42. Why should people call Greyhound for tickets in advance?
    A. To avoid waiting in lines at the booking office.
    B. To hand in necessary traveling documents.
    C. To get tickets from the nearest terminal.
    D. To fix the traveling destination in time.

43. What can we learn about the Greyhound tickets?
    A. They are not available for traveling outside the U.S..
    B. Travelers should buy their tickets in person.
    C. Babies can not travel free with their parents.
    D. They have the exact travel date on them.

44. When people are traveling to Canada or Mexico, a passport is a must for _____.
    A. American citizens   B. Japanese citizens
    C. Mexican citizens   D. Canadian citizens

45. This passage mainly offers information about _____.
    A. how to prepare documents for traveling with Greyhound
    B. how to purchase a Greyhound ticket and travel with it

C. how to make your trip with Greyhound interesting

D. how to travel from the U.S. to Canada and Mexico

Task 3

Directions: The following is an advertisement. After reading it, you should complete the information by filling in the blanks marker 46 to 50 in not more than 3 words in the table below.

December 10th, 2006

Dear Sirs,

  I know that your company has a reputation (声誉) for quality products and fairness toward its customers. Therefore, I'm writing to ask for a replacement for a lawn mower (割草机).

  I bought the mower about half a year ago at the Watchung Discount Center, Watchung, Nebraska. I'm enclosing a copy of a receipt for the mower.

  A month after I bought the lawn mower, the engine failed, and it was repaired under warranty (保修期). So far, I have had the engine repaired four times.

  Now the engine has broken down again.

  I have already spent more than $300 on repairs, and I am beginning to seriously question the quality of your mower.

  I am questioning that you replace this mower with a new one.

  I hope that you will live up to your reputation of the good customer service that has made your business successful.

Faithfully,

Rod Green

Letter of Complaint

Purpose of the letter: requesting a (46) _____ for a lawn mower

Time of purchase: about (47) _____ ago

Trouble with the machine: (48) _____

Times of repairs so far: (49) _____

Money spent on repairs: more than (50) _____

Task 4

Directions: The following is a list of terms frequently used in medical services. After reading it, you are required to find the items equivalent to (与……等同) those given in Chinese in the list below. Then you should put the corresponding letters in brackets on the Answer Sheet, numbered 51 through 55.

A --- employee turnover

B --- life-long employment

C --- role conflict

D --- profit sharing

E --- scientific management
F --- comparable worth
G --- flexible working hours
H --- social support
I --- survey feedback
J --- core competence
K --- public relations
L --- group culture
M --- wage and salary surveys
N --- honesty testing
O --- human resource planning

Example: (I) 调查反馈　　　　　　(A) 人员流动
51. 测谎　　　　　　　　　　工薪调查
52. 社会支持　　　　　　　　终身雇用制
53. 团队文化　　　　　　　　公共关系
54. 利润分享　　　　　　　　人力资源策划
55. 科学管理　　　　　　　　弹性工作时间

Task 5

Directions: There is an advertisement blow. After reading it, you are required to complete the statements that follow the questions (No. 56 to No. 60). You should write your answers in no more than 3 words on the Answer Sheet correspondingly.

Dear Sirs,

　　For the past 8 years I have been a statistician (统计员) in the Research Unit of Baron & Smallwood Ltd. I am now looking for a change of employment which would broaden my experience. A large and well-known organization such as yours might be able to use my services.

　　I am 31 years old and in excellent health. I majored in advertising at London University and I am particularly interested in work involving statistics (统计).

　　Although I have had no experience in market research, I am familiar with the methods used for recording buying habits and trends. I hope that you will invite me for an interview. I could then give you further information.

　　I am looking forward to hearing from you soon.

Yours faithfully,
Mike Smith

56. What's Mike Smith's present job?
　　He's working as a _____.
57. What was Mike Smith's major at London University?
　　_____.

58. What kind of work does he like to do?

    Working involving _____.

59. In what area does he lack experience?

    He has no experience in _____.

60. What's the purpose of the writer in sending this letter?

    To be invited for _____.

2006年6月高等学校英语应用能力A级试题(阅读部分)

Part III Reading Comprehension (40 minutes)

Task 1

Directions: After reading the following passage, you will find 5 questions or unfinished statements, marked 36 to 40. For each question or statement there are 4 choices marked A, B, C and D. You should make the correct choice and mark the corresponding letter on the Answer Sheet with a single line through the center.

When a rare disease ALD threatened to kill the four-year-old boy Lorenzo, his parents refused to give up hope. Doctors explained that there was no cure for ALD, and that he would probably die within three years. But Lorenzo's parents se tout to prove the doctors wrong.

The parents devoted themselves to keeping their son alive and searching for a cure. But doctors and the families of other ALD patients often refused to take them seriously. They thought the efforts to find a cure were a waste of time, and drug companies weren't interested in supporting research into such a rare disease.

However, the parents still refused to give up and spent every available hour in medical libraries and talking to anyone who would help. Through trial and error (反复实验), they finally created a cure from ingredients (调料) commonly found in the kitchen. The cure, named "Lorenzo's Oil", saved the boy's life. Despite the good results, scientists and doctors remained unconvinced. They said there was no real evidence that the oil worked and that the treatment was just a theory. As a result, some families with ALD children were reluctant to try it.

Finally, the boy's father organized an international study to test the oil. After ten years of trials, the answer is: the oil keeps ALD children healthy.

36. Doctors said that Lorenzo might die within three years because _____.

    A. they had never treated the disease before

    B. Lorenzo was too young to be cured

    C. no cure had been found for ALD

    D. ALD was a rare disease

37. The families of other ALD patients thought that _____.
    A. the research for the new cure would cost too much money
    B. the efforts of Lorenzo's parents were a waste of time
    C. Lorenzo's parents would succeed in finding a cure
    D. Lorenzo's oil was a real cure for ALD

38. Scientists and doctors believed that Lorenzo's Oil _____.
    A. was really effective   B. was a success story
    C. only worked in theory   D. would save the boy's life

39. Lorenzo's father organized an international study to _____.
    A. test Lorenzo's Oil   B. get financial support
    C. find a cure for the disease   D. introduce the cure worldwide

40. From the passage we can conclude that _____.
    A. doctors remain doubtful of the effectiveness of the cure
    B. many ALD patients still refuse to use the oil
    C. various cures have been found for ALD
    D. the oil really works as a cure for ALD

Task 2

Directions: This task is the same as Task 1. The 5 questions or unfinished statements are numbered 41 to 45.

Do you know how to use a mobile phone (手机) without being rude to the people around you?

Talking during a performance irritates (激怒) people. If you are expecting an emergency call, sit near the exit doors and set your phone to vibrate (振动). When your mobile phone vibrates, you can leave quietly and let the others enjoy the performance.

Think twice before using mobile phones in elevators, museums, churches or other indoor public places—especially enclosed spaces. Would you want to listen to someone's conversation in these places? Worse yet, how would you feel if a mobile phone rang suddenly during a funeral! It happens more often that you think. Avoid these embarrassing situations by making sure your mobile phone is switched off.

When eating at a restaurant with friends, don't place your mobile phone on the table. This conveys the message that your phone calls are more important than those around you.

Mobile phones have sensitive microphones that allow you to speak at the volume you would on a regular phone. This enables you to speak quietly so that others won't hear the details of your conversations. If you are calling from a noisy area, use your hand to direct your voice into microphone.

Many people believe that they can't live without their mobile phone. Owning a mobile phone definitely makes life more convenient, but limit your conversations to urgent ones and save the personal calls until you are at home.

41. What should you do when you need to answer a phone call during a performance?

    A. Call back after the performance   B. Answer it near the exit door

    C. Talk outside the exit door   D. Speak it in a low voice

42. Putting your mobile phone on a restaurant table may make your friends think _____.

    A. you prefer to talk to your friends at the table

    B. you value your calls more than your friends

    C. you are enjoying the company of your friends

    D. you are polite and considerate of your friends

43. When you are calling in a noisy area, you are advised to _____.

    A. use a more sensitive microphone

    B. shout loudly into your microphone

    C. go away quietly to continue the phone call

    D. use your hand to help speak into the phone

44. The author implies that the use of mobile phones in such places as museums should be _____.

    A. limited   B. expected

    C. discouraged   D. recommended

45. Which of the following is TRUE according to the passage?

    A. You should limit your mobile phone calls to personal affairs.

    B. You should speak quietly into your phone while in a church.

    C. You are supposed to turn off your mobile phone at a funeral.

    D. You are supposed to use your mobile phone as much as possible.

Task 3

Directions: The following is an advertisement. After reading it, you should complete the information by filling in the blanks marker 46 to 50 in not more than 3 words in the table below.

  The meeting is over. You're tired. Now will you get on a plane and rush back home to more work? Here's a better idea. Take a little time for yourself and relax at Holiday Inn.

  All our 1,642 hotels worldwide have the best leisure facilities available. And the best locations for relaxation.

  From the sun-bathed beaches of Thailand's Phuket to the unique scenery of Tibet. Or on a journey of discovery to Malaysia's Kuching and Penang, and beyond to the ski-fields (滑雪场). Holiday Inn makes it easy to relax.

  So does the American Express Card. It's the foremost business traveler companion. With no pre-set spending limit you can spend as much as you have shown us you can afford. You have the flexibility to quickly change your travel plans plus the spending power to make the most of your last minute holiday.

  Relax with confidence. Just one of the many benefits of being an American Express Card member and staying at Holiday Inn.

An advertisement

Items advertised:

1. Holiday Inn

2. American Express Card Number of Holiday Inn hotels worldwide: (46) _____

Services offered by Holiday Inn:

1. best (47) _____ facilities

2. best (48) _____ for relaxation

Advantages of American Express Card:

1. no pre-set (49) _____

2. flexibility in changing one's (50) _____

Task 4

Directions: The following is a list of terms frequently used in medical services. After reading it, you are required to find the items equivalent to (与……等同) those given in Chinese in the list below. Then you should put the corresponding letters in brackets on the Answer Sheet, numbered 51 through 55.

A --- abbreviated dialing code

B --- off-peak hours

C --- charging period

D --- access code

E --- identity number

F --- video conference

G --- operational status

H --- information subscription service

I --- Network User Address

J --- audio signal

K --- local user terminal

L --- file management

M --- response signal

N --- operating instructions

O --- charge of the battery unit

P --- function indicator

Q --- entry rejected

R --- external control

Example: (A) 缩位拨号码   (H) 预定信息业务

51. 计费时间   非高峰时间

52. 网络用户地址   标识码

53. 本地用户终端   音频信号

54. 文件管理   操作指令

55. 外部控制   功能指示

Task 5

Directions: There is an advertisement blow. After reading it, you are required to complete the statements that follow the questions (No. 56 to No. 60). You should write your answers in no more than 3 words on the Answer Sheet correspondingly.

The Singapore underground train system, known as the MRT, offers a speedy and easy way to get about our city. You'll need small change to buy an individual ticket. Alternatively, buy a special ticket designed with the tourist in mind. Costing S$6, it offers S$5.50 worth of rides; the extra 50 cents is for keeping the ticket as a souvenir (纪念品). Tourist tickets feature one of three designs: the Chinese Gardens, the Victoria Memorial Hall or a night skyline of Singapore.

You gain entry to the trains by inserting your ticket into the barrier machine (检票闸机). Wait for the ticket to reappear and put it away safely: you'll need it again. After your trip, you insert your ticket into the barrier in order to leave. Please note that each ticket is time coded on entry, and you are advised not to spend more than half an hour in addition to travel time, because tickets can expire (失效).

Moving stairs that take you to the platform and train destinations are marked clearly. Trains run frequently. Do remember, eating and drinking are forbidden in MRT stations and trains.

56. What purpose does the MRT serve?
    To provide a(n) _____ way to get about the city.
57. Why is there an extra cost of 50 cents for a tourist ticket?
    For the tourist to keep the ticket as _____.
58. Why should people keep the ticket after boarding the train?
    Because they will _____ when they leave.
59. What will happen if passengers stay in MRT over half an hour in addition to travel time?
    Their tickets will _____.
60. What is forbidden when people take the underground train?
    They are not allowed to _____.

2006年6月高等学校英语应用能力 B 级试题（阅读部分）

Part III Reading Comprehension (40 minutes)

Task 1

Directions: After reading the following passage, you will find 5 questions or unfinished statements, marked 36 to 40. For each question or statement there are 4 choices marked A, B, C and D. You should make the correct choice and mark the corresponding letter on the Answer Sheet with a single line through the center.

Unlike Britain, the U.S. does not have a national health care service. The government does help pay for some medical care for people who are on low incomes and for old people, but most people buy insurance (保险) to help pay for medical care. The problems of those who cannot afford insurance are an important political subject.

  In Britain, when people are ill, they usually go to a family doctor first, however, people in America sometimes go straight to an expert without seeing their family doctor first. Children are usually taken to a doctor who is an expert in the treatment (治疗) of children. In Britain, if a patient needs to see a specialist doctor, their family doctor will usually recommend a specialist.

  Doctors do not go to people's homes when they are ill. People always make appointments to see the doctor in the doctor's office. In a serious situation, people call for an ambulance (救护车), in America, hospitals must treat all seriously ill patients, even if they do not have medical insurance. The government will then help pay for some of the cost of the medical care.

36. Some medical care is paid by the U.S. government for _____.
  A. people living in the country   B. non-government officials
  C. people with insurance   D. the poor and the old

37. Most people in the United States buy insurance _____.
  A. to pay for their own medical care
  B. to help to live on their low incomes
  C. to improve the national health care service
  D. to solve one of the important political problems

38. What do British people usually do when they are ill?
  A. They go to see their family doctor first.   B. They go to see a specialist doctor first.
  C. They call for a specialist doctor.   D. They call for a family doctor.

39. In America, seriously ill patients will _____.
  A. be treated if they have an insurance
  B. make an appointment with a specialist only
  C. receive treatment even without insurance
  D. normally go to see an expert for treatment

40. Which of the following would be the best title for this passage?
  A. Types of Doctors in the United States
  B. Health Care in the United States and Britain
  C. Treatment of Sick Children in the United States
  D. Medical Insurance in the United States and Britain

Task 2

Directions: This task is the same as Task 1. The 5 questions or unfinished statements are numbered 41 to 45.

Dear sir or Madam,

  The MDC Company was established in 2001 and in four short years has become on of the most successful companies in the market place. For this, we are pleased, proud and grateful.

We are pleased because our customers have confirmed our belief that if the products we offer are new, exciting, innovative (有创意的) and of excellent quality, they will be purchased.

We are proud because we know we are a company that keeps its word to its customers; that guarantees that any product can be returned within 30 days if it proves to be unsatisfactory in any way; and that always lets our customers know if there is to be a delay in delivery.

We are grateful to customers like you, because you confirm our beliefs that good service and quality result in satisfied customers. Without you, there would be no reason for us to be pleased or proud. We thank you for orders and for giving us the opportunity to be of service to you.

Our special summer catalogue (商品目录) is at the printers and should be in your home soon. We hope that you will be pleased with the new selections.

Yours faithfully,

John Brow

41. From the passage we can learn that MDC Company always _____.
    A. keeps its promise   B. provides the same products
    C. sells it products at a low price   D. delivers its products without delay
42. MDC Company believes that its customers are satisfied because the company _____.
    A. gives them opportunities to order   B. provides good service and quality
    C. guarantees the quickest delivery   D. sends new catalogues to them
43. The customers will be informed if _____.
    A. the product can't be delivered on time
    B. the products is out-of-date and unsatisfactory
    C. the company doesn't accept the returned product
    D. the company can't send a new catalogue on time
44. The purpose of this letter is to _____.
    A. tell the customers about the quality of their products
    B. express the company's thanks to the customers
    C. prove the excellent service of the company
    D. inform the customers of a new catalogue
45. What can we learn about the company?
    A. It has the largest number of customers.   B. It is grateful for its employees' efforts.
    C. It is successful in the market place.   D. It charges the least for its services.

Task 3

Directions: The following is an advertisement. After reading it, you should complete the information by filling in the blanks marker 46 to 50 in not more than 3 words in the table below.

Thanks for using Metro (地铁)

Clean. Modern. Safe. And easy to use. No wonder Metro is considered the nation's finest transit (公交) system. This guide tells how to use Metro, and the color-coded map on the inside will help you use Metro to get all around the Nation's Capital.

Metro-rail fares

Each passenger needs a fare-card. (Up to two children under 5 may travel free with a paying customer.)

Fares are based on when and how far you ride. Pay regular fares on weekdays 5:30-9:30 a.m. and 3:00-7:00 p.m. Pay reduced fares at all other times.

Large maps in each station show fares and travel times. Please ask the station manager if you have any questions.

Fare-card machines are in every station. Bring small banknotes because there are no change machines in the stations and fare-card machines only provide up to $5 in change (in coins). Some machines accept credit cards (信用卡).

A Transit System Metro

Features of the system:

1) (46) _____,

2) modern _____,

3) safe, and

4) (47) _____

Fares for weekends: (48) _____ fares

Place showing fares and travel times: large maps in (49) _____

Change provided by fare-card machines: up to $ (50) _____

Task 4

Directions: The following is a list of terms frequently used in medical services. After reading it, you are required to find the items equivalent to (与……等同) those given in Chinese in the list below. Then you should put the corresponding letters in brackets on the Answer Sheet, numbered 51 through 55.

A --- Buses Only

B --- No Parking

C --- No Standing

D --- Police Cars Only

E --- No U-Turn

F --- No Admittance

G --- No Entry By This Door

H --- One Way Street

I --- One Lane Bridge

J --- Admission By Ticket Only

K --- Admission Free

L --- Keep Away

M --- House To Let

N --- Keep Order

O --- Wet Paint
P --- Line Up For Tickets
Q --- No Posting of Signs
R --- Seat By Number
S --- Wheelchairs Only

Example: (Q) 请勿张贴	(C) 禁止停车候客
51. 禁止停车	禁止掉头
52. 此门不通	不得入内
53. 房屋出租	单行道
54. 排队购票	凭票入场
55. 公交专用道	对号入座

Task 5

Directions: There is an advertisement blow. After reading it, you are required to complete the statements that follow the questions (No. 56 to No. 60). You should write your answers in no more than 3 words on the Answer Sheet correspondingly.

Letter 1

June 10, 2006

Dear Sir or Madam,

  Last night the central heating system that you installed(安装) in our factory exploded. The explosion caused a great deal of damage and our stock of fashion clothes has been completely ruined.

  We must insist that you replace the heating system immediately and pay for our damaged stock, valued at $400,000.

  We look forward to your reply.

Yours faithfully,
Bill Black
Assistant Manager

Letter 2

June 15, 2006

Dear Mr. Black,

  We are writing in connection with the recent explosion at your factory.

  We would like to point out that we have been manufacturing heating systems for over 25 years and we have never had a complaint before. We have asked a surveyor to find out the cause of the explosion.

  We are hoping that we can provide you with a satisfactory answer soon.

Yours sincerely,
Mary Miller
Service Manager

56. What happened in the factory last night?

   The central heating system _____.

57. What was the damage caused to the factory?

   The stock of _____ was ruined.

58. How much was the stock valued at?

   It was valued at _____.

59. What did Bill Black demand in his letter?

   To replace and pay for the damage.

60. What has been done by the heating system supplier?

   _____ has been asked to find out the cause of the accident.

参考答案 (Keys)

Unit One

Text 1

1. Definitions

1) applicant   2) admission   3) represent   4) hearsay   5) enroll
6) accurate   7) scholarship   8) identify   9) characteristic   10) consult
11) budget   12) realistic   13) competitive   14) available   15) frustrating

2. Sample Sentences

1) enrolled   2) identify   3) realistic   4) hearsay   5) characteristic
6) Admission   7) competitive   8) frustrating   9) applicants   10) consult
11) budget   12) accurate   13) scholarship   14) available   15) represents

3. Translation

A. 1) 在海外申请美国大学既激动人心又富于挑战。

2) 进入大学的竞争非常激烈，对于美国以外的申请者尤是如此。

3) 成功申请的关键在于对所要求的步骤进行严谨策划并且按时完成。

4) 一旦学年开始，即使对美国学生，也几乎不再提供经济资助。

5) 最好不要过分相信道听途说或他人的经验。

B. 1) Nowadays, many college graduates are rushing to enroll in MBA courses.

2) The rose represents England.

3) It's just not realistic to expect an economic recovery so soon.

4) You will be informed when the book becomes available.

5) Next year's budget will have to be drastically pruned.

4. Writing (略)

Text 2

1. Questions (略)

2. Multiple Choices

1) D   2) C   3) A   4) B   5) A

Text 3

1. True, False, Not Given

1) F   2) F   3) NG   4) T   5) T   6) T   7) T

2. Blank-Filling

1) situational appropriate   2) knowledge   3) the skills of using the situation

241

Unit Two

Text 1

1. Definitions
1) tutorial	2) amplify	3) motivation	4) available	5) undergraduate
6) tertiary	7) analyze	8) seminar	9) illustrate	10) parallel
11) vary	12) staff	13) timetable	14) option	15) engineering

2. Sample Sentences
1) tutorial	2) amplified	3) motivation	4) analyze	5) undergraduate
6) seminar	7) illustrate	8) parallel	9) vary	10) staff
11) timetabled	12) option	13) engineering	14) motivation	15) tertiary

3. Translation

A. 1) 国与国之间的医疗保障各不相同。

2) 该地区提供很多工作岗位。

3) 她用图表阐述了她的观点。

4) 这幅绘画作品达到了最高的艺术水准。

5) 金字塔是古埃及人工程技术精湛的丰碑。

B. 1) My experience in this matter is parallel to yours.

2) The course is timetabled for every Monday.

3) Genetic engineering will have revolutionary consequences for mankind.

4) He had no option but to agree.

5) What was your motivation for becoming a teacher?

4. Writing (略)

Text 2

1. Questions (略)

2. Multiple Choices
1) C   2) D   3) D   4) C   5) A

Text 3

1. True, False, Not Given
1) T   2) T   3) F   4) T   5) F   6) T   7) T

2. Blank-Filling
1) London has been established as a major trading port

2) 18th and 19th

3) 1970s and 1980s

Unit Three

Text 1

1. Definitions

1) harmonious	2) disquiet	3) circumstance	4) sophisticated	5) survival
6) indispensable	7) random	8) pursue	9) inhabit	10) nurture
11) diverse	12) advocator	13) ignite	14) deny	15) prosperity

2. Sample Sentences

1) denied	2) prosperity	3) diverse	4) survival	5) disquieted
6) Sophisticated	7) inhabited	8) nurtured	9) ignited	10) random
11) advocator	12) indispensable	13) circumstances	14) pursue	15) harmonious

3. Translation

A. 1) 我们随机调查了一些人们的想法。

2) 我们当务之急是设法生存下来。

3) 学生们在做好作业的同时，应该培养自己的兴趣爱好。

4) 奢侈商品销售量日增是一个国家繁荣的标志。

5) 目前计算机是很多公司不可或缺的工具。

B. 1) The student's interests are very diverse.

2) Many village children are denied the chance of going to school.

3) She is pursuing her studies at the university.

4) We hope to have a life of happiness and prosperity.

5) The sky and the sea make a harmonious picture.

4. Writing (略)

Text 2

1. Questions (略)

2. Multiple Choices

1) B 2) C 3) D 4) B 5) C

Text 3

1. True, False, Not Given

1) F 2) T 3) F 4) T 5) T 6) NG 7) T

2. Blank-Filling

1) the exception, the rule

2) three to six feet, a few inches

3) their concepts of individualism and personal boundaries beyond their current realms of thinking.

Unit Four

Text 1

1. Definitions

1) achievement　　2) justify　　3) evil　　4) conceal　　5) revolutionize
6) amazement　　7) typical　　8) numerous　　9) assume　　10) vital
11) persist　　12) major　　13) triumph　　14) docile　　15) contribution

2. Sample Sentences

1) evil　　2) numerous　　3) persist　　4) typical　　5) docile
6) amazement　　7) major　　8) conceal　　9) revolutionize　　10) justified
11) assume　　12) contribution　　13) triumph　　14) achievement　　15) vital

3. Translation

A. 1) 任何事情都不能成为你考试作弊的理由。

2) 这本书可谓是再现了过去那个邪恶社会的全貌。

3) 他的最大成绩就是将所有队员融为一体。

4) 我认为我们可以有把握地预测利率会提高。

5) 学校把培养对社会有贡献的学生视作自己的职责。

B. 1) Regular exercise is vital for your health.

2) Effort and achievement are always in full accord.

3) She persisted with her studies in spite of financial problems.

4) We always can not conceal our envy of others' success.

5) Computers have revolutionized office work.

4. Writing (略)

Text 2

1. Questions (略)

2. Multiple Choices

1) B　　2) A　　3) B　　4) C　　5) D

Text 3

1. True, False, Not Given

1) F　　2) T　　3) F　　4) F　　5) F　　6) F　　7) NG

2. Blank-Filling

1) Greeks　　2) March 1　　3) Catholic, Protestant

Unit Five

Text 1

1. Definitions

1) devoted　　2) represent　　3) immigrant　　4) origin　　5) worship
6) broadcast　　7) household　　8) occupy　　9) pattern　　10) host
11) freezing　　12) revel　　13) advertisement　　14) flock　　15) variety

2. Sample Sentences

  1) advertisement   2) worshipped   3) broadcast   4) pattern   5) hosted

  6) origin   7) household   8) devoted   9) reveled   10) occupies

  11) freezing   12) variety   13) flock   14) immigrants   15) represent

3. Translation

 A. 1) 该治疗方法代表了癌症研究领域的重大进展。

  2) 这个国家同化了来自许多国家的移民。

  3) 他既然已退休，如何打发日子呢？

  4) 可口可乐是全世界家喻户晓的品牌。

  5) 校方应该密切关注学生不断变化的行为模式。

 B. 1) Which country will host the next Olympic Games?

  2) She is a good wife and a devoted mother.

  3) Reading occupies most of my free time.

  4) The actress revels in all the attention she gets from the media.

  5) The social unrest has its origins in economic problems.

4. Writing (略)

Text 2

1. Questions (略)

2. Multiple Choices

  1) C   2) D   3) A   4) B   5) D

Text 3

1. True, False, Not Given

  1) T   2) NG   3) F   4) F   5) T   6) F   7) F

2. Blank-Filling

  1) the technical revolution

  2) 33% to 55%

  3) cooperate with colleagues, solve problems, and make decisions

Unit Six

Text 1

1. Definitions

  1) movable   2) attitude   3) beyond   4) strict   5) theory

  6) excitement   7) attentive   8) extend   9) fasten   10) separate

  11) thoroughly   12) contract   13) basic   14) social   15) restless

2. Sample Sentences

  1) excitement   2) beyond   3) attitude   4) attentive   5) theory

  6) strict   7) extend   8) fastened to   9) separated   10) contract

  11) thoroughly   12) basic   13) social   14) restless   15) movable

3. Translation

A. 1) 学生们会更加积极,所以焦躁不安的频率变低,注意力会更加集中。

2) 如果他对某一门课程,比如说对数学情有独钟,他可以将其学得比其他课程更加透彻。

3) 如今,我们努力地将教育的领域延伸到学校之外。

4) 他们在考察自己对警察的态度,并且将态度记录下来。

5) 除非可以激发自己,否则你不可能成为一个激发别人的老师。

B. 1) The ship made slow progress through the rough sea.

2) After only a month in the job, he felt restless and decided to leave.

3) We shall be landing (at Gatwick airport) shortly please fasten your seat-belts.

4) This word has three separate meanings.

5) The level of inflation has gone beyond 8%.

4. Writing (略)

Text 2

1. Cloze

to   when   who   for   themselves   but   that   as

2. Multiple Choices

1) A   2) A   3) C   4) B   5) A

Text 3

1. Questions (略)

2. Blank-Filling

1) Taste, flavorful   2) vitamins, nutrients   3) bio-engineered   4) particular program, law

Unit Seven

Text 1

1. Definitions

1) settler	2) aboriginal	3) encounter	4) exist	5) concept
6) independence	7) territory	8) contact	9) vast	10) phenomenon
11) diverse	12) apparently	13) throughout	14) roam	15) monarchy

2. Sample Sentences

1) encountered	2) Aboriginal	3) settlers	4) exists	5) territory
6) independence	7) concept	8) vast	9) contact	10) phenomenon
11) diverse	12) apparently	13) monarchy	14) roam	15) throughout

3. Translation

A. 1) 作为一个概念和一个国家,加拿大这个名称是近来才出现的。

2) 随后,法国和英国开始了对加拿大领土和贸易中心的争夺。

3) 它的真实来历并不确定,但人们对此却有很多解释。

4) 这些关于"加拿大"的故事表明了这个国家拥有多元化的文化背景。

5) "大熊湖"和"水牛峡谷"这些名字显示出危险的野生动物仍然普遍存在于加拿大。

B. 1) It snowed throughout the night.

2) They are the people from diverse cultures.

3) I encountered an old friend at Rome.

4) I can not understand the so abstract concept.

5) The experts are exploring every part of the island.

4. Writing (略)

Text 2

1. Questions (略)
2. Blank-Filling

  1) real life experience   2) Huiban   3) Martial art

  4) bottom   5) honesty; frankness

Text 3

1. Questions (略)
2. Blank-Filling

  1) Baseball   2) The World Series   3) east coast   4) Jackie Robinson   5) Baseball

Unit Eight

Text 1

1. Definitions

1) exactly	2) legislative	3) tyranny	4) majority	5) privilege
6) counteract	7) consist of	8) statement	9) guarantee	10) adopt
11) main	12) liberty	13) guard	14) provided	15) explicit

2. Sample Sentences

1) legislative	2) exactly	3) privileges	4) majority	5) attended
6) counteract	7) statements	8) consisted of	9) guarantee	10) liberty
11) main	12) adopt	13) explicit	14) provided	15) guard

3. Translation

A. 1) 有关政府的计划在非常简练的文字记录在了被称为美国宪法的文件中。

  2) 宪法同时号召对国家领袖，即总统进行选举。

  3) 编写宪法时，代表们不得不消除绝大多数美国人心存的两大忧虑。

  4) 一大忧虑就是一个由个人或由多数人组成的某个团体过于强大，或者控制整个国家并建立专制政权。

  5) 那些支持采纳宪法的人以口头和书面形式为此进行了长期而艰苦的辩论。

B. 1) The United Kingdom consists of Great Britain and Northern Ireland.

  2) Public opinion was moving strongly in favor of disarmament.

  3) Provided that circumstances permit, we shall hold the meeting next week.

4) Blue skies are not a guarantee of continuing fine weather.

5) I think we should work out a strategy to deal with this situation.

4. Writing (略)

Text 2

Cloze

    1) In   2) whether   3) in   4) to   5) from

    6) with   7) by   8) while   9) to   10) over

Text 3

1. True, False, Not Given

    1) NG   2) F   3) T   4) T   5) T

2. Blank-Filling

    1) permit   2) company; presence   3) abandoned; transform; inspire; bring together

    4) unusual   5) presidential

Unit Nine

Text 1

1. Definitions:

    1) promise   2) mention   3) ignore   4) absolutely   5) attractive

    6) advertiser   7) claim   8) subjective   9) equivalent   10) judgment

    11) pleasant   12) intimate   13) crush   14) smooth   15) horrible

2. Sample Sentences

    1) ignore   2) mentioned   3) promise   4) advertisers   5) attractive

    6) absolutely   7) claims   8) equivalent   9) subjective   10) judgment

    11) crush   12) intimate   13) pleasant   14) smooth   15) horrible

3. Translation

    A. 1) 新政府承诺将对权力进行平稳过渡。

        2) 医生们将全部精力集中在预防而非治疗上。

        3) 他把辞职的原因说得非常清楚。

        4) "如……一般"这个词使你忽视了产品本身，而将注意力集中在了广告宣传上。

        5) 一支香烟抽起来是好是坏属于主观判断，因为一个人感觉很好，或许另一个人感觉很糟。

    B. 1) Changing his job like that is equivalent to giving him the sack.

        2) I can't concentrate on my work when I'm tired.

        3) In my judgment, we should accept their apology.

        4) Her refusal crushed all our hopes.

        5) She smoothed out wrinkles out of the tablecloth.

4. Writing (略)

Text 2
Cloze
1) who 2) that 3) what 4) or 5) as
6) and 7) or 8) though 9) on 10) of

Text 3
1. True, False, Not Given
1) T 2) F 3) T 4) F 5) NG

2. Blank-Filling
1) Negroes 2) emancipator 3) re-invented
4) self-taught 5) surrendered; ended

Unit Ten

Text 1
1. Definitions
1) extent 2) given 3) suggest 4) adolescent 5) investigate
6) depression 7) service 8) socialize 9) interfere 10) attend
11) cause 12) sign 13) vote 14) total 15) journal

2. Sample Sentences
1) suggest 2) depression 3) extent 4) adolescent 5) investigates
6) Given 7) caused 8) socialize 9) interfere 10) attend
11) service 12) vote 13) sign 14) totaling 15) Journal

3. Translation
A. 1) 我越想越不喜欢这个主意。
2) 我对他知识之渊博感到惊奇。
3) 他面色苍白，说明身体不好。
4) 他尽量不让日常工作妨碍他的家庭生活。
5) 在我看来，恐怕这次演出不是完全成功的。

B. 1) The researchers have done a survey on adolescent health.
2) Listening to the music has claming influence on her.
3) The rail road gives free transportation for a certain amount of baggage.
4) A new study suggests that the more teenagers watch television, the more likely they are to develop depression.
5) I agree with you to a certain extent.

4. Writing (略)

Text 2
1. Comprehension
1) C 2) C 3) C 4) B 5) C

249

2. Vocabulary

    1) recover   2) willing   3) volunteers   4) removed   5) freshly

Text 3

1. True, False, Not Given

    1) NG   2) T   3) T   4) F   5) T

2. Blank-Filling

    1) exaggerated   2) details   3) beat   4) sick; died   5) do his best

Unit Eleven

Text 1

1. Definitions

    1) acquire   2) irritation   3) patience   4) desirable   5) charm

    6) vivid   7) induce   8) cooperation   9) live   10) sympathy

    11) dull   12) technique   13) principle   14) tolerant   15) capacity

    16) excitable

2. Sample Sentences

    1) dull   2) irritated   3) technique   4) live   5) sympathy

    6) acquired   7) cooperate   8) excitable   9) vivid   10) principle

    11) patient   12) tolerant   13) capacity   14) charm   15) desirable

3. Translation

    A. 1) 只工作,不玩耍,聪明孩子要变傻;尽玩耍,不学习,聪明孩子没出息。

        2) 自己的缺点在别人身上看到,最令我们讨厌。

        3) 要争取和平的环境,就必须同世界上一切和平力量合作。

        4) 天才出自勤奋。

        5) 酒精可使人信口开河。

    B. 1) He displayed a flawless technique in the competition.

        2) Some plants are tolerant of extreme heat.

        3) She uses her charm to manipulate people.

        4) Your sympathy has brought us great comfort.

        5) Imagination is sometimes more vivid than reality.

4. Writing (略)

Text 2

1. Questions (略)

2. Multiple Choices

    1) B   2) A   3) A   4) D   5) C

Text 3

1. True, False, Not Given

1) F 2) T 3) F 4) F 5) T 6) F 7) F

2. Blank-Filling

1) the sun   2) solar energy   3) seeing how the earth uses it

Unit Twelve

Text 1

1. Definitions

1) hatred   2) cure   3) distinction   4) cowardly   5) object
6) grumble   7) strike   8) watchword   9) sensation   10) principal
11) foul   12) notion   13) threefold   14) cheerful

2. Sample Choices

1) fouled   2) cheerful   3) object   4) grumble   5) hatred
6) cured   7) notion   8) watchword   9) struck   10) distinction
11) coward   12) threefold   13) sensation   14) principal

3. Translation

A. 1) 他很聪明,乐观,行动勇敢,举止文雅沉静。

2) 如果我们要保持身体健康,就必须记住预防重于治疗。

3) 爱情忽视缺陷,憎恨放大缺点。

4) 在罚球区内对方队员对他犯规。

5) 她在整个旅程中都兴高采烈、精力旺盛。

B. 1) They drew no distinction between right and wrong.

2) I felt a sensation of happiness.

3) Education has for its object the formation of character.

4) A courageous foe is better than a cowardly friend.

5) They claim to have discovered a cure for the disease, but this had not yet been proved.

4. Writing (略)

Text 2

1. Questions (略)

2. Multiple Choices

1) C   2) C   3) A   4) D   5) A

Text 3

1. True, False, Not Given

1) F   2) T   3) T   4) F   5) T   6) F   7) F

2. Blank-Filling

1) at rest, active   2) Non-REM sleep   3) straightforward, mysterious

Unit Thirteen

Text 1

1. Definitions

1) addled 2) disgrace 3) despair 4) aforementioned 5) paradox
6) obscure 7) revolutionize 8) daydream 9) indolent 10) prodigy
11) chuck 12) divinity 13) symptom 14) mess 15) inspiring

2. Sample Sentences

1) obscure 2) revolutionize 3) chuck 4) aforementioned 5) addled
6) symptom 7) paradox 8) despair 9) indolent 10) prodigy
11) daydreaming 12) inspiring 13) mess 14) divinity 15) disgraced

3. Translation

A. 1) 唯有上帝的宠儿,才能屡经挫折而不气馁。

2) 宁可玉碎,不为瓦全。

3) 自然美具有神性、类人性和社会性。

4) 贪睡、爱闲聊、毫无生气、懒散、急躁而没有耐心是导致堕落的原因。

5) 发病过程中出现的一种状况或症状,与该病没有必然的联系。

B. 1) She stared out of the windows, lost in daydreams.

2) Higher prices are often a symptom of scarcity.

3) If you cancel now you'll mess up all my arrangements.

4) It is a paradox that such a rich country should have so many poor people living in it.

5) The use of atomic energy will revolutionize the lives of coming generations.

4. Writing (略)

Text 2

1. Questions (略)

2. Multiple Choices

1) C 2) D 3) B 4) C 5) A

Text 3

1. True, False, Not Given

1) F 2) T 3) F 4) F 5) F 6) T 7) F

2. Blank-Filling

1) Lucy 2) wood 3) a very strange person walking toward her

Unit Fourteen

Text 1

1. Definitions

1) screen 2) intrude 3) seminar 4) clash 5) irritation

6) ultimate 7) architectural 8) remarkable 9) refuge 10) internalize
11) implication 12) barrier 13) typify 14) pattern 15) strain
16) contrast

2. Sample Sentences

1) strain 2) intrude 3) screen 4) typifies 5) irritation
6) implications 7) contrast 8) barrier 9) pattern 10) seminar
11) refuge 12) architectural 13) remarkable 14) clash 15) internalize
16) ultimate

3. Translation

A. 1) 这个地点的开发将会影响周围的乡村。
2) 窗帘的颜色和地毯的颜色不协调。
3) 你不能永远护住自己的子女,不让他们接触现实生活。
4) 暴力是无能者的最后手段。
5) 税收是自由贸易的最大障碍。

B. 1) His white hair was in sharp contrast to his dark skin.
2) The place is remarkable for its picturesque scenery.
3) The traffic noise is a constant irritation to city dwellers.
4) Our ultimate objective is the removal of all nuclear weapons.
5) I don't want to intrude on you if you are very busy.

4. Writing (略)

Text 2

1. Questions (略)
2. Multiple Choices
   1) B 2) D 3) C 4) C 5) B

Text 3

1. True, False, Not Given
   1) F 2) F 3) F 4) T 5) F 6) T 7) F
2. Blank-filling
   1) No one 2) highly explosive 3) They believe it brings bad luck

Unit Fifteen

Text 1

1. Definitions
   1) trifle 2) profound 3) preventive 4) exceedingly 5) initiative
   6) drudgery 7) tedium 8) innumerable 9) impair 10) provided
   11) zest 12) sufficient 13) idle 14) vigor 15) earthshaking
   16) agreeable 17) tiresome

2. Sample Sentences

1) initiative 2) drudgery 3) zest 4) profound 5) earthshaking
6) idle 7) impaired 8) exceedingly 9) tedium 10) sufficient
11) preventive 12) provided 13) tiresome 14) vigor
15) agreeable 16) innumerable 17) trifle

3. Translation

A. 1) 拥抱生活，创造生活，把握住每一个今天，让我们用全部的热忱去唤醒明天。

2) 这次的教训太深刻了，千万不可重蹈覆辙。

3) 索然无味的演讲似乎没完没了，几乎一半的听众都打起了瞌睡。

4) 技术进步减轻了我们生活中的许多劳作，我们应当得以轻松。

5) 并非每个人都得拥有惊天动地的特殊才能，其实人只要拥有一般的常识和爱心，也就够了。

B. 1) Time is life and when the idle man kills time, he kills himself.

2) They had food and clothing sufficient for their needs.

3) Human beings once created innumerable miracles.

4) It's a trifle thing not worth mentioning.

5) Garbage pollutes environment and impair the health of human.

4. Writing (略)

Text 2

1. Questions (略)

2. Multiple Choices

1) A 2) C 3) B 4) A 5) C

Text 3

1. True, False, Not Given

1) T 2) F 3) F 4) F 5) F 6) F 7) T

2. Blank-Filling

1) underwater insects, living with them in the pond or stream

2) getting its attention

3) dry and wet

Unit Sixteen

Text 1

1. Definitions

1) premium 2) risk 3) compete 4) stock 5) credit
6) replace 7) remain 8) expansion 9) available 10) specialty 11) target

2. Sample Sentences

1) completed 2) replaced 3) targeted 4) premium 5) available

254

6) risked　　　7) stocks　　　8) expand　　　9) remains　　10) credit　　　11) specialty

3. Translation

   A. 1) 世界快餐业巨头麦当劳和咖啡业巨头星巴克之间的竞争愈演愈烈。

   2) 麦当劳相信他们的新计划成功的机率是很高的。

   3) 把西雅图公司发展成为一个成功的国际连锁店，这是他的功劳。

   4) 但是一年前，他曾警告说星巴克的快速增长将会导致他所谓的星巴克掺水现象。

   5) 现在，星巴克将会减慢其在美国境内的扩张，同时加快其在国际上的发展步伐。

   B. 1) Welfare spending is being cut, so it should be targeted on the people who need it most.

   2) Can anything replace a mother's love and care?

   3) He's determined to remain loyal to the team whatever comes his way.

   4) The government is trying to claim credit for the fall in prices.

   5) The criticism has been watered down so as not to offend anybody.

4. Writing (略)

Text 2

1. Questions (略)
2. Multiple Choices

   1) C　　　2) B　　　3) D　　　4) D　　　5) D

Text 3

1. True, False, Not Given

   1) T　　　2) F　　　3) T　　　4) T　　　5) T　　　6) T　　　7) NG

2. Blank-Filling

   1) wasn't something they cared about

   2) be willing to do the work

   3) not a single one spends needlessly

Unit Seventeen

Text 1

1. Definitions

   1) injury　　2) resistant　　3) expose　　4) affect　　5) infection

   6) treat　　7) remove　　8) permanent　　9) weaken　　10) extreme　　11) minor

2. Sample Sentences

   1) permanent　　2) be exposed　　3) extreme　　4) infected　　5) minor

   6) been treated　　7) removed　　8) injuries　　9) weakened　　10) affect　　11) resistant

3. Translation

   A. 1) 如果深层组织受到影响，那么每次在这个部位变冷的时候，患者都会感到疼痛。

   2) 当身体产生的热量低于其损耗掉的热量时就会患上低温症。

   3) 避免受到严寒相关伤害的最佳方法就是出门前做好准备。

4) 穿上几层宽松的、质地轻盈的衣服要比只穿一层厚重的衣服要好。

5) 尽管喝酒可以使人感觉温暖，但事实上，喝酒会削弱身体保持热量的能力。

B. 1) What does the B stand for in his name "James B Clerk"?

2) If there is no coal, oil can be used instead.

3) She is the most likely girl to win the prize.

4) Keep indoors and don't expose your skin to the sun.

5) He was removed from his position because of that big mistake.

4. Writing (略)

Text 2

1. Questions (略)
2. Multiple Choices
   1) C   2) D   3) B   4) B   5) A

Text 3

1. True, False, Not Given
   1) F   2) T   3) NG   4) F   5) T   6) F   7) NG
2. Blank-Filling
   1) health conditions   2) living a healthier lifestyle   3) dietary supplements

Unit Eighteen

Text 1

1. Definitions
   1) assign   2) personality   3) progress   4) prediction   5) creative
   6) attachment   7) imaginative   8) fulfill   9) destiny   10) calculate
   11) affectionate 12) stubborn   13) significant

2. Sample Sentences
   1) significant 2) predicted   3) fulfilled   4) attachment   5) personalities
   6) progress   7) assigned   8) creative   9) destiny   10) affectionate
   11) imagine   12) calculated 13) stubborn

3. Translation

   A. 1) 数字命理学就是使用数字来描述一个人的性格并且预测未来事情的一种方法。

   2) 你的表达数字能够描述你的天分，还可以预测你该怎样利用天分来实现宿命。

   3) 在15号出生的人对家和家人都有很强的依恋。

   4) 如果我们计算出自己名字和出生日期的数值，数字命理学家们就认为我们可以了解更多关于性格的东西。

   5) 数字命理学家们认为拥有这个数字的人很安静、感情丰富、保守稳重。

   B. 1) They fulfilled their work ahead of time as we did ours.

   2) He challenged me to play another tennis game.

256

3) The scientists are able to calculate accurately when the spaceship will reach the moon.
4) The bus driver is responsible for the passengers' safety.
5) The two governments assigned a day for the next negotiation.

4. Writing (略)

Text 2
1. Questions (略)
2. Multiple Choices
   1) C   2) B   3) D   4) A   5) D   6) A

Text 3
1. True, False, Not Given
   1) F   2) F   3) T   4) T   5) T   6) T   7) T
2. Blank-Filling
   1) acting strangely   2) foreshocks   3) animal reactions

2007年6月高等学校英语应用能力A级试题答案(阅读部分)

Part III Reading Comprehension

Task 1
36. D   37. A   38. B   39. D   40. C

Task 2
41. B   42. A   43. C   44. B   45. D

Task 3
46. effective relief   47. the tongue   48. 12   49. every 4 hours   50. shortness of breath

Task 4
51. N D   52. O G   53. A H   54. K Q   55. J I

Task 5
56. reasonable cost   57. financial plan   58. An agent   59. family members   60. other debts

2007年6月高等学校英语应用能力B级试题答案（阅读部分）

Part III Reading Comprehension

Task 1

36. D   37. B   38. D   39. C   40. A

Task 2

41. B   42. A   43. B   44. B   45. B

Task 3

46. boss   47. information   48. memorandum   49. the subject line   50. body

Task 4

51. P N   52. J L   53. H D   54. A G   55. C B

Task 5

56. the clock   57. cold area   58. Minute Timer   59. The support   60. will not run

2006年12月高等学校英语应用能力A级试题答案（阅读部分）

Part III Reading Comprehension

Task 1

36. A   37. D   38. C   39. C   40. B

Task 2

41. B   42. D   43. C   44. D   45. B

Task 3

46. Macmillian Publishers Limited   47. original intended recipient   48. statements   49. viruses   50. e-mail communication

Task 4

51. M C   52. Q E   53. O G   54. L B   55. H N

Task 5

56. Waikiki Beach   57. 545   58. Prompt and reasonable   59. Half price   60. discounts

2006年12月高等学校英语应用能力B级试题答案（阅读部分）

Part III Reading Comprehension

Task 1
36. D   37. C   38. B   39. A   40. C

Task 2
41. D   42. A   43. D   44. B   45. B

Task 3
46. replacement   47. half a year   48. engine failure   49. four   50. $300

Task 4
51. N M   52. H B   53. L K   54. D O   55. E G

Task 5
56. statistician   57. Advertising   58. statistics   59. market research   60. an interview

2006年6月高等学校英语应用能力A级试题答案（阅读部分）

Part III Reading Comprehension

Task 1
36. C   37. B   38. C   39. A   40. D

Task 2
41. C   42. B   43. D   44. C   45. C

Task 3
46. 1,642   47. leisure   48. locations   49. spending limit   50. travel plans

Task 4
51. C B   52. I E   53. K J   54. L N   55. R P

Task 5
56. speedy and easy   57. a souvenir   58. use it again   59. expire   60. eat and drink

2006年6月高等学校英语应用能力B级试题答案（阅读部分）

Part III Reading Comprehension

Task 1
36. D 37. A 38. A 39. C 40. B

Task 2
41. A 42. B 43. A 44. D 45. C

Task 3
46. clean 47. easy to use 48. reduced 49. each station 50. 5

Task 4
51. B E 52. G F 53. M H 54. P J 55. A R

Task 5
56. exploded 57. fashion clothes 58. $400,000 59. the heating system 60. A surveyor

参考文献（References）

1. 林晓、卢睿蓉.《快乐 My Reading》.世界图书出版公司 2002.
2. 滕继萌、吴中东.《英语时尚阅读文选》.中国三峡出版社 2002.
3. 徐克容.《综合英语》.外语教学与研究出版社 1999.
4. 徐齐平.《现代英美散文选》.南开大学出版社 1992.
5. 史正永.《英语专业四级阅读理解》.世界图书出版公司 2004.
6. 韩志先、贺慧声.《英语阅读教程》.高等教育出版社 1995.
7. 朱永涛、王立礼.《英语国家社会与文化入门》.高等教育出版 2005.
8. 毛荣贵.《考试虫英语美文选》.开明文教音像出版社 2004.
9. Edward B. Fry.《英语快速阅读应试高手》.北京语言大学出版社 2008.
10. 英语学习杂志.《英语的门槛有多高》.外语教学与研究出版社 2004.
11. James Owen.《英语学习》.外语教学与研究出版社 1995.
12. E. Margaret Baudoin.《读者的选择》.世界图书出版公司 2000.
13. VOA 编辑部.《美国之音》.北京碟中碟软件科技发展有限公司 2008.
14. Neil J. Anderson.《积极英语阅读教程》.外语教学与研究出版社 2008.
15. 宣安.《大学英语快速阅读》.华东师范大学出版社 2008.

（按章节顺序排列）

新书推荐

《新编英语专业口语教程》(基础一、基础二)是"普通高等教育"十一五"国家级规划教材"《新编英语专业口语教程》系列的扩展教材,供高职高专英语专业学生使用,也适合成人教育学院、民办院校、广播电视大学、远程教育英语专业学生及自考生和广大英语自学者使用。基础一各单元涉及学生自我成长的话题,按话题的难易排序,例如:家人朋友、精神偶像、气候变化、饮食健康、价值观念、时间管理等。基础二各单元涉及职业发展相关话题,例如:社会服务、有效沟通、融入团队等,涵盖职前准备、初涉职场、应对工作变化等常见问题。

教材特点:

◎ 话题与学生生活、职业发展和社会环境紧密相关,易引起学生共鸣,让学生言之有物、言之有理,为跨文化交流打下坚实基础。

◎ 听说结合,随书配有光盘。听力水平和口语水平密不可分,教材将听说练习结合起来,让学生在提高口语水平的同时兼顾听力水平的提高。

◎ 口语材料新颖,实用。选材注重实用性和趣味性相结合,贴近生活,无过时用法。

◎ 练习形式多样,注重引导和启发。

| 新编英语专业口语教程(基础一) 齐乃政总主编 | 定价:28.00 元 |
| 新编英语专业口语教程(基础二) 齐乃政总主编 | 定价:29.00 元 |

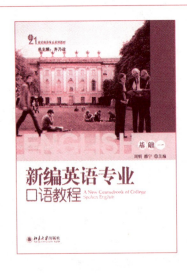 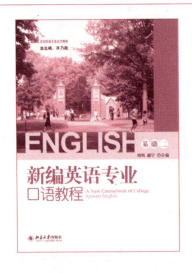